W9-CFT-602

LARRY E. FERGUSON

RED RIVER RISING

A Clear View Of 2,500-Year-Old Prophecy And Today's Headlines

xulon PRESS

Red River Rising
A Clear View Of 2,500-Year-Old Prophecy And Today's Headlines

Copyright © 2007 *by Larry E. Ferguson*

Printed in the United States of America

ISBN 978-1-60477-194-7

www.xulonpress.com

Contents

Introduction

These are, of certainty, troublesome times for America in general and the world as a whole. Events and national dispositions are so problematic the best description leads to one's greatest fears. There seems to be a *Red River Rising*. Politicians and courtrooms have stripped America of her foundational truths; then stand around scratching their heads as to the results of their very own waywardness. It seems they have lost their way and are still leading.

I have a take on how to get back on tract. It's a little old fashion. It is, however, grounded in truth, tested, tried and found faultless time and again. Its simple remedy is far beyond any imagination I could contrive. It is truth unaligned and unmaligned with or by today's left, center or right dogmas. It tells it like it is and is guaranteed to offend everyone at some point. At times I'm offended by it, and I agree with every syllable. It is the belief that the Bible is indeed the Word of God. The same Word that has never been proven wrong on any subject that it touches. It has also been impeccably right about its many projections of who's who and who is doing what in the very days in which you and I live.

This Guideline speaks of various crises in the weather and natural disasters, wars and rumblings of wars we read, see and hear about daily. It is even bold enough to name the nations and people groups along with their actions and the events we see in the headlines day after day. Would you believe it if I can show you what Scripture has to say about Russia, Iran, Turkey, Egypt, Ethiopia, Libya, China, the European Union the Arab/Muslim nations and even an unnamed but thoroughly described economic and military power of the last days? And it did so 2,500 years ago. It also speaks in great clarity and detail of a rising red river in our days. You will agree; I could not make these things up, for the events of these prophecies are playing themselves out in the headlines of papers and news networks daily.

Everywhere people are asking, "What are Russia and China doing? Do they plan to attack America? As you read through *Red River Rising* you will know exactly what they are up to and whether their actions impact America. By the way, Russia does; China doesn't. I'll prove it.

In *Red River Rising* the tough questions others refuse to answer are all on the table. Nations attached at the hips *today* in their various alignments (there are several) are often plainly named. At other times they are unmistakably described, and again as much as 2,500 years ago. Their military actions and plans are detailed. If God were anyone less than who He is guessing the nations that make up one of these alignments would be phenomenal. But to hit the nail on the head concerning every one of them is a God thing taking no less the deity He claims to be.

If the God of the Bible is who He says He is, and His projections of 2,500 years ago are correct as to the nations making up these end time national alignments, and He is also proven right as to the actions of each of these various alignments of nations, it stands to reason He may well also be right as to the result of each of these alignments of nations' actions.

That would offer to each of us, if we believe Him, the opportunity to know history before it takes place. It makes reading today's newspapers rather interesting too.

Chapter One

Man's Ultimate Destiny

Much Ado About Nothing?

"**G**ood grief, where in the universe is planet Earth heading?" In one use of selective words after another, that is the question on minds of not just Americans, but of humanity around the world. Well, sane humanity anyway. There is widespread insanity today. Some of it is being fomented by eastern-based religions in the name of their god, and others, such as in America and other first world nations, in the name of who knows what. Today's model of fascism has been around since A.D. 622 and has declared not just Israel's and the U.S.'s annihilation but hatred, envy and war on every tribe, nation, people, nook and cranny on this seemingly spinning-out-of-control planet. According to Islam you and I will either convert to their radical religion, be enslaved by it, or lose our head to it. There is nothing sane about Islamic Fascism. And despite political correctness, Islam is Fascist. And anything short of confronting fascism is lunacy.

Yet, an inevitable truth stands. Set aside Islamic ambitions. With or without war, this nation, you and I and everyone on this planet are hurling to an ultimate and predetermined appointment with destiny. Secularists, religionists and some of the more astute politicians (there are a few) agree upon one thing, this world is in a steaming heap of trouble with no foreseeable way of escape.

But to what destiny are we heading? Does death settle it all as some claim? You are born, you live, you die and you are dust. That's it? This perishable perishes. Death is the one and only victor. If that is true, the one with the most toys is as big a loser as the one with no toys. On what authority can such an inevitable and dreary doomsday claim be based? Is it reliable? Is there no alternative? Or must we resign to life's final vintage, one last choking gasp as cognizance and breath is expelled from mind and lungs?

Perhaps, on the other hand, there is life beyond earth's last gasp. That is a legitimate counterclaim! If a doomsday destiny can be argued, why cannot a heyday destiny be argued?

If there is life after death, it becomes an excellent rebuttal to the doomsayer's appointment with destiny from which no one can turn back and before which no one wins. But, if there is a haymaker's life after death, will eternity simply hold more of what we have known thus far, with the same results? If so, the doomsayers may be better off with their doomsday evaporation theory. Like a spray of fine mist you're gone! Here one minute and dust on someone's shoe soles the next. Get it over with! The little guy and the big guy, the good and the bad, the ugly and the beautiful are just gone in a puff and have nothing to repeat and no one to report to.

However, for the haymakers at death's beckon, I can see it being an individual's desperate lot to respond kicking, bickering and holding on for dear life; or possibly he is resigned to an indifferent Que Sera, Sera? For any individual to hold to either of these responses, it will be soon discovered not be an invitation but a demand; a demand cherished by no one, and from which bleak darkness and endless eternity no one escapes. I'm neither negative, nor am I pessimistic. I'm just painting the inevitable morbid negativity of a doomsayer's and the haymaker's reality — without Christ. Death, doubt-lessly, is a demarcation line drawn for the entire human race from the first Adam and Eve to the last Zelda and Steve. If life holds nothing more than any of the above, it is *"Much Ado About Nothing."* We may as well eat, drink and be merry while the sun shines and our bodies shrivel and perish over the years and before our eyes.

While the above wandering lost souls face a stacked and decidedly difficult future, there could be, if others are right, a third response to death's summons. This one offers neither a doomsayer's Grim Reaper nor a haymaker's destiny to repeat the sins of the past. So what is this third response to death's summons? These, we are told in the Bible, will experience a resurrection to eternal life (John 5:24-29), a life with no more death, mourning, crying or pain. Unfortunately for the above, this prognosis holds both the doomsayers and the haymakers responsible.

On what does this group base their beliefs? They are firmly embedded in one source; in the Bible's teaching based on the authority, reliability and finality of the Judeo-Christian God. The above statement of no more physical hardships finds its origin in the promise of Revelation 21:3-5. But how can we know it is true? Can God, if there is such a God, deliver on such a promise? Has He ever broken any promise or gone back on His word to friend or foe that we may have some measure with which to gage Him so as to determine His actions in the future? For these reasons, and certainly for our eternity's sake, you and I must be certain about what we believe and why we believe what we believe.

As we navigate in this book through the pages of history and historians, authors and literature, promised events and their fulfillment, or lack thereof, you alone must discover and decide the validity and reliability of a book referred to by many as the Word of God. Many others, to be certain, disrespect the Bible believing it to be the greatest hoax ever pulled on mankind. Obviously, both cannot be right. Be certain of this, one is and one isn't! It is my aim through the course of the pages of *Red River Rising* to build an argument based on the validity and accuracy of 2,500-year-old prophecies, and their fulfillment, before your eyes and those of the world today.

As you investigate the words and presumed truths I or anyone else bring to your attention, you alone must answer the question, "Is what is being espoused reliable? Have the truths presented ever been proven to be unreliable or false?" For heaven's sake you cannot trust anyone with your personal and eternal destiny. The security the God of the Bible gives is found in the reality of the truth He speaks, in the actions He takes, and in the changes He makes. Security can never be found in that which any fallible person believes or believes he believes. There are many who possess and adequately deliver truth. Yet, apart from Jesus Christ, not one has been perfect or had all the answers. There are many times more people who have not only skewed truth but long for you to be among their conquered adherents. Truth, on the other hand, liberates its adherents (John 8:32). How free do you want to be?

I am convinced God offers the only assurance that can be relied on. And He offers proof along the way. The neat thing about Him is He delights in revealing truth to those genuinely seeking Him. "I love those who love Me; and those who diligently seek Me will find Me," Proverbs 8:17. It is not easy to discover truth, especially when so many people have been taught and practiced falsehood from birth. Yet, truth eagerly awaits every honest soul's asking, seeking and knocking (Matthew 7:7, 8).

Solomon, attested to be the wisest man that ever lived, acquired his wisdom from God and passed on the secret of knowing God. Listen to this. This is great! "My son, if you will receive my sayings, and treasure my commandments within you, make your ear attentive to wisdom, incline your heart to understanding; for if you cry for discernment, lift your voice for understanding; if you seek her as silver, and search for her as for hidden treasures; then you will discover the knowledge of God. For the Lord gives wisdom; from His mouth comes knowledge and understanding," Proverbs 2:1-6. There can never be too "Much Ado" about that!

There must to be a longing before there can be a belonging. Far too many well-intentioned people today seek to give answers to questions no one around them is asking. We may as well offer keys to which no locks have been made. It is my hope that as you read the words of this book, be you part of the family of God or seeking that which is genuinely real, you will begin asking all the right questions. When you do, God will not sit still. He reveals Himself to every honest seeker so that he or she might respond in child-like faith to Him and to His love. I like to refer to Him as "His Foreverness". He is never far away, but very close. Yet, He will never force Himself on any man or woman. So read well! What have you to lose — eternity? This nation and this world are heading for their long foretold conclusion. You will discover that conclusion in the pages ahead. And you will discover how to be certain of where the getting-off platform is.

Earth – Man's Testing Ground

There are, of certainty, troublesome times upon us individually, America in general, and the world as a whole. So troublesome will be these times, the best description I can offer is they will be like a red river rising. The Bible speaks of this rising red river in great clarity and detail, as you will shortly discover. I prefer you see the clarity and detail of these days directly from the Bible, the Word of God. I could not make this up. As you go through these pages you will discover the foundation for all that is upon us clearly excavated in Scripture. Nations attached at the hips *today* in their various alignments (there are several) are either plainly named or unmistakably described, often as much as 2,500 years ago. If God were anyone less than who He is, guessing the nations that make up one of these alignments would be phenomenal. But to hit the target on the head for every one of them is a God thing taking no less the deity He claims to be. The actions these aligned nations will be taking were also clearly declared 2,500 years in our past, and will be seen to be exactly what these nations are doing and where they are heading today. The results of the actions of these nations are also divinely affirmed for all with eyes to see and ears to hear.

If God is who He says He is, the God of the Bible, and His projections of 2,500 years ago are correct as to the nations making up these end time national alignments, and He is also proven right as to the actions of each of these various alignments of nations, it stands to reason He may well also be right as to the result of each of these alignments of nations' actions. That would offer to each of us, if we believe Him, the opportunity to know history before it takes place. It makes reading today's newspapers rather interesting too.

I've often been asked, "Will there be another world war? Will it be a nuclear war? Will we destroy the earth?" The answers are yes, yes, and no. Although, Scripture does say we will come to the brink of destroying the earth. Armageddon is the coming war that has everyone's attention. Every household is familiar with the name of this coming war. Nevertheless, there are two more little-paid-attention-to wars sandwiching Armageddon. The war preceding Armageddon is called The First Battle of Gog and Magog. Seven years later the Battle of Armageddon takes place. Between these two coming wars one-half the population on the planet will perish. That's right! One half of earth's population will perish in a seven-year period that could easily begin any day now.

Of course, man is not the only one who perishes. Can't you imagine the outcry of environmentalists as the woods of the world melt from intense heat? We will visit both of these coming wars in the chapters that follow. Finally, the last war to envelop the earth is called The Second Battle of Gog and Magog. Each of these wars will be like no war any person on the planet at any time in all human history has ever witnessed. We can truthfully say today more so than at any other time, "No one is promised tomorrow."

On the Internet and on television I have repeatedly observed advertisements selling battery run radios and flashlights in case Al Qaida attacks. Make no mistake, battery run radios, flashlights and potluck deep fried fish dinners will be of little use when faced with what is, in all likelihood, just over the horizon for all mankind. We will see what Scripture says about these wars. We will also discover the facts and events leading up to them. Additionally, we will discover the alignments of nations I mentioned above, even the names of these nations, leading up to the first and second of these wars which are about to slam the planet. You will find the Bible's description of history immediately before us is like reading the headlines of today's papers and listening to the talking heads of newscasts from around the world.

Of these Biblical facts there can be little difference of opinion. The most informed politicians and seasoned investigative reporters are also mostly in one accord. Isn't that amazing! It is not a matter of "if," but "when and where" America will be hit, and hit hard by a nuclear weapon. As I write these words, the Secretary of Homeland Security, Mr. Michael Chertoff, is making an announcement similar to what I just wrote, that a nuclear attack on an American city or cities is a given. He has been harshly criticized for the term he used, "my gut feeling." Yet, the criticism he received from vastly knowledgeable men in the intelligence fields and in the investigative reporting fields agreed with his assessment of a soon coming simultaneous nuclear attack on from seven to ten American cities. (I believe they are shortsighted here, but will go into that later.)

Below is the report NewsMax.com placed on the Internet on July 16, 2007 entitled "Experts Agree: Major Terror Threats Loom," by Rod Proctor of NewsMax.com.

"Leading terrorism experts agree that Americans face a major Al-Qaida threat this summer, although several also slam Homeland Secretary Michael Chertoff for basing his recent threat-level analysis on his 'gut feeling.'

"'He better have more in the pit of his stomach, so we can react according to reason and not feeling.' Paul L. Williams of Homeland says. 'The American people right now don't need the feeling of anybody. They need the sound judgment of officials.'

"Although Williams disagrees with how Chertoff articulated his concerns to the media, he agrees that the threat from Al-Qaida in the months ahead will be very high. His nightmare scenario: An Al-Qaida dirty-bomb attack carried out against multiple U.S. cities simultaneously.

"The Center for Strategic and International Studies' Amaud de Borchgrave also objects to Chertoff's choice of words, 'I don't think you can assess the current terrorist threat by inflicting a case of gastric distress on the country,' he tells NewsMax. 'This is not a very serious way of handling the problem of terrorism.'

Yet, de Borchgrave cautions that Americans are getting too complacent about terrorism, adding, 'That's precisely when Al-Qaida will strike.'

"Here's what experts on terrorism have told NewsMax about Chertoff and the likelihood of a summer strike."

Arnaud de Borchgrave

"Senior adviser, Center for Strategic and International studies; editor at large, United Press International, and The Washington Times newspaper. Author of Open Source Information: The Missing Dimension of Intelligence, and co-author of Wild Atom: Nuclear Terrorism."

Prediction

"As for the next major terror attack, it's just a matter of time. My assumption is it will be a weapon of mass destruction. If Al-Qaida had used a small 10-kiloton nuclear weapon instead of two aircraft on 9/11, you would have had 1 million people killed."

How Dangerous Is It?

"No one can afford to relax their vigilance no matter what jobs they've got in the public security sector. I was on a flight recently where I didn't have the feeling an air marshal was aboard and the cockpit door was open. People forget what they should be on a constant lookout for. Six years since 9/11, people have become complacent. They don't think anything will happen. That's precisely when Al-Qaida will strike."

Dr. Marvin Cetron

Intelligence, technology and forecasting consultant; President, Forecasting International. Author of 'American Renaissance: Our Lives At The Turn Of The 21st Century.

Prediction

"The people who started Al-Qaida were engineers and doctors. They believe in technology. They made sure their attacks would be successful technologically.

"They are familiar with biomedical research. If they wanted to do a bioweapons attack they would be in a perfect position to do that.

"If they screwed up our food supply, say in Nebraska, we would be in big trouble. These people would have access to radioactive materials."

How Dangerous Is It?

"[Chertoff] had a "gut feeling" because he saw the intelligence report that said we were worse off – and we are worse off. The data and chatter we're hearing is as high, if not higher, than we had before 9/11… Data leads us to believe al-Qaida is getting stronger and will be back here whether we get out of Iraq or not. Summer is easier [for terrorists]. Students, who are generally the extremists, are not in school and can travel more easily. For the next month and a half, we ought to increase the threat level to red."

Steven Emerson

Executive Director, The Investigative Project of Terrorism. Author of <u>American Jihad: The Terrorists Living Among Us</u> and <u>Jihad Incorporated: A Guide to Militant Islam in the U.S.</u>

Prediction

"There are plenty of infrastructure possibilities (for attack). The list is endless – an exercise in futility.

"We've plugged some of (the border holes), but not all of them. The borders with Canada and Mexico could be tighter."

How Dangerous Is It?

"In general, I think [Chertoff's remarks] were helpful. They drew attention to the fact that Al-Qaida is mobilizing. There's always the risk of crying wolf, but again, in general he's trying to raise the alarm and he has good reason to."

Walid Phares

Director, Future Terrorism Project of the Foundation for the Defense of Democracies; Visiting Fellow, European Foundation for Democracy. Author of The War of Ideas: Jihadism Against Democracy.

Prediction

"If attacks are prepared they may come from either or both types of cells – those that have formed on their own inside the country and those receiving instructions from overseas. There are multiple scenarios for such attacks. It depends on what the cells have acquired inside the country in terms of targets, manpower, infiltration, types of weapons and materials."

How Dangerous Is It?

"I project that the Jihadists, not only Al-Qaida but also those connected to regimes, think that the next few months are crucial as they precede the presidential campaign year of 2008.

"They want to impact the choices made by the voters, but early in the process. They also want to impact the Iraqi ground report coming at the end of the summer."

Paul R. Pillar

Visiting Professor on Foreign Policy, Terrorism, and the Middle East, Georgetown University.

Prediction

"Al-Qaida proper – the group that did 9/11 and that is commanded by bin Laden and Zawahiri – probably is still weaker today than it was in September 2001, despite recent recouping of some of its losses in South Asia.

"The broader Islamist terrorist movement, however, has become larger and more threatening over the past five years."

How Dangerous Is It?

"I believe Secretary Chertoff is correct in gauging the chance of such an attack as significant. Al-Qaida's proven ability to use conventional means to inflict heavy casualties suggests that such means will continue to be more likely than the exotic methods. But the latter clearly have an appeal to terrorists as well, if for no other reason than that we focus so much attention on such means and are frightened of them."

Paul L. Williams

Journalist, author, and former terrorism consultant to the FBI. Author of <u>The Al Qaida Connection: International Terrorism, Organized Crime and the Coming Apocalypse</u> and <u>Dunces of Doomsday: 10 Blunders That Gave Rise</u>

to Radical Islam, Terrorist Regimes and the Threat of an American Hiroshima.

Prediction

"When our troops were combing caves in Kandahar during Operation Enduring Freedom, in those caves they found canisters left behind with Uranium 238, worth in the millions of dollars. It's not weapons grade, but it's perfect for a radiological bomb. Set one off in New York and you would have [expletive] to pay. Some of these substances, like cesium, when it hits a building, that material cannot be scraped off. It cannot be washed off. The building would have to be torn down and taken to a dedicated landfill. Just think what that would do to midtown Manhattan."

How Dangerous Is It?

"I believe the reason there have been no attacks here [since 9/11] is because [bin Laden] is planning to conduct an attack on seven to ten cities simultaneously... They're very patient."
© NewsMax 2007.

In respect of but contrary to the belief of each of these men, I do not agree such a devastating attack will come upon America this summer. By the time you read this we'll know. At least, not in the limited nuclear scale they have predicted. I do believe it will come. You will shortly discover why. But it will be on a much larger scale than these men have imagined or predicted. These days are beyond question America's most serious and dangerous times ever. These men, much wiser and with far greater resources than I, have evaluated events from the perspective of man's best intelligence gathering processes. Their assessments are right in line with what intelligence agencies around the world are saying. From my perspective, I seek to glean from what they have learned and passed on. Yet, my final analysis is based more on what God has given us in the Bible about the last days: the nations involved, their alignments, their purposes, their victories, and their failures. All of these have been revealed in the Word of God. You will discover each of these in the course of this book. It is amazing how Scripture's declarations and today's events match up in all of the above areas of concern. More amazing is the unfailing reality that the One giving us these match-ups is the infallible God who knows all things before they come to pass.

Banking on the truthfulness of the God of the Bible, in days ahead every individual on earth — not just America, will be severely tested. It is a test, a most severe test! Yet, with the test is also a way of escape.

Coming to earth is the Tribulation period the Bible has often spoken of. And with the Tribulation a long, wide and deep red river rises. The Bible describes for us the depth and length of this coming river of blood. Even more surprising than such an awesome river is all that has been prophesied and will come to pass *before* that terrible day.

What if I told you that as much as 2,500 years ago God, through His prophets Isaiah, Jeremiah, Ezekiel, Daniel, Zechariah, John and others, gave us all the startling details of the very battles that will engulf our planet in the very near future. In the details, He outlines for us the alignments of nations involved in world events *immediately before the first of these wars.* God's Word goes on to reveal the nations making up other strategic alignments. He uncovers for us when, where, how, who they are and who they are going to strike. You will discover all of them in the due course of this book.

It is amazing how God can look into the future and fore-tell tomorrow's events as if they were yesterday's realities. But do you realize that if He has ever been wrong or is presently mistaken, just once — on anything He says will come to pass, He is not a God who can be relied on? And, if He is not, no one can bank on anything else He says, now or concerning the future.

Though attacked by the most brilliant of human minds, in no instance in all these millennia has Jehovah God of the Old and New Testaments ever been proven wrong on anything He has said or done. His Word has an impeccable and perfect history of being kept. For many it is extremely hard to get along with someone who has all the answers. Perhaps that is why so many men and women in fields such as science, origins, related specialties and higher education have difficulty with even the thought of God, an all-knowing, all-present and all-powerful Creator looking over their shoulders. He hasn't anything to learn. Sadly, many of these I just named haven't learned they haven't anything to lose.

The Bible is not a book of science per se, but whenever it speaks of things relating to the field of science, it has forever been true. Every time one group of scientists believes they have debunked God, the next group proves them foolish. The Bible is not a book of origins, but in all that it says concerning the origin of all that has come into existence, it is invariably factual. The Bible is not a book of history, but all the details it lists concerning history past, present and future have either materialized when He said they would, or will at their appropriate time. Always! Without fail! In all areas of which the Word of God speaks, that which it says is infallibly and unassailably true. In no instance has His Word ever failed or proven to be in error.

I mentioned all that to state this. The passages in the Old and New Testaments, some written over 2,500 years ago, concerning the alignments of nations and who those nations are in the days immediately preceding the Lord Jesus' return, are like reading the headlines of today's newspapers and observing today's world events. The Bible has been unalterably right in the past. It is unshakably right in the present. So, for those who do not allow facts to affect decisions, buckle your seat belt and hold on. This is going to be quite an illuminating ride leading to the failure of every argument against Scriptural prophecy. If, on the other hand, you do take note of facts and have an inquiring mind as to how current events and ancient Scriptural prophecies can be so aligned before our eyes today, it is likely you will find the answers you seek. You will also discover additional hidden treasure leading to life's greatest questions.

God's Ultimate Purpose

Allow me in a few words to lay the foundation on which the Bible can be understood.

I mentioned man is heading to a certain appointment with destiny. That destiny is best understood by realizing God's ultimate purpose. He is extremely active in and through everything we have, are, and will experience. His purpose, decided long ago, is in constant progress toward its desired end. It cannot fail. God is active in the lives of people. But individuals are not the only ones targeted for His ultimate purpose. History itself is rapidly moving toward the intention of the Creator's design.

Ah, tipped my hand, didn't I? Creation, including mankind according to the Bible and good old common sense, was not a mass of bits, pieces and parts exploding in mid-air and perfectly falling into its intricate position and detail. Some dare call that science. Why hasn't the "big bang" theory been reproduced in a laboratory? So undeniable and unassailable is the Bible's teaching on creation, no argument is even offered in Scripture to defend the statement, "In the beginning, God created…" Take a look at Scripture's declarations in Genesis 1, John 1:1-3, and Romans 1:18-20. From that distant beginning down to this day, God foreknew and foretold the major events of history to come. Those events stare us in the face today as much as a hungry bear does its prey.

Yet God, in the midst of earth's chaos, is still in control. He is not the source of satanic or man-made chaos, although He has often been cursed for it. He does, nevertheless, wisely use it to accomplish His purpose. This earth is of His making, and it will be His when all is said and done. Listen to King David on this fact: "The earth is the Lord's, and all it contains, the world, and those who dwell in it," Psalm 24:1. Personally, I've just always figured if God was big enough to make it, He is big enough to keep it.

God chose Israel out of all the peoples of the world to be a special nation to Him. He blessed them with the greatest of privileges. They would be given His protection and guidance. Through them He gave the Law, the Word of God and eventually the Son of God. The Israelites were thankful at first, though slow to trust Him. They eventually, after great deliverances which their disobedience often seemed to require, began bringing their offerings to God, though not out of love, but out of obligation. In answer to His people's rebellious and cantankerous nature, God judged their deeds and testified against them saying, "I shall take no young bull out of your house, nor male goats out of your folds. For every beast of the forest is Mine, the cattle on a thousand hills. I know every bird of the mountains, and everything that moves in the field is Mine. If I were hungry, I would not tell you; for the world is Mine, and all it contains," Psalm 50:9-12. God has never relinquished the Title Deed to this spinning sphere we call home. Satan and sin may seem to be on the throne, but they and theirs are ever on a leash.

The God of earth and heaven has been in no rush to do away with sin and sinners. Sin is not of His making, but He certainly uses man's iniquities and Satan's contriving to drive many to Himself. I hope He has driven you and yours into the palm of His hand. Why? That is His purpose. He is "not wishing for any to perish but for all to come to repentance," II Peter 3:9. In working out that purpose, God established man's ultimate destiny — an eternal friendship with Him in a new heaven, on a new earth and in a new city.

In the midst of all the chaos, God is in control and working out His kind intention in the lives of men and women.

Let's see His plan to fulfill that purpose.

In infiniteness of wisdom, knowledge, and power God created the heavens, the earth and all that is in them. "Apart from Him nothing came into being that has come into being," John 1:1-3. In omniscience God knew from before the formation of the heavens, Lucifer, the highest of his created beings (Ezekiel 28:12-15; Isaiah 14:12-14), would rebel against His authority. Along with Lucifer, perhaps one third of the angels of Heaven fell (Revelation 12:3-9). God also knew before forming the earth for habitation that man, tempted by Satan, would follow the old serpent's example in thwarting the rightful place of his Creator. Yet, in omnipotence and unsearchable love God went forth with an indestructible purpose for the ages.

With a predetermined plan for accomplishing His purpose, He knew many men and women, convicted and drawn by His Spirit, would come to repentance and place their faith in His Son, Jesus Christ. Therefore, in eternity past He ordained *the way* to accomplish man's redemption. Peter speaks of this *way* in Acts 2:23: "... this Man, delivered up by the predetermined plan and foreknowledge of God, you nailed to a cross by the hands of godless men and put Him to death."

God foreknew man's rejection of the Lord Jesus Christ. Not withstanding, in infinite love and in consultation with His Son, God offered Jesus in payment for our sins. Doing so, He can be justified in redeeming and cleansing a repentant people coming to Him through faith in His resurrected Son, the sacrificial and risen Lamb of God.

Christ's selfless offering became the constant cause of the four living creatures and the twenty four elders of Revelation 5:9 to sing "a new song, saying, Worthy art Thou to take the book, and to break its seals; for Thou wast slain, and didst purchase for God with Thy blood men from every tribe and tongue and people and nation." The curse of sin can be lifted today, for the payment of sin has been made by Jesus Christ (Colossians 2:14). "(He) reconciled them both (Jews and Gentiles) in one body to God through the cross, by it (the cross) having put to death the enmity (the judgment of the Law upon sinners)," Ephesians 2:16.

The *"book"* mentioned above in Revelation 5:9 is the title deed to all creation, man included. It was purchased by the blood of Christ on the cross, fulfilling the role of the Lamb of God for Israel, and the substitute for the sins of all mankind.

Six Important Days

In working through His plan for the redemption of all things, God established six important "days" to help us see His hand moving toward that eternal purpose. There are other "days" mentioned in the Bible. There is the day of creation, the Sabbath Day, the Lord's Day, etc... Yet, I bring your attention to these six because they show the hand of God's movement from the "day of salvation" up to and including inheriting eternity, known as "the day of God." These "days" are keys to the Designer's blueprint concerning the events and facts and of all things present and future.

1. The Day of Salvation

"And working together with Him, we also urge you not to receive the grace of God in vain — for He says, 'At the acceptable time I listened to you, and on the day of salvation

I helped you, behold now is the acceptable time,' behold, now is 'the day of salvation,'" II Corinthians 6:1-2.

God has a calendar of events, the dates of which are determined beforehand in His own wisdom and grace. Hence, we find in Galatians 4:4-6, "when the fulness of time came, God sent forth His Son... that we might receive the adoption as sons... crying, 'Abba! Father!'" God knows the perfect timing for every event to be carried out and the perfect moment for His salvation to be brought forth in the hearts of all who will. He works on that schedule. Some of us, as we look at time *we've wasted*, have lamented, "If only I had come to Christ earlier." Yet, God never wastes time. He has always known just what it would take to get you where you are today, and He has worked on that timetable. Be thankful and go forward, rather than dwelling on an irrecoverable bygone past! Today and tomorrow (Lord willing) is where the action is, never yesterday.

Paul's compassion is seen in the words, "don't receive (the message of) the grace of God in vain." Esau did! Later he wept for he could find no place for repentance (Hebrews 12:15-17). The rich young ruler did not receive the message of God's grace either. He walked away sorrowfully. Many have been the men and women following such disastrous leads. Such sorrowfulness will know no limits in a bleak eternity future for those spurning Christ Jesus' willing offer of redemption today.

The day of salvation is that time in the heart and mind of a man or woman when the Spirit of the Lord Jesus convicts and draws him or her to Christ Jesus of Calvary. The author of Hebrews describes the Holy Spirit's conviction as a "scourging" (12:6). That Divine "scourging" is necessary in that it awakens the soul's consciousness to the sinfulness of sin and moves him to turn from sin and self to the reign of the Lord Jesus Christ. From that moment on in one's born again life, God's discipline becomes personal whenever we step out of line and go astray from the knowledge of His will. That's life in the family of God. Discipline is never fun, but rejoice in it for it is a certain way of knowing whose we are (Hebrews 5-8) and of growing up in the family of God. He loves His own too much not to discipline them. So, do you know Him by acquaintance with His Word or by personal experience (II Corinthians 13:5)? Be careful not to turn away from the Good News of God's grace when His Spirit comes calling.

The day of salvation concerns not just an individual's personal call to Christ. It also speaks of the duration in time known as the church age. There is coming a day when those who are alive on earth and members of the family of God will be caught up to meet the Lord in the air. Their Christian counterparts during this age having died "in Christ" will rise from the grave to also meet the Lord in the air. We'll see more of this later, but this event, called the rapture (I Thessalonians 4:13-18), brings the church age to a close. It also brings the opportunity of salvation to the "whosoever will" to a close. There will be many during the church age who heard the Gospel message and were convicted of sin and drawn to Christ by the Holy Spirit, but who rejected that call. For them will sadly be no more opportunity of redemption. II Thessalonians 2:7-12 makes this crystal clear. This is why the Apostle Paul wrote to the church at Corinth: "And working together with Him, we also urge you not to receive the grace of God in vain — for He says, 'At the acceptable time I listened to you, and on the day of salvation I helped you;' behold, now is 'the acceptable time,' behold, now is 'the day of salvation,'" II Corinthians 6:1, 2.

2. The Last Days For The Church

"But realize this, that in the last days difficult times will come. For men will be lovers of self, lovers of money, boastful, arrogant, revilers, disobedient to parents, ungrateful, unholy, unloving, irreconcilable, malicious gossips, without self-control, brutal, haters of good, treacherous, reckless, conceited, lovers of pleasure rather than lovers of God; holding to a form of godliness, although they have denied its power," II Timothy 3:1-5. See also I Timothy 4:1-5; James 5:3; II Peter 3:3, 4.

Among the many verses, this one passage adequately sums up the condition of the last days' church. By the words "last days," Scripture points to the days immediately leading up to the return of Christ.

A large number of passages in the New Testament detail the tarnished condition of the church in these last days. They speak of the overall corruption of *the* church in general, not *a* church in particular. There are in the last days churches that are pure, Bible believing, Spirit-filled, loving, evangelizing and Christ honoring. The general state of the church-at-large, however, is far different from those individual congregations where Christ is honored as head of the body. The former have departed from the Word of God, denying portions they cannot understand or that run contrary to their desired modern day ideals for the church. They are easily marked as the ecumenical churches of our day, and will be found in such worldly acceptable organizations as the World Council of Churches. The latter hold to the Word of God, in love they instruct others in the ways of God, and seek to reach out to those without Christ, whether at home or abroad.

A thorough study of Matthew 13 will reveal the Lord's assessment of His church as the end of the age draws near. This same desecrating and devastating development is seen in the Lord's letters to His churches in Revelation 2, 3. Most especially you will find this falling away in the last four of these letters. In them the Lord points these typical churches either toward the Tribulation or, by way of a promise, to deliverance from it. We will look into these letters to His churches a little later. They are revealing, correcting, instructive and come with a signed, sealed and delivered blessing for every overcomer.

3. The Day of Christ

"… Among whom you appear as lights in the world, holding fast the word of life, so that in the day of Christ I may have cause to glory because I did not run in vain nor toil in vain," Philippians 2:15f, 16.

With a personal experiential knowledge of God's salvation, Paul writes the Philippians of his confidence in that which God will do in them (1:6), of his prayers for them (2:9, 10) and of their being his cause for glory (2:16) — "in the day of Christ."

In his letter to the Ephesians, "the day of Christ" is Paul's reference to the Christians in the Ephesus Church as being "sealed for the day of redemption" (4:30). Again, in his first letter to the Thessalonians his reference to, "the dead in Christ shall rise first, then we who are alive and remain shall be caught up together with them in the clouds to meet the Lord in the air, and thus we shall always be with the Lord," (4:16, 17), also refers to "the day of Christ." Set before us in each instance where this term is found is the "day" when Christ Jesus comes "in the air" for His own. This is the gathering of Christ's own, or the catching up which is often referred to as the rapture of the church.

The "day of Christ" is the appointment day on God's calendar for the resurrection of the redeemed. This "day" finalizes the Christian's full redemption in the Savior's presence (see Ephesians 1:13, 14). "Christ" is the New Testament word for "Messiah." This "day" is called "the day of Christ" because it is the day when full salvation is realized in Christ the Savior. The redemption of each Christian's imperishable and immortal body and the total transformation of each person into Christ's likeness and glory will be realized in this day. In writing to the Corinthian believers, Paul explained it this way: "Behold, I tell you; we shall not all sleep but we shall all be changed, in a moment, in the twinkling of an eye, at the last trumpet; for the trumpet will sound, and the dead will be raised imperishable, and we shall be changed. For this perishable must put on the imperishable, and this mortal must put on immortality," I Corinthians 15:51-53. John adds this to Paul's teaching, "We shall be like Him, because we shall see Him just as He is," (I John 3:2). What a "day" the "day of Christ" will be!!!

4. The Day of The Lord

"But the day of the Lord will come like a thief, in which the heavens will pass away with a roar and the elements will be destroyed with intense heat, and the earth and its works will be burned up," II Peter: 3:11.

This "day" runs from the beginning of the Tribulation period, to the Lord's return to earth when "every eye shall see Him" (Revelation 1:7), through the millennium reign (Revelation 20:4-6) and until the end of all things temporal (Revelation 21:1-5).

"Lord" speaks of Christ's position as the coming "King of kings and Lord of lords." Two of the most vivid descriptions of the coming Lord Jesus Christ are found in Revelation 1:12-20; and 19:11-21. The Old Testament concludes with a sign and a warning of this "day" to Israel, "Behold, I am going to send you Elijah the prophet before the coming of the great and terrible day of the Lord," Malachi 4:5. Israel, religious Israel, has looked for Elijah to return since he was caught up in a whirlwind to heaven without seeing death (II Kings 2:11). Salvation for Israel, however, will spell disaster for many others. Joel 2:1-11 says of this time as, "The day of the Lord is indeed great and very awesome, and who can endure it?"

In II Thessalonians 2:1 Paul infers the "day of Christ" when he writes, ".... with regards to the coming of our Lord Jesus Christ, and our gathering together to Him" — that is, "in the air." He then corrects false teaching carrying his forged signature that "the day of the Lord" had already taken place and the church had been left behind. Paul dismissed that idea with these words: "... that you (the church) may not be quickly shaken from your composure or be disturbed either by a spirit or a message or a letter as if from us, to the effect that the day of the Lord has come," verse 2. He goes on to explain that "the day of the Lord" cannot take place until the "man of lawlessness is revealed, the son of destruction," verses 3-5. That cannot happen, says Paul, until "He (the Holy Spirit) who restrains... is taken out of the way," verses 6, 7. When the church is removed the Holy Spirit's restraining power on evil will be withdrawn so the "man of lawlessness" can do as he pleases. We may think things are bad now and getting worse. But you don't want to be here when the Holy Spirit withdraws His *"restraining power."*

I love the next verse: "And then that lawless one will be revealed whom the Lord will slay with the breath of His mouth and bring to an end by the appearance of His coming," verse 8.

"The day of the Lord" is the day Christ Jesus referenced when He mentioned His coming would be as "a thief in the night." That phrase simply means many will be caught unaware, unprepared and unexpectedly (see Matthew 24:43;

I Thessalonians 5:2, 4; Revelation 3:3; 16:15). "The day of the Lord," which includes His return to earth, also has a glorious reference to Christ's own: "When Christ, who is our life, is revealed, then you also will be revealed with Him in glory," Colossians 3:4. Won't some be surprised?

The "day of the Lord" encompasses not only the Tribulation, but also the binding of Satan, the judgment of Israel, the judgment of the nations, the one thousand year reign of Christ on earth, Satan's last revolt and, as mentioned above, the destruction of all things temporal.

5. The Day of Judgment

"Truly I say to you, it will be more tolerable for the land of Sodom and Gomorrah in the day of judgment, than for that city," Matthew 10:15.

"The day of judgment" refers to the trial of The Great White Throne Judgment. This "judgment" takes place during "the day of the Lord," but is so important the Author of Scripture gave it a name of its own. "That city" refers to the city where the testimony of Jesus Christ was rejected. Why? A messenger of Christ Jesus was in their midst with the Gospel. They saw truth concerning Him in all His glory, yet rejected all they saw. Though hearing of Him with ears they purposely shut Him out. The Scripture is ever true. "From everyone who has been given much, shall much be required," Luke 12:48. Sodom and Gomorrah will not be judged nearly so severely as "that city" that had received greater truth, thus greater opportunity. Judgment, according to Scripture, is always according to light given but refused, light received but rejected.

"The day of judgment" is in reference to the trial of the wicked, the unrepentant and unrighteous dead. Raised from the dead each unrepentant person will appear before God, kneel at The Great White Throne to be judged and sentenced to the degree of their everlasting punishment. This judgment occurs at the close of the Millennial Kingdom, after Satan's final revolt, and before things eternal. The sentence is final. "He who rejects Me, and does not receive My saying, has one who judges him; the word I spoke is what will judge him at the last day," John 12:48. See II Peter 2:9: 3:7. Jude reveals in his letter in verse 6 that this will also be the day of judgment for the fallen angels. Revelation 20:5, 11-15 describes the judgment of this terrible day.

6. The Day of God

"Since all these things are to be destroyed in this way, what sort people ought you to be in holy conduct and godliness, looking for and hastening the coming of the day of God, on account of which the heavens will be destroyed by burning, and the elements will melt with intense heat," II Peter 3:11, 12.

"The day of God" begins with entrance into and the longevity of eternity future. II Peter 3:13-18 describes this "day" as refocusing God's family from this present environment and pointing each of His own toward the *"new heavens and a new earth, in which righteousness dwells."*

In light of this coming day, Peter instructs us as to how to live in four areas. "Therefore, beloved, since you look for these things, be diligent to be found by Him in peace, spotless and blameless." "Peace" has to do with **our character**. "Spotless & blameless" refers to **our conduct**.

"And regard the patience of our Lord to be salvation." Here God encourages **constancy** in evangelism until He comes. Why would the Lord tarry after the last soul has been won? He won't! Since He won't, it is obvious there are still some around us who need to be brought into God's forever family. And that obviously means there is still time for personal repentance and faith. This passage closes with our being "on guard... steadfast... and growing in the grace and knowledge of our Lord and Savior Jesus Christ." That has to do with **continuance** in a walk of faith in the Lord Jesus today.

The day of God ushers in eternity future with the new heaven, the new earth, the New Jerusalem and endless ages in the brilliance of untainted glory. We'll glimpse more into this later.

The Necessity of Christ's Return

For God's Word to be true, *everything* He says *must* be true. It would not be possible to know Him or trust Him if He could be tainted with any untruth. Thus, Satan and his followers have made many a fruitless attack on the Word of God. Don't give the devil a toehold in your life. God's Word is literal Truth and is to be believed as such. He says what He means and He means what He says.

On the many occasions where Scripture employs figurative language, God reveals truth by painting pictures. Such a picture of truth is called typology. Whenever these types, figures or pictures are used they can be traced through Scripture where often times their meaning is clearly revealed. An example is the word *salt*. In Leviticus 2:13 we find with all Israel's offerings to the Lord *salt* was to be offered; no offering was to be made without *salt*. A study of the word *salt* in Scripture leads to Colossians 4:6 where we find, "Let your speech always be with grace; seasoned, as it were, with salt...." *Salt* represents *grace* without which it is impossible to offer anything pleasing to the Lord. One's service, sacrifices and offerings are all made possible by the grace of God. Where the meaning is not stated an orderly tracing of the type in Scripture reveals an ever-increasing revelation of that which the type represents. Once its meaning is understood, you can literally believe it to be truth.

In either case, when God states the meaning of the type, or when a type unveils itself, rest assured in the literal, believable, understandable and eternal Word of God on that matter.

The inerrancy of the Bible is authenticated by its proper interpretation. The saying, "If God's Word says it, I believe it and that settles it," is slightly erroneous. Certainly we ought to believe God. But if God's Word says it, that settles it whether we believe it or not. That established, consider the following essential reasons for Christ's return:

1. The second coming of the Lord Jesus Christ is the most mentioned truth in all Scripture. Let's just say it is mightily important to God!

2. For every mention of Christ's first coming, there are six references to His second coming. The law of frequency of mention is certainly of importance.

3. The second coming is the necessary completion of His work of redemption. The Lord's title deed to this world requires the redemption of all creation. He'll do that when He comes.

4. The Lord's second coming is necessary to fulfill Scripture — it is the most taught doctrine in the New Testament, where in its 216 chapters there are 318 references. Have you ever considered that while approximately 5% of Scripture is given to lead a person to the Lord Jesus Christ for salvation and eternal life, 95% has been given to instruct God's own in how to live, walk, honor and serve Him. With the second coming being the most mentioned truth in the

Bible, God must have considered it vitally important to the conduct and encouragement of His people in this day.

5. The second coming of Christ is necessary to fulfill scores of Old Testament prophecies. The Old Testament begins and ends with the promise of the reigning Messiah, God's provision for man's redemption (Genesis 3:15 and Malachi 4:1, 2, 5).

6. The New Testament begins and ends with the same promise (Luke 1:30-33 and Revelation 22:20).

7. The Lord's return is required to put down sin, sinners and Satan and to establish a reign of righteousness. Throughout seven millennia (should we have only one more) man will have proven success in two areas. He can neither stop the deathblow of sin, nor can he pay the debt of the broken Law and still live. This will be unquestionably proven in the most perfect of circumstances, the Millennial Kingdom. Christ Jesus, however, will bring to an end the deathblow of sin when He returns (Revelation 20). And, having fully paid the price for sin on His first coming, He will, at the close of the Millennial Reign, usher the redeemed into the eternal day of God.

Is man's ultimate destiny still "Much Ado About Nothing?" Far from it! The destiny of man has "Much Ado About Eternity."

Men question one thing more and more as the day of the Lord draws near, "What about the signs of Christ coming?" Are they real? Can they be relied on?

Jesus Christ has no desire for His own to be ignorant concerning the vicinity, or the season of His coming. Upon His disciples' request (Matthew 24:3) He listed a number of signs by which His people can know the vicinity of the time of His return.

Do these signs apply to us Gentiles as well? Or are they just for the Jewish people? Do all these signs appear to be present today? Are they increasing in number? Is the level of their intensity elevating like a hot air balloon? I hope you will agree one does not have to be a child of God to see the relationship of Jesus' words to today's realities. These signs are too plain, too stark and too real to be dismissed. Let's look at them.

Chapter 2

Signs Of Christ's Return

"Balderdash, Every Generation Claims That"

The Knowledge Of Christ's Return

Is it possible to know the nearness of Christ's return? Many sects of men and women down through the years, having more confidence in a trusted leader than a knowledge of the Word of God, have sold all worldly belongings and retreated to a mountaintop to await His return. Embarrassment and humiliation upon His failed return caused many of them to realize their directions were given by someone other than the God of the Bible. At best, they were greatly deceived. At worse, someone was a masterful thief and liar.

Matthew, Mark, Luke and others record the Lord's words concerning that which the Christian can know and that which he cannot know about the timing of Christ's return. Listen carefully, "Even so, you too, when you see these things happening, recognize that He is near, right at the door.... But of that day or hour no one knows, not even the angels in heaven, nor the Son, but the Father alone," Luke 13:29, 32; and Matthew 24:33, 36.

The exact timing of the Lord's return no one knows, not the day or the hour, and certainly not the minute or the second. But from Christ's own words it is evident we are to know the vicinity of the time of His return. During the Lord Jesus' earthly ministry the Pharisees and Sadducees strutted up to test Him, chest out and a smug look on their faces. Imagine that! They said, "Show us a sign from heaven as to who you are." To their Scriptural ignorance and spiritual arrogance, He gave one of His many brilliant answers. "When it is evening, you say, 'It will be fair weather, for the sky is red.' And in the morning, 'There will be a storm today, for the sky is red and threatening,'" Matthew 16:1-3. He then lowered the proverbial boom. "Do you know how to discern the appearance of the sky, but cannot discern the signs of the times?"

The Lord criticized Israel's religious leaders for not knowing the Scriptures well enough to know the signs of His first coming. There were many! He publicly and openly displayed them and disclosed Himself to everyone with eyes to see and ears to hear. The problem was He had not attended the schools on their accredited list and was not recognized by them as a man with any formal training. Added to Israel's leaders' growing list of incredulities He was an unemployed trouble-making son of a poor carpenter and, of all places, He was from Galilee (John 7:41, 52).

Again, the many signs recorded in Israel's Scriptures as to Christ's first coming accompanied Him everywhere He went. The Pharisees and Sadducees favored, however, things continuing as they had always been, rather than anything or anyone who might upset their religious applecart.

Now, imagine this. In the Bible there are six verses describing the Lord's second coming to every one verse pertaining to His first coming. Six times as many verses. If He pulled the rug out from under the feet of the religious leaders of His day for not knowing and recognizing His first coming, how much more guilt would we bear for not knowing and declaring the nearness of His second coming?

All this as dust settles on Bibles throughout our homes? Yes, we can and we are to know the general timing of the Lord's return.

Ignorance As An Excuse

Many have said, "Prophecy, and the book of Revelation in particular, need not be studied. I just teach and preach the practical parts of the Bible." Makes one wonder what other parts might not be practical in such a person's mind. There is no book in the Bible more practical and important to know and live the principles found within it than The Revelation of Jesus Christ.

Here are just a few of the reasons WE NEED TO STUDY PROPHECY and especially The Revelation:

1. The last book of the Bible is properly named The Revelation of Jesus Christ. Sure, The Revelation reveals things to come. But the primary purpose in giving us The Revelation is to reveal Jesus. On every page of this precious book, you will see Jesus Christ. How can we get to know Him more fully, love Him more dearly, honor Him more clearly and walk with Him more nearly if we neglect these invaluable truths?

2. The Bible says, "Be diligent to present yourself approved to God as a workman who does not need to be ashamed, handling accurately the word of truth," II Timothy 2:15. That would not be possible if we neglect the truths concerning the end times so clearly revealed in The Revelation of Jesus Christ. The Revelation is all about Him.

3. Some have said these truths cannot be understood. In that case the Holy Spirit is letting down on His job to reveal truth. See I Corinthians 2:14. Hum! Maybe the problems associated with comprehending truth lies within us. Heaven forbid!

4. Others have said these doctrines are seedbeds of heresy. Are we to relinquish other portions of God's Word to heretics because they misuse them, as well? Of course not! The Revelation is the crowning and closing Word of God to today's generation.

5. Still others contend too much confusion comes from studying The Revelation. There is too much typology, too many signs and too many symbols. Let me refer you to my comments on understanding typology in Chapter One under The Necessity Of Christ's Return. Prophecy was often shut up (that is, *sealed*) in Old Testament days (Daniel 12:4). God reserved these *sealed* passages and truths for no other generation than ours (Daniel 12:9; Rev. 22:10, 16).

6. Apart from The Revelation no other book of the Bible begins and ends with a blessing upon those who read, hear and heed the things written in it. See Revelation 1:3 and 22:7. Those who love the Lord would have to be lazy, crazy or deceived to ignore this book.

7. Prophetic truth is given to strengthen, encourage and enable God's forever family to live faithfully in light of our Lord's return. See II Peter 3:11, 14, 17, 18. Many other verses of Scripture speaking of these days encourage and challenge the child of God as well. One of the most memorable is the closing verse of "The Resurrection Chapter," I Corinthians 15:58: "Therefore, my beloved brethren, be steadfast, immovable, always abounding in the work of the Lord, knowing that your toil is not in vain in the Lord." Nothing causes God's people to live in light of eternity more than knowing Him and understanding what He is up to in our day.

8. Finally, in closing this unique book, this testimony of Himself, the Lord Jesus said, "I, Jesus, have sent My angel to testify to you these things for the churches," Revelation 22:16. Our lives take on a whole new meaning as we see these life changing revelations of Jesus Christ. Look upon it as a love letter to His family. It was specifically written to those called by His name.

These and many other reasons are given in Scripture for the purpose of equipping, preparing, training and leading the child of God into a manifested walk of faith and usefulness in the kingdom of heaven. That term, "the kingdom of heaven," is a phrase and, too often, a little known reality among God's own. It speaks of a sphere wherein the will of God can go on. It only takes two to make a kingdom. If He is King and you are His servant, the will of God can go wherever you go. That doesn't mean everything will be hunky-dory. It might be and it might not. God's will going on in your life could get you strung up today. Nevertheless, for such a willing and loving spirit with a servant's heart there are great and eternal rewards.

As of yet, we have not even begun mentioning the rewards, the glory and the eternal position promised those who read, comprehend and heed these truths. It is enough to say for the present, however, one cannot give back to the Lord more than he or she has received.

The Time Of Christ's Return

Since the ascension of Jesus Christ every generation of Christians has lived expectantly and excitedly in hope of His return in their day. Every generation has also witnessed

Biblically based signs bringing with them the hope of His soon return. Christ Jesus Himself proclaimed His sure return on several occasions. Naturally, every faithful generation of Christians for the past 2,000 years has exercised good faith in that promise, declared the fact of His coming, and manned the watchtowers for Him in their day.

On coming out of the Temple with His disciples the Lord's understudies pointed out various Temple buildings. I wonder if, with a chuckle, He ignited the conversation with a question as to the purpose of these buildings. In any case, with their eyes fixed on wrong values, "He answered and said to them, 'Do you not see all these things? Truly I say to you, not one stone here shall be left upon another, which will not be torn down,'" Matthew 24:2. That was the year A.D. 33. He foretold the destruction of Jerusalem and the Temple. The Roman army, always willing to oblige with carnage and destruction, fulfilled His prophesy by over-throwing the Temple and the city. Not one stone was left on top of another. The year of Rome's invasion and Israel's captivity was A.D. 70.

The purpose of Israel's scattering was due to God's judgment upon the nation. "When the house of Israel was living in their own land, they defiled it by their ways and their deeds... Therefore, I poured out My wrath on them... I scattered them among the nations... when they came to the nations where they went, they profaned My holy name," Ezekiel 36:16-20.

The disciples, however, were more caught up in the signs that would accompany His return than in the intervening history of Israel's fate. The Lord, of course, obliged their curiosity by detailing several signs indicating the certain nearness of His return. Knowing many false religionists would seek to lead His children astray, Jesus sought to blunt the deceiver's deception with this comment, "For just as the lightning comes from the east, and flashes even to the west, so shall the coming of the Son of Man be," Matthew 24:27. False leaders have arisen and will yet arise in spite of His warning. They have deceived many, and many more will follow these wolves in sheepskins in the days ahead. In fact, Scripture teaches false prophets and teachers will explode on the scene in days ahead. "Don't go following after them," is Christ's warning to those who find themselves caught in the coming Tribulation period. The mad hunt for His replacement is unnecessary. His return to earth will be seen and known by all in that coming great day. The manner of His coming and the purpose of it we will see later in this book.

Jesus On The Time Of His Return

The timing of the Lord's return has been in the minds, on the hearts and across the lips of every generation. On more than one occasion, the Lord Himself answered questions as to the time of His return for His disciples. In every instance He left it an undated event. "But of that day and hour no one knows, not even the angels of heaven, nor the Son, but the Father alone," Matthew 24:36. "Therefore, be on the alert, for you do not know which day your Lord is coming," Matthew 24:42. "The master of that slave will come on a day when he does not expect him and at an hour which he does not know," Matthew 24:50. "Be on the alert then, for you do not know the day nor the hour," Matthew 25:13.

On the Lord Jesus' last day on earth, the day of His ascension, He was once again asked the question: "'Lord, is it at this time You are restoring the kingdom to Israel?' He said to them, 'It is not for you to know the times or epochs which the Father has fixed by His own authority; but you shall receive power when the Holy Spirit has come upon you...'" Acts 1:6-8. Establishing an earthly kingdom was not their concern. Their business was to *"receive power."* *"Power"* for what? *"Power"* for wisdom, service and faithfulness. The Lord knew the difficulty of leading people with a view only of this world toward investing themselves in eternal values. Things have not changed much since then. Therefore, it is best for us also to leave the timing of His return to a certain and unknown day. If you hear of someone predicting a date, go ahead and plan a picnic. It probably won't even rain!

Every generation has had signs of the Lord Jesus' return. And what did they do? Some prepared, most didn't. What are we doing? Some diligently worship the Lord with every breath, word and deed. They race through His fields scattering seed, cultivating and harvesting, ever attentive to the trumpet's sound. Most, however, do not and will not. What do you believe past generations would have done knowing the day and the hour of the Lord's return? I'll take an accurate stab at it. Less than what they did then and less than what most do now. I am guessing the Lord knew that, too! Without question, God has chosen to leave His Son's return an undated event, yet one to be expected at any time. And for more good reasons than you can probably imagine now.

The Apostles On The Time Of Christ's Return

The Apostles Paul, Peter and John all vouched for the return of Christ Jesus and taught many aspects concerning His coming.

While the Apostles often amplified Christ's return, and with much teaching, yet none sought to fix a date. Paul in his first letter to the Thessalonians wrote, "Now as to the times and the epochs (i.e. seasons and dates), brethren, you have no need of anything to be written to you. For you yourselves know full well that the day of the Lord will come just like a thief in the night," (I Thessalonians 5:2). The *"day of the Lord"* is in reference to the Tribulation period. *"Like a thief in the night"* is a description of how the lost in and out of the church will be caught when God's judgment comes upon the world. Though speaking often on the subject, no date was ever set by Paul. His hearers, therefore, had no indication of the timing of the Lord's second coming.

Peter's teaching was identical. "But the day of the Lord will come like a thief," II Peter 3:10. This picture of the Lord's coming *"like a thief,"* is used on several occasions. It is a picture of an intruder catching someone unaware. Had the homeowner known when the thief was coming, he would not have been taken by surprise.

To His mostly *"dead"* and dying church in Sardis John penned the words the Lord Jesus gave him: "Remember therefore what you received and heard; and keep it, and repent. If therefore you will not wake up, I will come like a thief, and you will not know at what hour I will come upon you," Revelation 3:3. Again, *"like a thief"* designates certain people being caught unaware.

Paul, in I Thessalonians 5:4-6, makes it clear God's people will not be overtaken as by *"a thief."* Those taken unaware at the Lord's return will be engulfed in the Tribulation period, a time of God's wrath on the world. What a horrible way to be caught. What a nightmare to try and live through, and for one's family to be drug into. Though God's children know neither the day nor the hour, *they will be ready.* But, we also ought to be found *"doing"* when He comes (Matthew 24:46).

The Signs Of Christ's Return

Has there ever been a generation that has witnessed *all* the signs of Christ's return since the completion of Scripture? No, not one! Though some may have come close. Now combine *all* the signs being present with a convergence and an escalation in intensity of each of the signs as we are witnessing to today. This acceleration and escalation is in itself a sure indication of the Lord's coming season. Before a volcano erupts there is always a pressure packed buildup leading toward its predictable explosion. The same is true concerning the signs of Christ's return. Every sign must be present and there must be a growing intensity in each of them if they are heralds of His return.

Will He come in your lifetime or mine? Until He *"shouts,"* only God knows. But don't invest your life savings in things remaining as they have always been. Until the Lord returns our responsibility is to be looking for that great day, hastening it and being busy in the Master's fields.

Some of the greatest signs of the Lord's return will be seen throughout the remainder of this book: the minor signs in this chapter, and Israel in the next. Others we will encounter shortly include: a revival of the old Roman Empire; the rise of the kings of the north; an end time economic Babylon; and a two hundred million man army from the east. We will see all these and more in detail. I'll categorize these just mentioned as the *major signs*.

But there are a number of other signs that are the early indicators. We will just briefly mention some of them here. These I will take the liberty to call the *minor signs* of Christ Jesus' return. Though their buildup is anything but minor.

The Minor Signs

These "minor" signs, given by our Lord and recorded in Matthew 24, were spoken to His disciples in answer to their question, *"... what will be the sign of Your coming?"* verse 3. But don't let my entitlement of them as *minor* distract you from how devastating each of these will be. These signs will find their unequaled fulfillment during the Tribulation also called: the Time of Jacob's Trouble and the Time of Israel's Travail. However, they are greatly relevant to us as well. Signs may or may not occur overnight. Two things are to be diligently looked for in reference to the days of Christ Jesus' return. First, are *all* the signs mentioned in Scripture present? Second, is there *a build up* intensifying each of these predicted signs? In other words, is each of the signs increasing in intensity in our day? Let's see!

1. False Religions

"See to it that no one misleads you. For many will come in My name, saying, 'I am the Christ,' and will mislead many," Matthew 24:4, 5.

False religions from cults to occults, from sects to "me-to" groups, from denominations to non-denominations, some of which once held to the Word of God but who have since departed from it, proliferate the planet. Just check America's daily filings of new 501(c) (3) groups claiming, "we've found the truth." Truth has certainly been obscured today, but it has never been lost. Yet, it is understandable with church buildings on every corner that confusion dramatically increases with the number of varying "groups." Even more confusing to the lost all around us is the departure from the faith by seemingly mainline denominations.

In addition to wandering "Christian" groups has been the tendency of many to change the Word of God to "update" its relevance to our changing mores. Therefore, practices abhorred by God in the "ancient" days, are now deemed common practices in certain churches. Adultery is permitted. Child molesters are protected. Homosexuality is an acceptable lifestyle. Women are ordained to ministry. How do we explain to past and future generations that a woman can be *"the husband of one wife,"* I Timothy 3:2? It's easy! You either change the Scriptures, or you deny them. Teachings that would have caused past generations to run in stark amazement from the church before lightening strikes are the norm in pulpits across America and around the world.

Signs of decay in the moral fabric of America should be sounding the loudest and most condemning alarms on the disintegrating reality of American Christianity. And those warnings should begin in the pulpits and resonate through the pews. But alas, the world is far more likely to condemn us before most "spiritual leaders" will. I refer to America here because the churches of most every other nation parted with truth long before America began sinking to her lowest levels of apostasy. The greatest problems among ministers today are jealousy and fear — jealousy of another minister's accomplishments, and fear of comparison. With those realities in leadership positions, what are we to believe of those in the pew.

The difficulty in talking with many about Christ today is due not just to cowardice but also to religious dogma camouflaging truth. Even Jehovah's Witnesses and Mormons call themselves Christian today. To our shame the world doesn't know the difference. The only good characteristic of Islam is they will never call themselves Christian.

A childhood friend recently said, "Everyone claims to have truth. My way is the only way; everyone else is wrong. Who really knows what truth is?" If you were the devil and wanted to discredit God's way, what better arsenal could you draw from than to instigate many religions, sects and denominations?

The Christian church is still Satan's enemy, but only so long as it takes him to get them fighting about stained glass windows or the color of new carpeting. Satan is crafty and deceptive. Most especially will that be true during the Tribulation. Many will look for a savior, and any savior will do.

Dr. M. R. DeHaan, in his book The Second Coming of Jesus (page 9, published in 1944), said this. "Never before in the history of the world has there been so much deception practiced by those who claim to be the saviours of civilization and of the world. It is said that in the last one hundred years there have been no less than thirty-six men who have claimed to be the Messiah, and these have deluded millions. Today there are an undetermined number of men and even women who claim deity. They call themselves by divine titles and say they are messiahs or a savior."

Those numbers have skyrocketed in the intervening sixty-three years, Dr. DeHaan. While there are still a good number of Bible believing, Bible teaching and Spirit-filled churches around, the silly little commercial in the late 1980s for Life Alert Emergency Response seems to best state the sad condition of the vast majority, "Help, I've fallen and I can't get up."

2. Wars and Rumors of Wars

"And you will be hearing of wars and rumors of wars; see that you are not frightened, for those things must take place, but that is not yet the end. For nation will rise against nation, and kingdom against kingdom..." Matthew 24:6.

Here again, there is little value in elaboration. All one needs to do is turn on the news. Since the beginning of recorded history man has risen against man, family against family, nation against nation. Conflicts and wars will continue until the Lord's coming. They will also continue growing in fierceness and frequency. Though wars have always been horrifying, yet only in the last few decades has man had the ability to destroy every living thing on Earth.

Recently a radio talk show host commented. "Don't worry folks, God made this planet and He made it unique. It is impossible for man to destroy the Earth." Sorry sir, but you are wrong. The only reason man will not be able to destroy the planet is because the Lord Jesus will step in and cut Armageddon short, just in a nick of time (Matthew 24:22).

Keeping up with the wars and saber rattling around the world today could drive a person mad. Multiplied numbers of fingers and toes are needed just to count them. But, consider this! Wait until the water and food wars begin.

Christ's words to His own are comforting and encouraging: "Don't be overly concerned." Besides, we have the advantage of knowing the beginning from the end, "... see that you are not frightened, for those things must take place, but that is not the end."

3. Famines

"... and in various places there will be famines," Matthew 24:7f.

Through the millennia of human history, famines have come and gone. No more! In our day, famines in a world of plenty are the cause of 35,000 deaths a day, every day of the year. That's right. Every day! More than 1/3 the world's population is malnourished. The United Nations Food and Agriculture Organization estimates one in six people on earth are suffering from acute to chronic hunger.

Every decade world hunger grows more grave and desperate. The trend is set in concrete. Yet, some of the world's religious and political groups are the greatest culprits in causing hunger, malnourishment and starvation. Famines, once caused by war or nature, are now more the result of personal greed, selfishness, hatred and strife. But don't rule out present and coming wars wreaking continuing havoc on the hungry bellies of infants, children and adults of all ages.

America has been the breadbasket of the world. To what do you suppose the present hunger levels will rise when America's grain crops, and those of other developed nations, are diverted to making fuel for transportation rather than offering families a meal a day? Why is this? Is it because oil is running out? No! Oil will never run out. It is because Congress will not allow the drilling of America's vast oil resources. All in the name of two of the greatest hoaxes ever perpetrated since man set foot on Earth, global warming and (whacko) environmentalism. This is the generation of fools at the helm.

4. Earthquakes

"... and in various places there will be... earthquakes," Matthew 24:7f.

The most nature shaking earthquakes will rattle the Earth during the Tribulation. Today's growing intensity and frequency of earthquakes, however, is surprising everyone. Little needs be said. Simply look over the below seven year chart of worldwide earthquakes reported by the U.S. Geological Survey National Earthquake Information Center for the startling facts. The following is for all magnitudes. (* Indicates incomplete results.)

YEAR:	2000	2001	2002	2003	2004	2005	2006
Number:	22,256	23,534	27,454	31,419	31,194	30,478	*29,534

Scientists, who generally hold back nothing, tell us the number of earthquakes over the past 100 years is on the rise and far out number those of any other corresponding time period. The phrase in the above verse, *"in various places,"* is a Greek expression meaning there will be earthquakes in several places at the same time. Ask the Japanese. They recently experience not one, but two jolting earthquakes in the same day from different ends of their nation. Go to the above earthquake information center to see the dates, times and magnitudes listed for all earthquakes by year. This old globe is indeed rocking and rolling.

After the Lord's forecast of escalations of false Christs, wars, famines and earthquakes we find these amazing words, "But all these things are merely the beginning of birth pangs," Matthew 24:8. As a woman experiences birth pangs prior to giving birth, these above named catastrophes are merely the beginning of troubles. These events occur in increased velocity, strength and numbers prior to the Tribulation on earth.

The world will be subjected to these pre-tribulation diffi- culties we've just listed from Matthew 24:4-8. Most espe- cially, however, these early problems will affect the people of Israel (Matthew 24:9) with "hatred by all nations." Have you taken into account the attitudes and hatred of the vast majority of countries that compose the United Nations? Antichrist will at this time "confirm a (peace) covenant" for Israel (Daniel 9:27), possibly The Road Map To Peace In The Middle East, brokered by the infamous Quartet (U.S., E.U., U.N. and Russia). Difficulties grow worse and worse for God's beleaguered people. Many will be caused to stumble and begin to hate one another (Matthew 24:10). More false prophets come out of the woodwork (Matthew 24:11) as hope and help is searched for from every quarter of earth. As bad as this is for Israel, these trials will cause her to eventu- ally seek Jehovah God, the Lord Jesus Christ.

More tribulations are on the way.

5. Lawlessness Increases And Love Is Lost

"And because lawlessness is increased, most people's love will grow cold," Matthew 24:12.

Could anyone two or three decades ago have imagined the degradation of morality and law that is commonplace today. Indeed, these are the days of the good being considered bad, and the bad being considered good. From the highest courts in the land to the man down the street sin has been enthroned and decency hidden in the closet. Sexual desires cannot be satisfied. Alcohol and drug use is deemed common and acceptable behavior. When addiction develops it is no longer the result of sin, but sickness. Mothers are given the right to kill their unborn, even at the moment of birth around the globe. Numbers reaching one and a half million abortions a year in America feed the pocketbooks of greedy doctors, nurses and attorneys throughout the land. Rather than an atrocious and wicked sin against humanity, killing of the unborn is a choice, a protected right. Hitler never slaughtered so many innocents. Responsibility is a thing of the bygone past and less enlightened generations! Problems and accidents are always the fault of another. Homosexuality, once shunned in dark alleys, is acceptable lifestyle. Speak out against such lawless and unnatural God-condemned behavior and it could well be off to jail most any day now. Quoting Scripture on homosexuality is a "hate crime" punishable by astronomical fines and jail in Canada — and parts of America The No Longer So Beautiful. Sodom's sins today dim in light of America's pernicious and promiscuous behavior, whether practiced or permitted.

Lawlessness increasing invariably leads to love growing cold. How else could mothers and fathers beat up, rape, drown and grind up their small children? In part, abortion validates butchering of the defenseless. How can children kill children? "Foolishness is bound up (always has been) in the heart of a child; (but, I thought) the rod of discipline will remove it far from him," Proverbs 22:15. What has happened? Oh, I nearly forgot. Parents aren't allowed to punish, correct and discipline with the rod any longer due to the wisdom of our courts and legislators. From where does road rage come, ball game rage, and all the rages of the world? It derives in hearts where love is colder than the polar cap.

Though each of these signs reach their zenith in the Tribulation period, they do not begin and mushroom to Tribulation levels overnight. There is a build up we have witnessed since the days of World War II that has over the past few years accelerated beyond anyone's comprehension. But there is some good along with the bad. Nevertheless, they too are signs.

6. Increase In Knowledge And Travel

"But as for you, Daniel, conceal these words and seal up the book until the end of time; many will go back and forth, and knowledge will increase," Daniel 12:4.

It is interesting to note that while Daniel is told to *"conceal these words and seal up the book,"* John is told the opposite: *"Do not seal up the words of the prophecy of this book,"* Revelation 22:10. The reasoning is simple. Daniel was to "conceal and seal ... **until** the end of time." John was "not to seal... **for the time is near**."

We have the good fortune of living in the days for Daniel's book to be *revealed* and *unsealed?*

"Many will go back and forth." "Back and forth" speaks of vast travel as a sign of "the end of time." In Daniel's day, and up until about the mid-1800, travel was unchanged: a horse, or a horse and a buggy were the only choices. Six horse-power transportation was a cart with six horses. I'm sure that was fun, but talk about the maintenance! For the first nearly 6,000 years of human history, the ability to go from one place to another was essentially the same – the speed of the animal. (I beg the pardon of any carbon-testing whacko that may perchance read this.) In only a little over one-hundred-fifty years the ability to "go back and forth" has moved from the horse and buggy to the steam engine, to the automobile, to airplanes and now to spacecraft. To say

land, air, sea and space travel has dramatically increased is a vast understatement. And, it is not by just a few people, but by *"many"* the Scripture says. It is the masses today that "go back and forth." Thus, we have another sure sign the Lord's coming is not far away.

Not only does travel increase, but Daniel was informed *"knowledge"* in these last days will increase as well. This is mind-boggling to anyone trying to keep up with the increase of knowledge. From the time of the flood until the 19th Century *"knowledge"* doubled only about once. From the beginning of the 19th Century until the 20th Century *"knowledge"* doubled again. From the beginning of the 20th Century until 1950 it doubled about every ten to fifteen years. By the end of the Century *"knowledge"* was doubling every six months, or less. Today human *"knowledge"* is doubling at unprecedented speed.

Consider this. Well over ninety percent of all medicines ever developed have been developed since 1945. Ninety percent of all scientists that have ever lived are living today. It has been said that computers duplicate in a few minutes today the life work of all engineers who ever lived prior to a decade ago.

The rapid increases in "travel and knowledge" are God-given signs Jesus is coming — shortly! Very, very shortly!

7. The Universal Preaching Of The Gospel

"And the gospel of the kingdom shall be preached in the whole world for a witness to all the nations, and then the end shall come," Matthew 24:14.

Godly Christians and denominations are seeking to fulfill this sign in our lifetime. And the means are all available today. Yet, it will not be the Christian church that succeeds in this noble venture. Worldwide evangelism will find its fulfillment during the second half of the Tribulation. At the midpoint of the seven years of Tribulation 144,000 signed, sealed and delivered Jewish evangelists will deliver the Gospel message to every tribe, nation, tongue and people. We'll see more of this amazing group of worldwide evangelists soon. As with all signs, there is a build up or an increasing movement toward the ultimate fulfillment of world evangelization. Maybe satellite TV paves the way? Huh? What do you think? Think about it! The depths of degradation preached by Imas and his like could be hijacked during the Tribulation to preach the Gospel of Jesus Christ in the hearing of every ear around the globe.

Never before in the history of the world has there been the ability to instantaneously broadcast to the entire earth. There is now! Through landlines, airwaves and satellites the preaching of the Gospel is readily available to virtually every speck on the planet. Many of these means will be limited during the Tribulation, but that won't stop the work of God in a final outreach to the unsaved. The Internet may help. But don't minimize the efforts of 144,000 amazing evangelists.

Well, that's it for what I've termed "minor signs" of the Lord Jesus' return. The minor signs all in place point us to greater indicators of God's work in our day bringing about His people's full redemption and the greatest, most cataclysmic changes since the creation of Genesis 1 and Noah's Ark of Genesis 7.

Let's now begin a closer look at the "major signs."

Chapter 3

Israel

The Critics Unanswerable Dilemma!

ISRAEL — The Infallible Sign Of Christ's Return

Other than the signs previously listed that I dubbed "minor signs," there are other signs, or indicators of the Lord Jesus' second coming. These I dubbed as "major signs." That is because they are bigger indicators as to where we stand today in reference to the end times. These are enormously gigantic, mammoth signs! Add the end time signs of false religions, wars and rumors of wars, famines, earthquakes, lawlessness, the increase in knowledge and the explosion of travel together and they will not measure up to what you are about to see. I call it, "The Infallible Sign of Christ's Return." But this is not the last major signpost we will discover.

The reality of spiritual warfare will be found nowhere pronounced more clearly than in the people and in the history of Israel. From her calling out as a nation she has been God's *"special treasure."* But, allow me to allow Scripture to speak for itself.

A Special Treasure

To Israel, upon her exodus from Egypt, God declared, "Now then, if you will indeed obey My voice and keep My covenants, then you shall be My special treasure among all the peoples, for all the earth is Mine," Exodus 19:5. Moses, on many occasions, reminded Israel of her special place in the heart and plan of God. "For you are a holy people to the Lord your God; the Lord your God has chosen you to be a people for His special treasure out of all the peoples who are on the face of the earth," Deuteronomy 7:6.

This same statement in its exact words was used again by Moses in Deuteronomy 14:2. In Psalm 135:4 the psalmist wrote, "For the Lord has chosen Jacob for Himself, Israel for His special treasure." The Old Testament concludes with these same words, even in a day of Israeli apostasy, "'And they will be Mine,' says the Lord of hosts, 'on the day that I prepare My special treasure, and I will spare them as a man spares his own son who serves him,'" Malachi 3:17. This same promise and quote is echoed again in the New Testament.

In Matthew 13, in parabolic form, the Lord Jesus declared His future intention for the nation of Israel. "The kingdom of heaven is like a treasure hidden in the field, which a man found and hid; and from joy over it he goes and sells all that he has, and buys that field," verse 44. This parable is one, not the only one, but one, of the most misinterpreted parables in the Bible. Those misinterpreting it generally do so to protect another error. The first error is in teaching this parable and the next parable of a merchant seeking fine pearls as both teaching the same truth. They do have similarities, but they are vastly different. The first is in reference to Israel, and the second parable references the church. This group's second error is based on their first error. It is to protect their belief, or desire, to write off the Israel of today as descendents of the Israel to whom God made a special promise: "I will bless those who bless you, and the one who curses you I will curse," Genesis 12:3. That promise, by the way, has been unaltered by God for four millennia now. Let me recommend to you William Koenig's book, *Eye to Eye*, published by About Him Publishing, Copyright © 2004. Nations that have blessed Israel, even in her dispersion, have been blessed. And nations that have cursed her have been likewise cursed. This group's erroneous doctrine is called "replacement theology." It replaces Israel with the church as descendents of the promise, and leads to dangerous nation destroying beliefs and actions through cursing Israel. We'll get more into that and its devastating results later, especially in reference to America and her changing political persuasions.

Parables are spiritual truths clothed in down-to-earth stories. In the parable of the treasure hidden in the field national salvation for Israel is procured as the *"man... goes and sells all that he has, and buys that field."* The *"man,"* of course, is the Lord Jesus Christ. The *"field"* is the world. He *"found and hid"* again the *"treasure"* within it. Buying the *"field"* He assured the *"treasure hidden in the field"* would be His at the time of His choosing. That *"treasure"* is Israel, God's *"special treasure"* throughout the Old Testament. The time of His revealing this *"special treasure"* forever will occur at the midpoint of the Tribulation as Israel recognizes Him as her Messiah and Lord.

Paul, teaching on Israel's present spiritual condition, informs us of this very thing, "For I do not want you, brethren, to be uninformed of this mystery, lest you be wise in your own estimation, that a partial hardening has happened to Israel until the fullness of the Gentiles has come in; and thus all Israel will be saved," Romans 11:25, 26a.

Of course, God has an archenemy. Should a people or a nation be His *"special treasure,"* rest assured fire from the dragon will be directed toward that group. This, too, is seen throughout the Bible and in modern day history. Addressing their situation in Egypt, from which Israel received God's deliverance, Moses reminded them, "But the Lord has taken you and brought you out of the iron furnace, from Egypt, to be a people for His own possession, as today," Deuteronomy 4:20.

The fierce pressure Israel faced, would often face and continues to face is described as an *"iron furnace"* on numerous occasions in Scripture. Satan is alive and well and savagely contesting God's purpose in heaven and on earth. Prayer, faith and perseverance are the chief weapons of the people of God. Never forget the practical reality of spiritual truth; while this war is fought in heaven, Satan's battles are directed on earth toward the people of God. Again, prayer, faith and perseverance are the only keys to victory.

This truth has never escaped the minds of God's people in the past or present. Listen to Solomon's dedicatory prayer over the house of God. In reference to Israel he prays, "... for they are Thy people and Thine inheritance which Thou has brought forth from Egypt, from the midst of the iron furnace," I Kings 8:51. Later Jeremiah would refer to Israel's deliverance from Egypt when God told him to speak to the men of Judah and Jerusalem, "Thus, says the Lord, the God of Israel, 'Cursed is the man who does not heed the words of this covenant which I commanded your forefathers in the day that I brought them out of the land of Egypt, from the iron furnace, saying, "Listen to My voice, and do according to all which I command you; so you shall be My people, and I will be your God,"'" Jeremiah 11:3, 4.

Satan's strongest assaults are against those God desires to bless and use. Because of that God told Abraham and his descendants, "I will bless those who bless you, and the one who curses you I will curse," Genesis 12:3. Being on God's side can be costly— then and now. Nevertheless, accept it by faith; coming rewards are worth the price of victory won through diligence. But be assured, if God gives the promise of a blessing, understand Satan has other designs. Against no one has this been more real than Israel, the *"special treasure"* of God. It was through her the Word of God came to all men. It was through her that Messiah the Lord and Deliverer came on behalf of all men. It is for her the Lord Jesus is coming to earth again for all men. With God's love and purpose for Israel, expect the dragon's fury toward her to be ruthless and vile. Israel has incontestably paid the price, and it is a price that continues to be exacted from her to this day.

Daniel's Seventieth Week, the Tribulation period, will be Satan's all out attack on Israel. He must thwart the purpose of God. The ethnic cleansing of Israel was his strategy in the past and continues to be so today. In this and the following chapters are the nations and their rolls Satan purposes to use in his attempt to dash God's plan for the ages. I call the evidence of them the "major signs" of Christ Jesus' return. The magnitude of their significance today is found in comparing 2,500-year-old prophecy concerning the end times with today's on-the-ground realities.

A Secular History Of Israel's Rebirth

As a nation, Israel was overthrown and taken captive by Rome in A.D. 70. Her people were scattered among the nations of the world. As little as 55 years ago, with the exception of a few Bible believing men and women, the thought of Israel becoming a nation again was cause for derision and laughter. Ask any historian how long a nation can remain in captivity and still become a nation again, and they have one answer. "Any nation taken captive and scattered among other nations of the world must find a way to reconstitute within two generations. After that through death, adapted lives and intermarriage a re-nationalization is impossible."

Israel, however, broke the mold. Scattered in the first century, her people were persecuted and despised throughout the entire world. Many intermarried with those in their adopted cultures. Others found it impossible to blend into society. Yet, today in the 21st Century since Israel was scattered among the nations, the Jewish bloodline has been supernaturally kept intact. Explain it away as some seek to do, Israel's existence remains a God-thing. I am finding more and more people today, many claiming to be Christian, who dispute Israel's right to Palestine with the excuse, "This Israel is not the Israel of the Old Testament. Even if they were what right do they have to reclaim that land after all these years. Who do they think they are that after nearly two thousand years they can walk in and say, 'This land is mine?'" Let me be plain and kind and explain it in a way such individuals can understand. "God gave the land of Palestine to Israel and has continued to preserve it for her throughout her great dispersion! Argue with Him, if you will!"

Here is the short story of Israel's literal and miraculous reformation. World War I was fully engaged. England was desperate for a rapid method of producing TNT and a smokeless gunpowder. A Jewish Englishman named Chaim Weizmann invented both. His discoveries changed the course of the war. Prime Minister David Lloyd George asked Mr. Weizmann to name his reward. His request was for Palestine to be named a national homeland for the Jewish people.

Palestine, taken from the Ottoman Turks, was under English rule. Therefore, the Balfour Declaration was drawn up and signed on November 2, 1917. Below is England's concession to the rights of the Jewish people to occupy and develop the land.

The Balfour Declaration

Dear Lord Rothchild,
I have much pleasure in conveying to you, on behalf of his Majesty's Government, the

following declaration of sympathy with Jewish Zionist aspirations, which has been submitted to, and approved by, the Cabinet.

His Majesty's Government views with favor the establishment in Palestine of a national home for the Jewish people, and will use their best endeavors to facilitate the achievement of this objective, it being clearly understood that nothing shall be done which may prejudice the civil and religious rights of existing non-Jewish communities in Palestine, or the rights and political status enjoyed by Jews in any other country.

I should be grateful if you would bring this declaration to the knowledge of the Zionist Federation.

Sincerely Yours,

Arthur James Balfour

The stage was set for Israel to reclaim a portion of her God-given land for a homeland. Thirty years down the road she would constitute as a nation with international backing.

In 1918 the Jewish population of Palestine increased to 50,000 people. By 1932 it had risen to 175,000. In 1935 Israel had grown to a 375,000 population. At the outset of 1948 Israel boasted of having 850,000 Jewish citizens in residence. By the year 2000 there were over 6,000,000 Jewish people living in the land of God's promise to Abraham, Isaac and Jacob. That was better than 1 out of every 3 Jews in the world and was rapidly increasing. Today's Israeli population is estimated at 7,100,000 residents.

With her 1918 bequest bestowed, hatred for the Jewish people rapidly multiplied as was evident by the events of

World War II. Thus, on May 15, 1948 a group of Jewish renegades, terrorists in the eyes of many, walked into the United Nations in New York City, threw a map of the world on the desk and demanded, "Give us our land back."

"What right do you have to it?" the august World Council asked. "God gave it to our father, Abraham," they replied. A line was drawn around a small portion of the actual God-given land of Palestine. Israel became a nation for the first time since A.D. 70 with the granting of *a small share* of her God-given inheritance.

Arab nations quickly united to destroy this speck of a new nation on three occasions — each occasion to their own defeat. Jerusalem, the West Bank and the Gaza Strip were won in these battles and held onto due to their defensive positions necessary for Israel's protection, and indeed her survival. There seems to be something strange about this smallest of nations among the nations of the world and her ability to survive and prosper. There definitely is! No one else has ever caused that desert area to blossom like a rose. Such blooms, however, faded back into desert sands with the return of Gaza to the so-called "Palestinians."

The Psalmist stated God's purpose in the reconstituting and building up of Israel:

> *"When the Lord has build up Zion,*
> *He shall appear in His glory."*
> *Psalm 102:16*

Israel, God's Timepiece

To birth the nation of Israel, God called out Abram from Ur of the Chaldeans (Acts 7:2, 3). In doing so, He shifted from dealing with the nations and began to deal with a man and his family. From this family God would transform Jacob the son of Isaac, the son of Abraham, rename him Israel and birth the nation. Through the descendents of Israel God gave the commandments, the ordinances and at the appropriate time His Son. The nation He chose, however, would reject Jesus, God's Son and Israel's Messiah. From Genesis to Revelation we find the double-edged sword of rejection on one side and salvation on the other. "He came to His own, and those who were His own did not receive Him. But to as many as received Him, to them He gave the right to become children of God, even to those who believe in His name," John 1:11, 12.

Thus, after her rejection of Christ, Israel was *"broken off for (her) unbelief,"* Romans 11:20. Israel's being *"broken off"* allowed *"a wild olive"* branch to be grafted in (Romans 11:17). That *"wild olive"* branch is the church of the Lord Jesus Christ made up of Jews and Gentiles alike throughout the world. But what about Israel? What happens to the nation God chose, the special treasure He sat aside? The Scriptures teach throughout, "... if they do not continue in their unbelief, (they) will be grafted in; for God is able to graft them in again," Romans 11:23.

In setting Israel aside, and promising to deal with her again, Israel has become God's timepiece in dealing with the entire human race. Should you desire to discern God's calendar of events for this world, keep your eye on Israel. That is why she is called *"the center (or, navel) of the world,"* Ezekiel 38:12. She is the polestar of all God's dealings with mankind and His program for the ages.

So, what does the Bible forecast for Israel's future? Does she have one? Does God's Word speak of a national rebirth for Israel after nearly two millennia of dispersion? Let's see!

The Biblical History Of Israel Foretold

Among many Scriptural passages to select from one in particular mentions five main points concerning Israel and the land God gave her. In doing so, He outlines Israel's "history to come." This passage from **Ezekiel 36** is over 2,500 years old. The prophecy it contains, as you will see, is rapidly moving to fulfillment before our eyes today.

1. The Nations' Insults Of Israel Will Cease To Be (verses 1-7)

In this passage God declares His purpose for the land He gave to Abraham and to his descendents through Isaac. These verses need to be tacked to the walls of every Christian church and seminary in the world.

"And you, son of man, prophesy to the mountains of Israel and say, 'O mountains of Israel, hear the word of the Lord. Thus says the Lord God, "Because the enemy has spoken against you, 'Aha!' and, 'The everlasting heights have become our possession,' therefore, prophesy and say, 'Thus says the Lord God, "For good cause they have made you desolate and crushed you from every side, that you should become a possession of the rest of the nations, and you have been taken up in the talk and the whispering of the people."' Therefore, O mountains of Israel, hear the word of the Lord God. Thus says the Lord God to the mountains and to the hills, to the ravines and to the valleys, to the desolate wastes and to the forsaken cities, which have become a prey and a derision to the rest of the nations which are round about, therefore, thus says the Lord God, "Surely in the fire of My jealousy I have spoken against the rest of the nations, and against all Edom, who appropriated My land for themselves as a possession with wholehearted joy and with scorn of soul, to drive it out for a prey." Therefore, prophesy concerning the land of Israel, and say to the mountains and to the hills, to the ravines and to the valleys, "Thus says the Lord God, 'Behold, I have spoken in My jealousy and in My wrath because you have endured the insults of the nations.'

Therefore, thus says the Lord God, 'I have sworn that surely the nations which are around you will themselves endure their insults.'"""

Today, being willfully ignorant of the Word of God, the Arab/Muslim nations all around Israel continue to ask, "What right do you have to this land?" The answer as always is, "It is God's land. He apportioned it to Israel." Because of this land and because of Israel's being the chosen people of God, the descendents of Ishmael continue to this day to broadcast their unveiled threats of the annihilation of Israel and the possession of her land. The Islamic nation's ravings will continue for a little while longer. But they will cease to exist.

2. Israel Will Come Back Into The Land of Promise (verses 8-15)

In these verses God informs the world He will bring Israel back into the Land of Promise after a great dispersion. Scorned, insulted and disgraced by the nations of the world, Israel will "stumble (no) longer," verse 15.

"But you, O mountains of Israel, you will put forth your branches and bear your fruit for My people Israel; for they will soon come. For, behold, I am for you, and I will turn to you, and you shall be cultivated and sown. And I will multiply men on you, all the house of Israel, all of it; and the cities will be inhabited, and the waste places will be rebuilt... Yes, I will cause men — My people Israel — to walk on you and posses you, so that you will become their inheritance and never again bereave them of children," verses 8-10, 12.

That is God's promise and stated purpose.

3. God Tells Us Why He Scattered Israel Many Years Ago (verses 16-20)

Her many acts of unfaithfulness were the reasons for Israel's scattering among the nations.

"Son of man, when the house of Israel was living in their own land, they defiled it by their ways and their deeds; their way before Me was like the uncleanness of a woman in her impurity. Therefore, I poured out My wrath on them for the blood which they had shed on the land, because they had defiled it with their idols. Also I scattered them among the nations, and they were dispersed throughout the lands. According to their ways and their deeds I judged them. When they came to the nations where they went, they profaned My holy name, because it was said of them, 'These are the people of the Lord; yet they have come out of His land.'" verses 17-20.

God does judge the sins of a nation, including His *"special treasure."* If He will judge Israel, what right do we as Americans have to believe He will not judge us?

4. God Will Bring Israel Back In Unbelief (verses 21-24)

Israel's return to the Land is not for any righteous acts or merits of her own. Nor is it that she has been punished long enough. Her restoration is for God's righteousness sake.

"I had concern for My holy name, which the house of Israel had profaned among the nations where they went. Therefore, say to the house of Israel, 'Thus says the Lord God, "It is not for your sake, O house of Israel, that I am about to act, but for My holy name, which you have profaned among the nations where you went. And I will vindicate the holiness of My great name which has been profaned among the nations, which you have profaned in their midst. Then the nations will know that I am the Lord," declares the Lord

God, "when I prove Myself holy among you in their sight."'
'For I will take you from the nations, gather you from all the
lands, and bring you into your own land," verses 21-24.

All this will be accomplished for God's namesake, even
though Israel does not yet acknowledge Jesus as the Son of
God, her Redeemer.

5. God Makes A Promise To Israel *After* She Returns To Her Land (verses 25-27)

Points 1-4 above have already taken place with #4
continuing to this day. *The promises of Ezekiel 26:25-27 have
not yet come to pass.* They are relegated to the Tribulation
period, the time of Jacob's Trouble, the time of Israel's
Travail. At this soon appointed time God promises Israel He
will do three things for her. This is after she returns to her
God given Land in unbelief, and after she comes to a saving
knowledge of the Lord Jesus Christ.

In parenthesis and in italics, after each of these state-
ments of things God will do for Israel, you will find a New
Testament parallel, a counterpart, experiences of the child of
God today — Jew or Gentile.

Verse 25 — *"Then"* He Will Cleanse Israel

"Then (after Israel is brought back into Palestine in
unbelief) I will sprinkle clean water on you, and you will be
clean; I will cleanse you from all your filthiness and from all
your idols."

After returning to her land (during the Tribulation) Israel
will come to a saving knowledge of the Lord Jesus Christ.
She will be cleansed from all her *"filthiness."* Here is the
fulfillment of God's promise, "'Come now, and let us reason
together,' says the Lord, "'though your sins are as scarlet,
they will be as white as snow; though they are red like

crimson, they will be like wool,'" Isaiah 1:18. The first thing God does when Israel comes to a saving knowledge of her Redeemer is He cleanses her of all her sins. Sins past, sins present, sins future — God *"cleanses her of all her sins."*

(New Testament parallel: John 1:29; Romans 8:1; I John 3:5.)

Verse 26 — *"Moreover"* He Will Give Israel A New Heart

"Moreover, I will give you a new heart and put a new spirit within you; and I will remove the heart of stone from your flesh and give you a heart of flesh."

Not only is Israel going to be cleansed of her sins, but she will no longer have a Covenant of righteousness by doing righteously — that is, by keeping the Ten Commandments, which neither she nor anyone else could ever do. She will be given a new heart, a new nature and new desires within herself. God's laws will be written across her *"heart of flesh."* She will do righteously because she is righteous. Born again in her *"heart"* she will possess the righteous nature of God.

(New Testament parallel: II Corinthians 3:3-5; Romans 8:11; I John 2:4.)

Verse 27 — *"And"* He Will Indwell Israel By His Spirit

"And I will put My Spirit within you and cause you to walk in My statutes, and you will be careful to observe My ordinances."

Israel will be cleansed of every sin. She will receive a new heart patterned after God's own heart. And the Holy Spirit of God will indwell her. His *"Spirit within"* her will give her the ability to accomplish her God given desires. He comes to live within her in order to do through her the will of God for her — that, my friend, is grace.

(New Testament parallel: Romans 8:9; II Corinthians 3:6; 6:16; Philippians 2:13; 4:13; I Thessalonians 5:24.)

So 2,500 years ago, five hundred years before Christ, God forewarned Israel He would scatter her for an untold number of years. He tells us why He scattered her. He notifies the world He is going to bring her back to her Land in unbelief — thereby, beginning the process of vindicating the holiness of His great name. He then shares with Israel and us what He is going to do after she returns to the Land of Promise in unbelief.

During the Tribulation period God will bring Israel through much sorrow to her Messiah, the Lord Jesus Christ. She will be cleansed. She will be given a new heart. And the Holy Spirit will inhabit her. God will impart to her His will and the power to accomplish that God given will. That is salvation from A to Z for Jews and Gentiles alike today, and for the nation of Israel collectively in a day soon to come.

Ezekiel's Valley Of Dry Bones

Israel's scattering over the centuries has made her regathering a mind-boggling, reason-defying miracle. Her vast and seemingly endless dispersion brought ridicule from the world on her and on the truth of God's Word for two millennia. Many within the church, unable to comprehend Israel's dispersion of nearly 2,000 years, spiritualized Scripture in substituting the church for Israel, the people of God the Father's own possession. Such thinking by the world and in the church is dead wrong, contrary to Scripture, and leads to ill attitudes and acts toward the Israel of God, the nation on behalf of whom God blesses those who bless her and curses those who curse her (Genesis 12:3; 27:29; Numbers 24:29). Israel is Israel, the wife of Jehovah (Isaiah 54:5). And the church is the church, the bride of the Lord

Jesus Christ (Revelation 19:7). The two are never the same — except that the redeemed of both are members of God's forever family.

Ezekiel 37 sheds additional light on vital information as to how Israel comes together as a nation. God points Ezekiel to a valley of dried, parched, and scattered skeletal remains. He then asks His servant, "Son of man, can these bones live?" verse 3. Ezekiel's answer makes you wonder if he wasn't chuckling in unbelief under his breath. He said, "O Lord God, Thou knowest," verse 3f. In other words, "What? Not by any logic or human imagination can these bones ever live again."

God then tells Ezekiel to preach to the bones, "Prophesy over these bones, and say to them, 'O dry bones, hear the word of the Lord.' Thus says the Lord God to these bones, 'Behold, I will cause breath to enter you that you may come to life. And I will put sinews on you, make flesh grow back on you, cover you with skin, and put breath in you that you may come alive; and you will know that I am the Lord,'" verses 4-6.

Ezekiel preached as God commanded and suddenly, "There was a noise, and behold, a rattling; and the bones came together, bone to its bone. And (Ezekiel) looked, and behold, sinews were on them, and flesh grew, and skin covered them; but there was no breath in them," verses 7, 8.

Again, Ezekiel was told to preach. "Prophesy to the breath, prophesy, son of man, and say to the breath, 'Thus says the Lord God, "Come from the four winds, O breath, and breathe on these slain, that they come to life,"'" verse 9. Ezekiel did as commanded, and they "came to life, and stood on their feet, an exceedingly great army," (verse 10).

To make certain no one mistakes, wrenches or distorts the meaning of this phenomenal incidence to come, God plainly gives the meaning. "Son of man, these bones are the whole house of Israel; behold they say, 'Our bones are dried up, and our hope has perished. We are completely cut off (to our unity as a nation).' Therefore prophesy, and say to them, 'Thus says the Lord God, "Behold, I will open your graves and cause you to come up out of your graves, My people; and I will bring you into the land of Israel. Then you will know that I am the Lord, when I have opened your graves and caused you to come up out of your graves, My people. And I will put My Spirit within you, and you will come to life,""" verses 11-14

Most often overlooked is the fact that that which is humanly impossible is Christ-possible when God is in it. This passage speaks of the gathering of Israel from the Balfour Declaration to the present day, and beyond. Bone has come to bone. Sinew (muscles) for strength and a governmental skin has covered the rebirthed nation of God's chosen people. But there is no life in Israel to this date. Her new life comes only when she acknowledges her crucified Messiah at the midpoint of the Tribulation. The message of the "two witnesses" (Revelation 11:1-13) during the first half of the Tribulation will resoundingly ring home to the hearts and minds of Israel when she witnesses the Abomination of Desolation. She will then turn in saving faith to her long ago crucified and resurrected Messiah, the Lord Jesus Christ, God Almighty.

Daniel's Seventy Weeks

Once again allow me to stress, God's dealings with the nations of the world revolves around His dealings with the nation of Israel. Daniel's Seventy Weeks, often mentioned yet scantily comprehended, is the key to understanding the timetable God has instituted to bring in everlasting righteousness. Here is what the Bible says about that which should be referred to as *Israel's Seventy Weeks*. In **Daniel 9:24-27** we find the angel Gabriel bringing Daniel the answer to his concerns for God's testimony on earth because of Jerusalem's reproach and Israel's sins.

Verse 24: Seventy weeks are appointed for Israel to run the course of her nation's history in several areas. First, she is "to finish the transgression" (against God). Second, she is "to make an end of sin" (before men and God). Third, she is "to make atonement for iniquity" (sacrifice the Lamb of God). Fourth, she is "to bring in everlasting righteousness" (that is, bring back the Messiah through acknowledgment of Jesus Christ). Fifth, she is "to seal up vision and prophecy" (to complete what is lacking in God's promises concerning her). And sixth, she is to "to anoint the most holy place" (the everlasting throne of God). Toward these goals Daniel is given **three timetables** foretelling Israel's history from the Persian King Artaxerxes' "decree to restore and rebuild Jerusalem" and on to the establishment of Christ's kingdom on earth.

1. First Time Table – Verse 25: "So you are to know and discern that from the issuing of a decree to restore and rebuild Jerusalem... there shall be seven weeks..." Here is the first of the three timetables. The first timetable is a *"seven week"* period. Nehemiah 2:1-8 gives the decree of King Artaxerxes' authorizing of Nehemiah's rebuilding of Jerusalem. According to historians from the time this decree was issued until Jerusalem was rebuilt was a literal period of 49 years. Yet, Scripture says it would be *"seven weeks."* Before us are a puzzle, a riddle and a mystery. The *"seven weeks"* Daniel is *"to know and discern"* and the 49 actual years it took from the decree's issuing and Jerusalem's rebuilding equal the same thing. Here is the answer to the mystery. The *"seven weeks"* represent the 49 years. (That was hard, wasn't it?) If this is correct each *"week"* represents a 7-year period; *"seven weeks"* divided into 49 years equals 7 years per *"week."* If we have the proper under-standing, each *"week"* of this prophesy must also be based on the same formula or timetable: seven years in historical reality per week in the prophesy.

Let's see if our formula for the mystery pans out.

2. Second Time Table – Verse 25: *"...* until Messiah the Prince... sixty-two weeks...."* The second timetable of *"sixty-two weeks"* begins with Jerusalem rebuilt and ends with Messiah's first coming. A chronological study of family ancestries in Scripture and historical records reveals this time period to have been 434 actual years. To see if our formula is accurate we simply divide the 434 years by *"sixty-two weeks."* Once again we find each *"week"* is representative of 7 years. The formula fits. Anyone surprised? Of course not! God's Word is literally and eternally without error. That means it's pretty accurate.

These first two prophesied time periods of Israel's future are now historical fact: *"seven weeks"* and *"sixty-two weeks"* equals a total of **sixty-nine weeks**. These match the actual historical record of 483 years from King Artaxerxes' decree until *"Messiah the Prince."* Yet, Daniel's revelation is for Israel to have a total of *"seventy weeks"* equaling 490 years.

Verse 26: "Then after the sixty-two weeks the Messiah will be cut off and have nothing..." That has a historical date as well. In fact, what happened on that date was often prophesied in the Old Testament and attested by the Lord Jesus Himself during His earthly ministry. He was *"cut off,"* rejected, crucified and had no kingdom. Well, no visible kingdom anyway! The Romans, the Jews and Satan himself all overlooked one important matter. Jesus had the authority and the ability to lay His life down, and He had the authority to raise it up again. Oh, bad and upsetting news reached Hell that day. Heaven rejoiced! The netherworld grieved, its fate being sealed.

"... And the people of the prince who is to come will destroy the city and the sanctuary." *"The people"* refers to the Roman Empire in A.D. 70. It was they who destroyed Jerusalem, dispersed the Jews and dissolved the nation of Israel. It will be from this empire **revived**, *"the prince who is to come"* will come. The anticipated antithesis of Christ will rise out of a revival of the old Roman Empire. *"The prince who is to come"* refers to Antichrist and his kingdom — revived in the last days from the historical area of the old Roman Empire. The revival of that empire we have been witnesses to over the last few decades. We know this conglomerate of nations today as the European Union. We will see more concerning her very shortly.

3. Third Time Table – Verse 27: "And he (Antichrist) will make a firm covenant with the many (Israel) for one week (7 years), but in the middle of the week (at the three and a half year point of the Tribulation) he will put a stop to sacrifice and grain offering; and on the wing of abominations will come one who makes desolate, even until a complete destruction, one that is decreed, is poured out on the one who makes desolate." The *"one who comes on the wings of abomination... who makes desolate,"* and will come to *"a complete destruction"* is Satan Himself. He duplicates the Holy Spirit's work by indwelling Antichrist. The hordes of fallen angels reserved in Hell break loose on earth from this point of the Tribulation until the end. Their time to act, however, is short. And Satan angrily knows it! That's putting it mildly.

After the *"seven weeks"* and the *"sixty two weeks"* the Messiah was *"cut off."* Israel was dispersed. The timepiece of God (Israel) paused with her Messiah being *"cutting off."* Yet, she is the one who cut Him off. Be assured though, the cross of Christ took into account her sins as well.

The church, unforeseen prior to this time, was birthed and continues until today. This third time period of *"one week,"* presently suspended in time, is the final week of **Israel's** *"seventy weeks."* This *"week,"* as the other *"weeks,"* must also be seven years in length. It is and corresponds with the seven year Tribulation (Daniel's Seventieth Week) that is to come upon the earth. At the midpoint of this *"week"* Satan comes *"on the wings of abomination."* This three and a half year point of the Tribulation, until the end, is called the Great Tribulation. It is referred to by various time designations, all equaling three and a half years. *"Forty-two months"* (Revelation 11:2 and 13:5) designates Antichrist's absolute rule during the second half of the Tribulation. *"One thousand two hundred and sixty days"* (Revelation 12:6) refers to Israel's protection by God during the last half of the final *"week,"* — that is, after she accepts Christ Jesus, her Messiah. Finally, the term *"time, times and half a time"* (Revelation 12:14; Daniel 7:25; 12:7) also refers to these last three and a half years of Israel's history.

Israel's re-gathering today in the Promised Land is the prelude to the Seventieth Week of Daniel. She must be in the land for the Seventieth Week to begin. And Israel *is* in the land! The week begins when she turns to the European Union, to confirm a previously unconfirmed covenant of peace, that is, protection for her (Daniel 9:27). If she only knew, her revived Roman Empire's strongman is her Antichrist. She'll learn again and again over the next three and a half years.

Hastening The Coming Of The Day Of God

In his teaching, Peter mentions that when time-designated history has run its course, the present heavens and earth will be destroyed with intense heat (II Peter 3:10). As members of God's forever family, however, "... according to His promise we are looking for new heavens and a new earth, in which righteousness dwells," II Peter 3:13.

Sandwiched between these verses is the marching order of Christ for our day, verse 12: "... looking for and hastening the coming of the day of God...." Yes, we should look for and hasten *"the coming of the day of God." "The day of God,"* if you remember, is eternity future laid up for all God's children on the other side of time. Evil is past and blessedness reigns forever — then! But we've not yet come to eternity future. And, in fact, there's a whole lot coming down the pike between now and then.

So the question begs an answer. How can we *"hasten"* this great day?

The words *"looking for"* denote an expectation sought after. The same Greek word is found in Luke 3:15 in the phrase, *"... the people were in a state of expectation."* Peter is saying, "Live in a state of expectation of the Day of God." Additionally, he tells us to *"hasten"* that great day.

Now, man can neither hinder nor speed up the kingdom of God. Yet, we are told to *"hasten"* it. This Greek word linked with the words *"looking for"* denotes *"earnestly striving for."* We are to live in a state of expectation, striving earnestly for the Day of God. Why? Well, there are many reasons. And here is a good one to begin with. What the Christian does in time determines position, responsibility and glory throughout eternity. It is the storing up of treasures in heaven that results in bringing greater glory to the Lamb of God. Anyone with great expectation striving earnestly for a goal works hard to attain it.

Peter's thought on this matches John's, "And now, little children, abide in Him, so that when He appears we may have confidence and not shrink away from Him in shame at His coming," I John 2:28. In the verses around Peter's urging us to *"hasten"* are found the secrets of hastening well.

In verse 11, Peter brings out the "... sort of people (we) ought to be in *holy conduct*...." That has to do with our **behavior**, what we do with our lives, the deeds done in our body. Obviously behavioral conduct vastly determines the credibility and value of who we are and what we say.

In the same verse he goes on to say, "... *and godliness.*" That has to do with our **character**, what sort of people we are. *"Godliness"* is the inner quality of God's life as seen in us. The deeds we do are the result of *"godliness"* exemplified through us in the presence of God and others. *"Godliness"* can be measured in the way we conduct ourselves when we are alone, and speaks loudly when with others.

In verse 13, Peter's encouragement to be, "... looking for new heavens and a new earth, in which righteousness dwells," is similar to Paul's, "... keep seeking the things above, where Christ is, seated at the right hand of God. Set your mind on things above, not on the things that are on earth. For you have died and your life is hidden with Christ in God. When Christ, who is our life, is revealed, then you also will be revealed with Him in glory," Colossians 3:1-4. The one who succeeds here is a heavenly-minded person with his or her feet firmly grounded on earth. His value can be calculated in heaven, but is immeasurable on his way to heaven.

In verse 14 and following, Peter shares the practical life of godliness. "Therefore, beloved, since you look for these things, be diligent to be found by Him in peace, spotless and blameless, and regard the patience of the Lord to be salvation...." In these qualities are found the practical outworking of Christ in one's life. Peace, spotlessness, blamelessness and patience are byproducts of the Word of God worked in and *"diligently"* worked out.

The Lord's *"patience"* is intended to motivate the child of God toward the work of ministry and the wisdom of soul winning.

Chapter 4

A King, A Bride And
A White Horse

Heaven's Undefeatable Champion

God's Blueprint For The Revelation

We begin now taking a closer look at some of the key players and events that, as foretold in the Revelation, will be acted out live on this world's center stage in the very near future. No suspense or action book has ever been printed matching the drama, the mystery and the love found on the pages of this crowning book of the Bible. There is only one place to go for information on all earth's coming events. They are right before us in The Book of Revelation, coupled with other Old and New Testament passages, as you will discover throughout the remaining chapters of this book. You are about to discern how to interpret these passages and where to find each of the key players, their actions and their results.

The book of The Revelation has been diagnosed, dissected and diagramed from almost every imaginable angle. Numerous outlines of John's vision have been devised and designed with an effort to interpret the message of this closing book of the Bible. Yet, the vast wealth of information in this marvelous volume defies all man contrived ways of tampering with its meaning. Well-intended approaches continue to come only to go the way of obscurity. The Apostle John, banished to the Isle of Patmos, did not even try to outline and arrange what he saw and heard. In his words, "I was in the Spirit on the Lord's Day, and I heard behind me a loud voice like the sound of a trumpet, saying, 'Write in a book what you see,'" Revelation 1:10, 11.

John stuck with the script and allowed the Author of the Book to dictate as He wanted us to have it. I am convinced that to be the best posture to follow without faltering. My utmost imaginative outline of this Book would fall as short of the Author's as the finite does of the Infinite. I hope you will agree with me that after seeing the Author's overview of The Revelation, no other outline compares. But an outline alone will not suffice. Wait until you see and experience first hand all the visible future holds in store before it occurs. It is as if you are now on center stage and the curtain is about to be drawn.

You might want to read fast as this action is coming soon to the world nearest you.

Three Major Divisions

As mentioned above there is a Divine order given for The Revelation. "The Revelation of Jesus Christ, which God gave Him to show to His bond-servants, the things which must shortly take place; and He sent and communicated it by His angel to His bond-servant John, who bore witness to the word of God and to the testimony of Jesus Christ, even to all that he saw," Revelation 1:1, 2.

God gave The Revelation to the Lord Jesus who delivered it by His angel to John who *"bore witness... to all that he saw."* The God of the universe is a God of orderliness. He not only delivers truth in an orderly fashion, He freely gives understanding to all with ears to hear and eyes to see. So pay attention as to whom the truths in this book are intended, they were given — *"to show to His bond-servants."* A *"bond-servant"* is a love slave of the Lord Jesus Christ. It is those who lovingly serve Him with all their heart, mind and soul who discovers the true wisdom of the ages as is revealed in The Revelation.

Therefore, if you and I want to understand this Book, our first order of business is to accept that which God has passed down to us concerning the entirety of its structure, its contents and the future events it unveils. God is jealous of what He has given, both of His outline and overview of The Revelation. He wrote it. He ought to know the best way to interpret it. But mark this down, you are about to see Jesus as never before imagined. Shortly after presenting a sobering view of Himself to His beloved Apostle John (Revelation 1:9-18), the Lord Jesus had to resuscitate him (vs. 17).

Know this first of all. The Revelation is of Jesus Christ. It is *all* about Him. Prophecy is of second importance. A proper understanding of this book is found by following the three major divisions God has given us as a roadmap to follow. The mile markers for these three divisions are given in Revelation 1:19. Here, John was told to, "Write therefore the things which you have seen, and the things which are, and the things which shall take place after these things."

The First Division Of The Revelation

"Write... the things which you have seen," (verse 19a) composes the first division of the Revelation of Jesus Christ. These are the *"things"* which John saw (1:12) having *"... heard behind (him) a loud voice like the sound of a trumpet."* Verses 12-18 are a description of *"one like the son of man"*

whom John *"turned to see."* A little more *"turning"* to Him and a lot of folks might *"see"* more clearly.

In verse 12 there are "seven golden lampstands." The meaning of these *"lampstands"* is explained for us in verse 20. They represent the *"seven churches"* of Asia Minor to which John would shortly address seven letters. *"Seven"* is the number of completeness or perfection and declares the thorough revelation common to all churches and members belonging to Christ Jesus. *"Golden"* stands for the purity before God in which these churches stand having been redeemed by the blood of the Lord Jesus Christ. We stand in imparted righteousness. The *"lampstand,"* representative of each of the *"seven"* churches, is not the light in and of itself. The *"lampstands"* are the bearers of the light. Such is God's intention for churches in proper relationship with their risen Lord.

John then noticed, "in the middle of the lampstands one like a son of man," verse 13. A description of this *"One"* awaits us in the next several verses.

In verse 13 we find He is, "clothed in a robe reaching to the feet..." This *"robe reaching to the feet"* is that of a priest in John's day. As our High Priest He is merciful and forgiving and interceding before the Father on behalf of every repentant sinner or saint. He is about to be seen as being no mere Priest!

"... And girded across his breast with a golden girdle." The *"girdle"* with which He is *"girded"* is the judge's *"girdle."* *"Golden,"* remember, stands for purity. Together the *"gold"* and the *"girdle"* represent the righteous judgment executed by the *"One"* John sees. There is no escaping His righteous judgment!

Before us is our moral and blameless Priest standing in the presence of God interceding on behalf of the churches and the individuals thereof. Notwithstanding, pictured comingled with our Priest is also the Judge. He represents the holiness of God before the churches. Jesus holds both positions, our Priest and our Judge. Humility is not in view here! He is who He is! He is our interceding Priest and our righteous Judge. Grace has been declared for whosoever will; but grace runs its course in time, and judgment surely follows.

In verse 14 notice, "His head and His hair were white like wool, like snow." The description given here matches that of the *"Ancient of Days"* found in Daniel 7:9-14. Look it up. Get to know Him better — if you dare. It will be a liberating experience.

No simple Man is this! He has been around a long, long time. And nothing, not a thing, escapes His dutiful notice. He's Alzheimer proof. Nothing is forgiven or forgotten that is not cleansed by the blood of the Lamb. Perhaps this is why so many people want nothing to do with Him. Fear is the real reason many fail to get to know Him, and for some to even acknowledge His existence. Yet, the reason for shunning Him is also the reason to get to know Him. Yes, He is omniscient! He knows you like the back of His hand. If He has a hand, that is! Get over it! He knows you thoroughly and loves you supremely. Did you know? He is the originator of love, mercy, grace and peace. One only experiences and understands the balance when by faith he or she spends a little time with Him. Pay the price of quality time and you will find love grows through getting to know Him.

But do it in the acceptable time, the day of salvation, when "fear" is more accurately defined as reverence toward Him. There is coming a time when "reverence" reverts to fearful fretfulness of the One on the throne. The fearful then will be left with nothing but the gnashing of teeth at Him.

"His eyes were like a flame of fire." These *"eyes... like a flame of fire"* stand for omniscience, the all-knowing, nothing escaping, terrifying wisdom of God. They burn through *all* the dross in one's life, consuming the clutter and exposing the intents of the mind and heart. "For the word of God is living and active and sharper than any two-edged sword, and piercing as far as the division of soul and spirit, of both joints and marrow, and able to judge the thoughts and intentions of the heart. And there is no creature hidden from His sight, but all things are open and laid bare to the eyes of Him with whom we have to do," Hebrews 4:12, 13.

God's infinite wisdom coupled with the refining fire of judgment is in view here. Nothing is hidden from His sight, and there will be, in the Day of Judgment, nothing that will not be brought out into the light. See I Corinthians 4:5. The Apostle Paul's personal testimony to King Agrippa speaks expressly of this very thing — get it out into the light with God today (Acts 26:14-18). May I remind you? Judgment for sinful actions and thoughts, as well as sins of commission and omission, are removed forever from the lives of those coming in simple childlike faith to Him.

John had seen these tender eyes filled with tears. No longer! They are now aflame with the fire of judgment!

In verse 15 we see, "His feet were like burnished bronze, when it has been caused to glow in a furnace." *"Burnished bronze"* represents judgment, tried and proven. This is what Calvary's cross is all about. He took His perfect, precious and sinless life and laid it down in payment for our sins. "And He Himself is the propitiation (the offering set forth) for our sins; and not for ours only, but also for those of the whole world," I John 2:2. Ah! Yes! The *"feet"* of the One before us were qualified to *"stand"* the test and the refining power of holy judgment. He went into the fire and came out unscathed. The *"burnished bronze"* feet of Jesus Christ symbolically declare righteous judgment has been paid in full for those coming to Him.

"His voice was like the sound of many waters." The *"sound of many waters"* speaks of the majestic power of His voice. When He speaks His reverberating voice sounds like the strength of the majestic sea. Yet, not quite! That's still short of the coming reality. Multiply the crashing mighty waves of the most storm-tossed sea many times over by all the waters of the world. There is great, terrifying power in the sound of this *"One's"* mighty voice. He is the all-powerful One! The pounding of His voice, however, is only toward those who reject His love and forgiveness offered through the "propitiation" of His Son. Israel of old heard and trembled at the sound of His voice. They asked God to tell them what He required of them to be His people and for Him to be their God. He gave them the perfect Law. Without the Law's demands met in full, terror would reign in eternity. Yet, terror also rose in the hearts of all who heard Him. For who could keep the perfect Law? They had already broken ever syllable of it. There is simply nothing one can do to earn God's favor. Yet, His grace is freely offered to all coming to Him through faith and faith alone. Salvation was, is and will be freely given.

What we see in the first division of The Revelation is the coming again of the King of kings. This is The Revelation of the One the world scorned as the Lamb. He will shortly be seen as the Lion.

In verse 16 we find, "In His right hand He held seven stars." These *"stars,"* are explained for us in verse 20. They are "the angels of the seven churches." *"Angel"* is the word for "messenger." These messengers are God's ministers among His churches. He holds them *"in His right hand."* The *"right hand"* is the *"hand"* of acceptance, strength and authority. God's ministers are in the *"right hand"* of the Lord Jesus Christ. Don't mess with His men! It is a dangerous thing to rebel against God's anointed and appointed messengers. Rebellion against them is rebellion against the One who placed them.

"Out of His mouth came a sharp two-edged sword." This *"two-edged sword"* is, of course, the Word of God. See

Hebrews 4:12 and John 12:48. There will be no fleeing this sword! We study for years to have a meaningful and profitable place in society. Wouldn't it be a good idea to occasionally pick up and read one of the Bibles scattered throughout our homes. It would be wise if we got our lives correctly aligned with His Word. In all likelihood it will require a little divine surgery here and there. But why not do it now when it leads to salvation, rather than later when it leads to damnation.

"And His face was like the sun shining in its strength." Such language describes the radiance and glory of His righteousness. The closing book of the Old Testament refers to this reality and makes this verse understandable. "But for you who fear My name the sun of righteousness will rise with healing in its wings; and you will go forth and skip about like calves from the stall," Malachi 4:2. The power of God's holiness is in view — blinding and terrifying to His enemies, healing and refreshing to His own.

When John saw this vision of the coming again Lord, he "fell at His feet as a dead man." John, the youngest of the Apostles, was the closest to the Lord Jesus Christ. It was into John's hands the Lord entrusted His mother at the cross. So close was John to Jesus that when other disciples had a question they dared not ask, John was sought to take it to Jesus. He is the one who laid his head upon the Lord's shoulder at the last supper. Yet, when John saw His precious Savior for whom he had suffered and was now banished to Patmos, he was so startled and frightened he *"fell at His feet as a dead man."*

Here is the coming again picture of the Lord Jesus. When He comes again, He will not be a babe in a manager. Mercy has been scorned and grace has been rejected. The Judge is back in town and judgment day has arrived. No wonder "kings... great men... commanders... the rich... the strong... every slave and free man, hide themselves in the caves and among the rocks of the mountains; and say to the mountains and to the rocks, 'Fall on us and hide us from the presence of Him who sits on the throne, and from the wrath of the Lamb; for the great day of their wrath has come; and who is able to stand,'" Revelation 6:15-17.

At His first coming he was Jesus the Christ, the Savior. The procurement of salvation was necessarily first. At His second coming, He is the Lord Jesus Christ. Put the emphasis on Lord. It is not as a humble servant the Lord returns to earth. As Priest, King and Judge He reclaims all things made by the voice of His commands. What, do you ask, is the extent of all things made? "All things came into being by Him, and apart from Him nothing came into being that has come into being," John 1:3. That leaves out nothing inanimate or living.

To be certain there is no misunderstanding of who this *"One"* is, He instructs John, "Do not be afraid; I am the first and the last, and the living One; and I was dead, and behold, I am alive forevermore, and I have the keys of death and of Hades," verses 17, 18. To John and all who know Him, He is the risen Lord Jesus Christ. There is no need for fear among His own, He is our victorious Lord, Savior, Redeemer and God. And, He *"has the keys of death and of Hades"* hanging at His side. See I Corinthians 15:55-57. He locks and no one can open. He opens the door and no one can lock it. Today it is open wide. It's closing, however, will be fast and final.

The above verses encompass the first division of the Book of The Revelation of Jesus Christ. Terrifying is He to all on Satan's side. Today testifying to the world He says, "Whosoever will may come." Joyful are all looking forward to the King's return.

The Second Division Of The Revelation

The second division of The Revelation is designated by "... and the things which are," Revelation 1:19. *"The things which are"* are the *"things"* that were going on in John's day and continue to this day. This second division contains seven letters to seven specific churches and to the church age as a whole.

These letters are addressed to seven literal churches of John's day as to their character and the things going on in them — good and bad. Their content, however, encompasses much more than just the goings on in these seven individual churches.

Additionally, in the chronological order of these letters an amazing history of the church since birth will be found. Each letter powerfully describes a time period through which the church has lived.

In their turn, as well, each of these letters will represent *the general attitude and characteristics* of the overall churches of their day.

It is also true that there are and have been in every period, churches pictured by each of these letters. Each of us can find our church today described by one of the Lord's seven letters. We can know what the Lord has to say to us, our attitudes, our hearts, how to right any wrongs, how to get on track and how to reap the rewards of faithfulness. We also discover the consequences of not *"hearing what the Spirit says to the churches."*

Just as important, one of these letters, at any given time in your life and mine, will let us know where we stand in fellowship with the Lord Jesus Christ. For every child of God living in light of the truths in these letters blessings are promised to flow unlimitedly throughout time and into eternity.

The following is *a very brief* synopsis of each of The Revelation's seven letters.

Ephesus (Revelation 2:1-7)

The letter to Ephesus pictures the first century church and translates, "the girl of My choice." Ephesus has many wonderful traits, and in them she "*has not grown weary.*" The Lord is pictured as walking among "*the seven golden lampstands,* of which Ephesus is one. As did the priests in their day, the Lord walks among the "*Lampstands*" trimming the wick of each lampstand that its light might continually shine brightly. He sees in her one serious error. She has left her first love! The things she used to do out of love for her risen Lord, she now does out of habit, obligation. To get back where she belongs, Ephesus is told to, "*remember... repent... and repeat the deeds (she) did at first.*"

Failing to return to her "*first love*" could cause her "*lampstand*" to be removed. That's serious! No "*lampstand*" for her day means no light for her or the coming generation. Along with the Lord's single condemnation, He also gives correction as to how to get the wrong right and the light bright: "*Remember therefore from where you have fallen, and repent.*" In other words, "get back to the first things, "*your first love.*"

She is also given a great compliment. She "*hates the deeds of the Nicolaitans.*" That God likes. He hates them, too. These are those seeking to rule over others in the church of the Lord Jesus Christ. This will come out more clearly in the following letters.

As in all the Lord's letters, a promise is given Ephesus' "*overcomers.*"

Smyrna (Revelation 2:8-11)

Smyrna means suffering. Smyrna represents the Lord's persecuted church. Historically, the Smyrna church era was from A.D. 100 to A.D. 312. Having been taken captive in

A.D. 70, the Smyrna church endured ten Roman Emperors who persecuted her relentlessly for more than 200 years. This became the era of the underground and suffering church.

The Lord has no critical word or correction for the Smyrna congregation. He encourages her to *"be faithful until death"* with the promise, *"and I will give you the crown of life."* The death of the saints through torture, persecution and terror would be swallowed up in victory. As individuals and entire families were cruelly martyred alongside one another for their faith in and testimony of Christ Jesus, this was the promise that enabled them to stand and die for their risen Savior and Lord. She will never have a reason to *"be ashamed"* when she stands before her risen and enthroned Sustainer.

The Lord makes an interesting statement in closing out the letter to Smyrna. *"He who overcomes shall not be hurt by the second death."* The world's church of the day promised the battered Smyrna church the fires of Hell. In contrast, the Lord promises Smyrna, "To the contrary, you shall not be hurt by the second death." That would remain reserved for her detractors.

Pergamum (Revelation 2:12-17)

Pergamum means "objectionable." The Pergamum historical era ran from A.D. 312 to A.D. 500. She is complimented for *"holding fast"* Christ's name *"where Satan's throne is."* Yes, the Lord intends for His people to *"hold fast"* no matter the day or circumstances in which she finds herself. Many religions had sprung up, and it was a tough day for these supposedly narrow minded Christians.

Pergamum's problem resulted from her marrying the world. It all began when Constantine was seeking to win the throne of the Roman Empire. He used the debased and persecuted Christians to win his crusade and title. Afterwards, he declared Christianity to be the religion of Rome. Baptizing all his army and much of the citizenry of the Roman Empire, he married the church to the world. He made the church an acceptable and highly favored religion. Not a good idea in the eyes of God.

There are a *"few things"* the Lord chose to address in the Pergamum church. The first was her being married to the world and lifted to a place of prominence and worldly acceptance. The true Gospel has a stinging, biting effect on the world in that its very nature points out the sinfulness of man and the necessity of repentance toward God. The second is what God calls *"holding to the teaching of Balaam,"* which meant she became a stumbling block to others by loose living. That generally follows being married to the world. The third problem God has with the Pergamum church then and now is she holds, *"to the teaching of the Nicolaitans."* This doctrine allowed a class of "clergy" to rise up and rule over the church, and the individual members of it. They became intermediaries between God and man. God requires *"repentance"* from Pergamum or He promises, "I will, *'make war against them with the sword of My mouth.'"* Any person depending on a priest, rather than direct reliance on God, quickly takes his or her eyes off the One true Savior and God. This was the beginnings from which the Catholic Church sprung.

Again, wonderful promises are made for *"overcomers."*

Thyatira (Revelation 2:18-29)

Historically the Thyatiran era began in 500 A. D. and continues on into the Tribulation period. Thyatira means, "a continual sacrifice" and refers to the continual sacrifice of the mass in Rome. This continuing sacrifice denies the finished work of Christ at Calvary. Thyatira pictures the Roman Catholic Church where the doctrine of the Nicolaitans is in full sway. The priests have power over the people with the perceived ability to forgive sin, grant individuals entrance into heaven and to "excommunicate" individuals, therefore sealing their eternal doom.

God recognizes and compliments the Thyatiran church's many good deeds, but immediately rips into her for her tolerations. He accuses Thyatira of *"tolerating"* Jezebel by *"teaching and leading (His) bond-servants astray."* Whether the church was in sympathy with the evil of Jezebel, or lacked the moral fiber to resist it, it is all the same; it was *"tolerated."* Toleration of that which God condemns is never acceptable. Jezebel was extremely proficient at the art of mixing. She undertook to unite into one the religions of Phoenicia and that of Israel. She blended a personal relationship with Jehovah God, immoral behavior and the bowing of one's head to foreign gods. This is what Catholicism portrays. It is a mixture of Heathenism, Christianity and Judaism. It is not Christian, although there is much about it that appears Christian.

Repentance is needed or says God, "I will cast her upon a bed of sickness, and those who commit adultery with her into great tribulation." She has some, though, who do not hold to her teaching. To these God says, *"Hold fast until I come."* During the 1,000-year reign of Christ *"overcomers"* will be given the very thing the Romanists have sought for hundreds of years, *"authority over the nations."*

Sardis (Revelation 3:1-6)

Sardis means "remnant" and refers to the Protestant movement, the remnant that parted ways with Catholicism. Historically the Sardis era runs from A.D. 1520 and continues into the Tribulation. Now I know, there is going to be some gnashing of teeth over what follows by some of my Protestant friends. Well, you may have to settle for the scraps after the Catholics are finished.

God begins this letter with, "I know your deeds, that you have a name that you are alive, but you are dead." Throughout this letter, God has no good word for Sardis. None! Instead, He jumps right into the middle of her problem with words of correction.

"Excuse me! Hold on a minute. Dead? God, do you not see all our wonderful deeds?" Perhaps Sardis' problem lies right here; she has a "profession" but lacks the reality of a changed life (Matthew 7:21-23). She has a "testimony," but when tried she is lacking the reality of the Person of Christ within (II Corinthians 13:5). She knows about Him, but her life denies the *"power"* of the Holy Spirit (II Timothy 3:1-5). This is the church that has all the programs and enjoys great respect throughout her community. Her deeds are ongoing, but spiritually she is *"dead."*

What a contrast between the insight of God and that of man! We dare not compare the church, or a Christian, with any model other than the one given by the Holy Spirit at Pentecost. God never does! And compared with the blood-bought, Christ-indwelled, Spirit-empowered church or Christian, "Protestantism" has a name, but is *"dead."*

The Person and work of the indwelling Christ is the *only* assurance one has of salvation. God gives no other. The reality of the Person of Jesus Christ, when two or more gather together in His name, is the only guarantee that any congregation has gone beyond the feigned acts of worship found in the *"church in Sardis."*

She is told to "wake up, and strengthen (set fast, establish) the things that remain, which were about to die." They are to "remember... what they have received and heard; and keep it, and repent." If not, says God, "I will come like a thief;" that is, she will be caught unaware and left behind.

Again, God assures the faithful. "You have a few people who have not soiled their garments; and they will walk with Me in white; for they are worthy." There is a remnant even among the remnant. Overcomers "hear what the Spirit says," and are given enormous promises.

Philadelphia (Revelation 3:7-13)

Philadelphia means "brotherly love." This is the church where brotherly love is evident to all. The historical time period of this precious church is about A.D. 1750 up to the time of the rapture. There is no rebuke of this church, just praise and encouragement. This is the church of the great missionary movements.

She is not exceptionally strong, but is greatly complimented, "I have put before you an open door which no one can shut, because you have a little power, and have kept My word, and have not denied My name."

She does have hecklers, of course. God refers to them as, "the synagogue of Satan, who say that they are Jews, and are not, but lie." These *"synagogue of Satan"* adherents are other religious groups surrounding and criticizing her for her narrow-minded and intolerant Christianity. But, God promises her victory. "Because you have kept the word of My Perseverance, I also will keep you from the hour of testing, that hour which is about to come upon the whole world, to test those who dwell upon the earth." She is pledged deliverance from the Tribulation and other wonderful promises belonging to — you guessed it, *"overcomers."*

Laodicea (Revelation 3:14-22)

Laodicea, the last days' church, means "the people rule." Historically the Laodicean era is from the early 20th Century and goes into the Tribulation.

This is the second church for which God has no compliments. He begins His letter to Laodicea by saying she is, "lukewarm, and neither cold nor hot." She is therefore in danger of being, "spit out of My mouth." *"Cold"* refers to being belligerently hostile toward spiritual things. "Give me that old time boring religion, but don't get spiritual on me." Let me add that being *"cold"* is bad in itself, but at least *"cold"* is an attitude, and an attitude with which God can deal. It was the *"cold"* spiritual atmosphere of the Church of England that set John Wesley ablaze, causing him to seek for, find and preach the unchanging, yet ever refreshing Word of God. It was the cold atmosphere of the Methodist Church that drove William Booth to become the mighty Salvationist. Think what you might of today's Salvation Army, it was in its earliest days a red-hot evangelistic iron in the hands of God. But, this Laodicean church is not *"cold."*

Nor is the Laodicean church *"hot."* There is no zeal, no evidence of fire and no burning passion for her absent Lord. There is no burning desire for work in His fields. This church is not *"cold,"* nor is she *"hot."* She's somewhere in between.

A *"cold"* church may demonstrate an atmosphere of ice, whereas a *"hot"* church may be accused of being overly zealous, intolerant or legalistic. Nevertheless, God was able to deal with either of these conditions, had they only existed. Laodicea, however, was neither *"cold nor hot!"*

She is plain and simply, *"lukewarm."* Lukewarmness produces a nauseating condition. Laodicea is not *"cold"* to the things of God. But neither is she *"hot"* for Him. She lacks moral conviction and enthusiastic fervency. She just doesn't care! She is indifferent and unconcerned. A "could not care less" attitude holds her in death's grip. Its clammy fingers are wrapped tightly around her throat. She is halfhearted, unresponsive and non-committed. Her adherents will often (or at least, occasionally) attend church on Sunday mornings. But generally they are too busy with life or are just too lazy to be bothered with Sunday evenings, Wednesday nights or weekday ministries. "What's the point in all these meetings anyway? We need more *family time.*" In fact, many such churches have found Sunday evening services to be highly impractical, unimportant and terribly inconvenient, not to mention — unattended, in these days of Laodicean apathy.

Lukewarm is a condition so abhorrent to the Holy Spirit of God that not even He can do anything about it. The great 20th Century theologian, John R. W. Stott, concerning the Laodicean church, said this: "It describes vividly the respectable, sentimental, nominal, skin-deep religiosity which is so widespread among us today."

"So because you are lukewarm, and neither hot nor cold, I will spit you out of My mouth." What a horrific judgment of this church straight from the heart of God! The Spirit and character of Christ cannot tolerate such a condition; thus, his determination to *"spit out,"* not just "throw up," but to *"spit out of My mouth"* this last days' church. *"Spit out"* denotes "projectile vomiting." This church is foreign to God's love and character.

She is told she needs the perfect righteousness of Jesus Christ — rather than tradition or religious acts. She needs *"white garments,"* — the purchased garments of heaven washed in the blood of Jesus. She also needs *"eyesalve to anoint (her) eyes."* This eye-opening eyesalve is the enlightenment of the Holy Spirit, the revealer of truth. Since she does not have the correction of God upon her, she is encouraged to, "be zealous therefore, and repent." The invitation to *"open the door"* carries with it the strong promise of, *"sitting with (Christ) on (His) throne."* Will she, *"Hear what the Spirit says to the churches?"*

Far more truths are to be found in these seven letters to the churches than are portrayed in the above brief descriptions. Study them thoroughly. You will be enriched from the knowledge of them and their many, many truths. You will find the Lord's disposition toward each church as you discover how He describes Himself in the opening comments of each letter.

These two chapters, Revelation 2 and 3, detailing the church age, form the second division of The Revelation, *"the things which are."*

The Third Division Of The Revelation

The third division of The Revelation is "... the things which shall take place *after these things,"* (1:19). As we have seen, the church age is detailed in the seven letters of Revelation 2 and 3. Notice carefully how chapter 4 verse 1 begins and ends. *"After these things* I looked, and behold, a door standing open in heaven, and the first voice which I heard, like the sound of a trumpet speaking with me, said, 'Come up here, and I will show you what must take place *after these things,'"* Revelation 4:1. The words, *"after these things,"* appear at the beginning and at the end of this first verse of chapter 4, and refers to "things after" the church age, that is, *"after"* the things of chapters 2 and 3. The phrase, a *"voice... like the sound of a trumpet,"* and *"Come up here,"* certainly calls our attention to a great promise. "For the Lord Himself will descend from heaven with a shout, with the voice of the archangel, and with the trumpet of God; and the dead in Christ shall rise first. Then we who are alive and remain shall be caught up together with them in the clouds to meet the Lord in the air, and thus we shall always be with the Lord," I Thessalonians 4:16, 17.

The Lord's promise of His own being *"caught up"* is referred to by many as "the rapture" and is described in the Bible as *"the blessed hope,"* Titus 2:13. These descriptions refer to the event of Christ Jesus' return *"in the clouds,"* also referred to as *"in the air."* Each of these terms describes the same event. This is part one of a two-part return of the Lord Jesus. He comes first *"in the air"* to resurrect all His deceased saints and to call to Himself all the living saints. In the above words to Titus, Paul mentions the *"catching up"* of the saints, deceased and alive, and then the second part of the Lord's return in the phrase, *"and the appearing of the glory of our great God and Savior, Christ Jesus."* This *"appearing"* is in reference to Christ's return to the earth along with all His gathered saints. There is a time period of seven years between *"the blessed hope"* and the *"appearing of... Christ Jesus."* He comes first for His saints, and then, seven years later He returns with His saints. We'll get back to what the Bible says of these events shortly. At the sound of His trumpet, the church age is over and the Tribulation is about to begin on earth.

This third division of The Revelation covers chapters 4 – 22, the end of the book. These chapters include more than just the Tribulation judgments. You will find many parenthetical chapters and passages intertwined with the narrative. These parenthetical portions go back and forth in time to describe characters, events and nations involved in the running narrative. They fill in the gaps making The Revelation understandable. They add rich insight and give added detail to the narrative. There are also three chapters dealing with future eternal things, chapters 20-22.

Following is a chapter-by-chapter overview of the main characters and events of The Revelation. The (parenthetical) chapters and passages are marked. Each of the remaining chapters and passages are the chronological narrative of The Revelation.

Chapter 4: The throne of God; twenty-four elders; four living creatures and the song of the redeemed (parenthetical).

Chapter 5: The seven-sealed book; a Lamb standing as if slain; a new song by the four living creatures; the elders; the angels and created things (parenthetical).

Chapter 6: The first six seals releasing judgments upon earth; one fourth of mankind killed.

Chapter 7: 144,000 sealed; a great multitude from the Tribulation (parenthetical).

Chapter 8: The seventh seal; silence in Heaven; first four trumpet judgments.

Chapter 9: The fifth trumpet judgment and the first woe; the sixth trumpet judgment; one third of mankind killed.

Chapter 10: The angel with the bitter/sweet little book (parenthetical).

Chapter 11: The two witnesses and the second woe (parenthetical); the seventh trumpet judgment.

Chapter 12: The woman (Israel) clothed with the sun; the red dragon; the male child; Michael and his angels waging war with the dragon; the dragon cast down; the third woe (parenthetical).

Chapter 13: The beast (Antichrist) out of the sea; the beast out of the earth (false prophet) (parenthetical).

Chapter 14: The Lamb on Mount Zion with the 144,000; the wine press of God's wrath (parenthetical).

Chapter 15: The angels with the seven plagues; the victorious ones and the Song of Moses (parenthetical).

Chapter 16: The plague judgments; the Tribulation comes to an end (chapters 17-20).

Chapter 17: The great harlot; a scarlet beast; and the religious Babylon (parenthetical).

Chapter 18: The end time economic Babylon (parenthetical).

Chapter 19: The bride; the marriage supper of the Lamb; the Word of God; the armies in heaven; the return of the King.

Chapter 20: The binding of Satan; the first resurrection; the thousand-year reign of Christ; the great white throne judgment.

Chapter 21: The new heaven; the new earth; the holy city.

Chapter 22: The river of the water of life; the throne of God and of the Lamb; final testimony.

The Church And The Tribulation

The question most often asked about the church and the Tribulation period is, "Does the church go through the Tribulation?" Many have wondered, "Why should the church be exempt? Others have suffered much for Christ's sake, why should the church escape the Tribulation?"

These and many other questions we will seek to answer from Scripture. There are many good and scholarly men who have varying opinions on the events of the last days. They, too, base their beliefs on Scripture. While we may disagree on doctrines nonessential to the foundational truths of faith in Christ, it is my aim we always seek to do so respectfully and in Christian love. If I am not mistaken, none of us are yet perfect, so we seek to let love reign.

Certainly there are verses in the Bible that seem to support differing viewpoints. There is, however, a proper method that leads to understanding Scripture on any given topic. First, all Scripture on any topic must first be taken in its context. Second, it must be interpreted in light of all Scripture on that topic to grasp the meaning as God intends it. No doctrine is ever to be built on any one verse without comparing all verses on the matter at hand. Then, and only then, can truth be seen and understood in light of all the will and Word of God.

In reference to the question often asked as to why the church should not suffer along with everyone else, let me simply say this. The church *has* suffered in every generation, and none more than this current generation. Millions of Christians around the world are suffering for their faith in Christ at this very moment. In fact, more Christians have been martyred for their testimony of Christ over the past one hundred years than in all previous centuries. Deliverance from the Tribulation period has nothing to do with escaping tribulations, trials and sufferings that accompany godliness. Should Christians be removed prior to the Tribulation, their deliverance has nothing to do with "what right have they," but everything to do with the plan and purpose of Almighty God as revealed in the Word of God. It is His plan and purpose alone we seek to learn from Scripture.

What we believe is important. Our beliefs dictate how we live. Knowing why we believe what we believe is vital to live and witness for Christ Jesus today, and to be unashamed when you approach Him on that soon coming day. So let's get started looking at Scripture on the church and the Tribulation.

The Wise And The Foolish Virgins

Matthew 25:1-13 gives the account of the Lord's parable of *"ten virgins,"* and pictures the day of His coming for His bride. Those whom the ten *"virgins"* represent become so increasingly evident that even a child can understand.

Each of the *"virgins"* was looking for the *"bridegroom."* This cannot be said of Israel, as she is *not* looking for a *"bridegroom."* It is not written to the unchurched, for they certainly are *not* looking for a *"bridegroom."* It *is* written to the redeemed and to the unredeemed within the church. They *are* all looking for the *"bridegroom."*

Other elements in this parable also declare it points to those professing faith in Christ Jesus at the time of His return, such as *"oil"* in their *"lamps." "Oil"* is a type or picture of the Holy Spirit who indwells believers today. The Holy Spirit did not indwell Israel, and neither are those without a profession of faith in Christ. So I'll not belabor the point. This parable has as its theme the Lord's coming for His bride, her preparation at the time He *"shouts"* (I Thessalonians 4:16), and the disposition of those professing faith in Christ without possessing the life of Christ.

Notice the *"virgins"* all *look alike.* You'd be hard pressed to tell the *"foolish"* from the *"prudent."* They are all *expecting* the *"bridegroom."* They all knew he was coming. Throughout the professing church today most everyone knows the Lord's promise of His return. All signs point to the approaching day of His coming. So the Bridegroom is expected.

All the *"virgins"* also had *"lamps."* All ten of them! A *"lamp"* in Scripture is representative of one's living testimony, the life we live as made real by the Holy Spirit. We are to bear light as to the testimony of our Bridegroom. Every member of a local church has a testimony of his or her confession of Christ. The same was true of these *"ten virgins."* They not only expected the *"bridegroom,"* they each had a *"lamp,"* a testimony. Yet, as we are all aware, some testimonies are false professions of faith in Christ alone.

You might notice, also, the *"foolish"* and the *"prudent"* both grew weary while waiting, *"and began to sleep."* That is all too often the case in the church today. Is it not? The many seem to grow tired and weary of waiting, watching and working. Suddenly, however, the midnight shout rings out, *"Behold, the bridegroom! Come out to meet him."* By the way, *"Behold"* is a term of startlement, amazement. They were expecting Him. They all had testimonies. But they were startled when He came. To their awakened amazement the *"virgins"* were called to *"come out."*

Of the ten, five were *"foolish"* and five were *"prudent."* The *"prudent"* took *"oil"* in their *"flasks."* They each had *"oil"* with which their *"lamp"* could be lit. The *"foolish"* took their *"lamps"* as well, but they had no *"oil."* *"Oil"* throughout Scripture is a picture of the Holy Spirit. How loudly Paul's words should echo through Christ's churches today, "But if anyone does not have the Spirit of Christ, he does not belong to Him.... For all who are being led by the Spirit of God, these are the sons of God," Romans 8:9f, 14. It seems the *"foolish virgins"* had enough knowledge to deceive their minds, but not enough truth to change their hearts. They had no *"oil."*

The *"five foolish virgins"* lit their *"lamps,"* but their *"lamps"* continually went out. Of course, they would; they had no *"oil."* Immediately, they requested the *"prudent virgins"* to give them some of their *"oil."* The answer was obvious: *"No, there will not be enough for us and you too; go instead to the dealers and buy some for yourselves."* Seriously now, no one has the authority to give the life of God, the Person of the Holy Spirit, to anyone. That is an individual transaction between God and man. The *"oil"* cannot be borrowed! The *"virgins"* with *"lamps,"* yet without *"oil,"* affirm the sad reality of lost within the church. We should not be surprised. Scripture informs us there are tares mixed in with the wheat. There are bad fish swimming around with the good in every pool. There are wolves dressed in sheep's clothing among God's flocks. Has it struck you yet? In this parable the Lord chose to represent His coming for His bride, a full 50% had no *"oil."* Huh!

The *"foolish"* were told, *"go instead to the dealers and buy some for yourselves."* And, of course, it was *"while they were going away to make the purchase, the bridegroom came."* Then it is said, *"and those who were ready went in with him to the wedding feast; and the door was shut."* Happy day, for them!

"And later the other virgins also came, saying, 'Lord, lord, open up for us.' But he answered and said, 'Truly I say to you, I do not know you.'" It was too late. They came back *"later"* desiring entrance, but no entrance could be had. Paul, in writing to the church at Thessalonica, mentions individuals who hear and comprehend truth but reject it, receive after the door has been shut, *"a deluding influence so that they might believe what is false, in order that they may be judged who did not believe the truth, but took pleasure in wickedness,"* II Thessalonians 2:8-12. That is exactly why it is so important for a man or a woman, a boy or a girl, to respond to the Lord Jesus when the Holy Spirit comes knocking on the door of their heart.

I have two points in closing out this short look at the *"ten virgins."* The Lord ended this parable with, *"Be on the alert then, for you do not know the day nor the hour."* Point one, we need to be on *"the alert"* daily. How and for what are we looking? We are to look expectantly for His coming. Expectancy leads to holy living. If there is no expectancy, one's holy living needs an examination. If there is no holy living, one's expectancy of Christ's coming ought to be carefully examined (II Corinthians 13:5; I John 2:4).

The second point is, the *"prudent virgins"* are taken. The *"foolish virgins"* are left behind. The Lord's parable runs parallel with Paul's teaching mentioned above in II Thessalonians 2. In this passage Paul corrects false teaching that *"the day of the Lord"* (the Tribulation period) had already begun and the Thessalonians were left behind. In both, we have a picture of the true church being removed and the false church being left. We cannot build doctrine though on one or two passages of Scripture. So let's go on.

The Gathering Of The Church

The church will be gathered to the Lord when He comes *"in the clouds."* This coming *"in the clouds"* is separate and completely different from His "coming" to the earth. There is a time span separating the Lord's *calling out* of this world His own, and His *coming back* to this world *with* His own. The difference in these two phases of Christ's return can be found in several passages.

1. The Rapture And The Appearing

There are seemingly conflicting passages on the return of Christ. These passages harmonize, however, when we realize the Lord's return is in two distinct phases. One is The Gathering of the Church, often referred to as the Rapture, and is filled with mercy and grace. The other is The Appearing of Christ, and is filled with judgment and blood.

At the rapture of the church Christ comes *"in the air"* for His own (I Thessalonians 4:17). At the appearing of Christ, He comes back to the earth with his own (II Thessalonians 2:8).

At the rapture of the church Christ comes *"as a thief."* Those without Christ are caught unaware (I Thessalonians 5:2, 4). At the appearing of Christ, *"every eye shall see Him"* (Revelation 1:7).

At the rapture the saints will be *"comforted"* (I Thessalonians 4:18). At the appearing of Christ *"people... shall mourn"* (Matthew 24:30).

At the rapture Christ's own shall be *"caught up"* (I Thessalonians 4:16-17). At the appearing of Christ the saints will be *"revealed with Him"* (Colossians 3:4).

2. The Rapture And The Appearing Are Both Seen In...

Both are seen in one Book of the Bible: Revelation 4:1, *"... come up here"* — the rapture; and in Revelation 19:11-16, *"He judges and wages war"* — the appearing with His own to earth at Armageddon.

Both are seen in one Chapter of the Bible: II Thessalonians 2:1, *"our gathering together to Him;"* — the rapture; and in II Thessalonians 2:8, *"the appearance of His coming"* — to the earth.

Both are seen in one verse of the Bible: Titus 2:13, *"the blessed hope"* — the rapture; and *"the appearing"* — on His return to the earth.

3. The Old Testament Examples

The Old Testament gives examples of the New Testament church being removed before the Lord's judgment falls on earth, and of Israel being saved through the Tribulation.

1. Enoch – Genesis 5:24. One minute Enoch was here, the next he was not. Enoch's sudden removal pictures the *"catching up"* of the church. The disappearance of Enoch prior to the flood pictures God removing the church *prior* to the Tribulation.

2. Noah – Genesis 7:1. Noah and his family, as a picture of Israel, were brought into the ark for deliverance *through* the flood to populate the world afterward. In the same way the hand of God through the Tribulation will deliver Israel.

3. Lot – Genesis 19:22. God removed Lot, a righteous man in a sin soaked city, from Sodom *prior* to the destruction of the city. Lot pictures the church's removal before judgment is poured out upon the earth. It is interesting to see what a shallow child of God Lot was, yet were he a Christian today he would still be delivered from the Tribulation.

4. The Tribulation Period Refers To Israel's Future History

The Tribulation period is referenced by several names, all of which refer to God's dealings with Israel.

1. **The Time of Jacob's Trouble** – Jeremiah 30:7. Jacob, though he was always having trouble, was renamed Israel after struggling with God. He had trouble with his brother, trouble with his father and trouble with his father in-law. In each instance he wrestled with God in prayer and prevailed.

The Tribulation is called The Time of Jacob's Trouble, and is appropriately so named. As in Jacob's life, Israel's troubles force her into turning to her Lord and Messiah, Jesus Christ, during the Tribulation.

2. **The Time of Israel's Travail** – Jeremiah 6:24; 13:21. The Tribulation is referred to as The Time of Israel's Travail since it is then she will travail as if *"she was with child... being in labor and in pain to give birth,"* Revelation 12:1-6. Compare this passage with Isaiah 66:7, 8: "'Before she travailed, she brought forth; before her pain came, she gave birth to a boy. Who has heard such a thing? Who has seen such things? Can a land be born in one day? Can a nation be brought forth all at once? As soon as Zion travailed, she also brought forth her sons. Shall I bring to the point of birth, and not give delivery?' saith the Lord." Israel's travail in the Tribulation period results in her salvation.

3. **Daniel's Seventieth Week** – Daniel 9:24-27. The Tribulation is Israel's final week of the seventy given her by God. This *"week"* comes after a long dispersion, the gap known as the church age that occurs between Israel's sixty-ninth and seventieth weeks. Again, Daniel's Seventieth Week refers to the Tribulation period God will use to bring Israel to Himself.

In each of these above designations, referring as each does to the Tribulation, the reference is always to the nation of Israel. The church is nowhere mentioned or seen. This is Israel's time of rebirth, after the church age (Revelation 4:1 – 16:21). Each designation refers to the travail, the trouble or the tribulation Israel goes through in coming to her rejected Messiah of Calvary.

5. The Scriptures' Testify Of The Rapture

Many Scriptures testify as to the saints of the church age being caught up from earth to meet the Lord in the air prior to the Tribulation's coming upon the world.

1. Luke 21:35 – "But keep on the alert at all times, praying in order that you may be accounted worthy to escape all these things that are about to take place, and to stand before the Son of God."

2. Romans 5:9 – "Much more then, having now been justified by His blood, we shall be saved from the wrath of God through Him."

3. Philippians 1:6, 10 – "I am confident of this very thing, that He who began a good work in you will perfect it until the day of Christ Jesus... so that you may approve the things that are excellent, in order to be sincere and blameless until the day of Christ." Remember, the *"day of Christ"* is in

reference to the rapture and full salvation. If God's children were going into the Tribulation, Paul would have said, *"the day of the Lord."*

4. I Thessalonians 1:9 – "... to wait for His Son from heaven, whom He raised from the dead, that is, Jesus, who delivers us from the wrath to come."

5. I Thessalonians 5:9 – "For God has not destined us for wrath, but for obtaining salvation through our Lord Jesus Christ."

6. Revelation 2:22 – "Behold, I will cast her upon a bed of sickness, and those who commit adultery with her into great tribulation, unless they repent of her deeds." The point is if this church repents she will *not* experience the Tribulation.

7. Revelation 3:3 – "If therefore you will not wake up, I will come like a thief, and you will not know at what hour I will come upon you." Here again, if this false church wakes up she will *not* be caught unaware as by *"a thief,"* and be left behind.

8. Revelation 3:10 – "Because you have kept the word of My perseverance, I also will keep you from the hour of testing, that hour which is about to come upon the whole world." The Philadelphian church will not suffer *"the hour of testing,"* for she has God's blessed promise she will be kept from it.

6. The Early Church Was Expectant Of The Rapture

The early churches expected the Lord to return and were in constant vigil for His coming. Paul often spoke in his letters and obviously in his messages of the Lord's second coming. In his first letter to the Corinthians he wrote, "... in a moment, in the twinkling of an eye, at the last trumpet; for the trumpet will sound, and the dead will be raised imperishable, and we shall be changed," I Corinthians 15:52. Indeed, the entirety of I Corinthians 15 is Paul's great discourse on the resurrection of the saints.

Some Bible students have attributed *"the last trumpet"* Paul refers to in the above verse as the *"seventh trumpet"* in the final moments of the Tribulation (Revelation 11:15). Using this interpretation they wrongly attribute the *"catching up"* of the church as belonging at the close of the Tribulation. There are three good reasons refuting Paul's *"last trumpet"* and John's *"seventh trumpet"* as being the same.

1. Paul had no knowledge of John's *"seven trumpets"* as his letter to the Corinthians was written 37 years before John wrote The Revelation.

2. Paul certainly expected the Corinthians to understand his usage and meaning of the words *"the last trumpet."* They could not have understood were his comment in reference to a book that was nearly four decades from being written.

3. Paul knew the Corinthians were, however, very familiar with the Roman Army and their procedures. Roman soldiers often camped all around the outskirts of Corinth. The Corinthians were well acquainted with Rome's military routines. Roman soldiers made use of three trumpet sounds for gathering their forces. The blowing of the first trumpet signaled the soldiers to pack up camp, roll up their sleeping pad and take down their tent. The second trumpet sound meant to fall in line; they were soon leaving. And the third Roman trumpet was the signal to move out.

Paul was using an illustration they well understood to communicate a spiritual truth. The meaning to the Corinthians is a good one for us as well, spiritually. Picture the *first trumpet* sound calling God's people to pull up their stakes in this world. This place is no longer their home. In God's army we are looking for a much better home in that we have been bought by a price and brought into God's forever family. *That's justification!*

The *second trumpet* beckons the child of God to fall in line with the purpose of God today. We are to be busy in His army, in His fields and wherever He places and leads us. We have been set apart for this special time and are to be useful to the Master. *That's sanctification!*

The *"last trumpet"* is the longed for and sought after call to move out. This is the one for which the church has long waited, the blessed hope. With the Lord's *"shout"* we will be *"caught up"* to be with Him in the air. *That's glorification!*

7. The Church In The Revelation

Throughout the New Testament, beginning with the book of Acts, the church is the focal point of God's dealings with man. That focus continues in the New Testament up to Revelation 2 and 3. These chapters describe *"the things which are;"* that is, the *"things"* of the church age, the *"things"* that were going on when The Revelation was given, and the *"things"* which continue to this day. In fact, Revelation 2 and 3 is a summing-up of the churches' history on earth from birth to vanishing. Suddenly with the first verse of Chapter 4 she is gone from the remaining pages of the Bible. Look hard and look long. She is not seen again until she is mentioned in the Lord's closing comment: "I, Jesus, have sent My angel to testify to you these things for the churches," Revelation 22:16.

The Revelation was specifically written to inform, encourage and equip the church in her witness for Christ to a lost world, especially during these closing days. Many will doubtlessly come to the Lord Jesus during the Tribulation due to the churches' work prior to the rapture. They will see the events of The Revelation unfolding around them, read the literature left behind, find the Bibles stored away for her sake, and remember the testimony of former and now absent Bible believing Christians.

When it comes to Christ's church on earth from Revelation 4:1 on, there is no more mention of her. She has disappeared; literally she has vanished. Searching for her in the mountains and valleys would be as foolish as the sons of the prophets searching for Elijah after he was caught up. Oh, there will still be church meetings, but the evangelical, Bible believing, Spirit-filled and soul-winning churches and Christians are absent from earth and absent from Scripture. She is AWL, Absent With Leave, from her preserving influence and presence on earth.

So many suddenly disappear from the planet. In Revelation 4:1, twice the words are found, *"After these things."* That phrase designates the beginning of the third division of The Revelation (1:19). It draws a demarcation line between the "things which are" — the *"things"* of the church age, and "what must take place after these things" — *"after"* the church age.

As soon as the church is no longer mentioned in Scripture as being on Earth, we find a never before mentioned scene in Heaven. *"Twenty four elders"* are called to our attention in Revelation 4:4. They are sitting on *"twenty four thrones"* and "clothed in white garments." *"White garments"* are the clothing of the righteous, and given only to saints. These *"elders"* also have "golden crowns on their heads." *"Gold"* stands for purity, the preciousness of the purity of God. *"Crowns"* are promised in the Bible as rewards for the faithfulness of saints. These *"crowns"* declare the degree of one's ability to glorify Christ Jesus and rule in eternity with Him. Most Bible scholars agree; these *"twenty four elders"* are representative of the saints of the Old and New Testaments. The church is no longer on earth. The *"church"* is *"the elders,"* and they are with the Lord. And, He is in the air!

Trace the *"elders"* throughout the book of Revelation. She is almost beside herself in worship, praise and adoration — and, doubtlessly, in taking in the sites. Who wouldn't be? Listed below is every mention of the *"elders"* in the Revelation. Look these verses up. See what the *"elders"* observe and do; see what their occupation is. The *"elders"* are seen in Revelation 4:4, 10; 5:5, 6, 8, 11, 14; 7:11, 13; 11:16; 14:3; 19:4.

Have you looked up each of those verses? Certainly, we should do more today of what they do every time they look into His face.

The Judgment Seat Of Christ

"The judgment seat of Christ" has nothing to do with being called before a judge after having committed a crime. Just the opposite! The word, *"judgment seat,"* is the Greek word, *"bema."* The *"bema"* is in reference to the judge's seat at the Roman coliseum. The runners in a race were not condemned for losing; they were rewarded for winning. It is the same with the *"bema of Christ."*

Paul introduced this truth in II Corinthians 5:10 when he wrote, "For we must all appear before the judgment seat of Christ, that each one may be recompensed for his deeds in the body, according to what he has done, whether good or bad." The word *"appear"* has the connotation of everything being revealed, motives as well as deeds. We will be *"recompensed."* That is, our *"deeds in the body"* will be rewarded. It's payday! Someone has said there are no rewards for posthumous acts. I believe they are right. Of a deceased lady leaving her church a million dollars it was said, "Oh, won't her reward be great!" No, it won't. If she were still *"in the body"* she would *still* be clutching her million dollars. Rewards are for *"deeds (done) in the body... whether good or bad."* *"Good"* deeds, those done in the name of Jesus, those accomplished in the Spirit of mercy and grace, and those done through God's leading and calling will be recompensed. The word *"bad"* is not bad in a malicious, evil sort of way. This word translated *"bad"* is best understood to mean, "good for nothing." In other words, there will be no reward for those in God's forever family who have lived their lives invested in works that are "good for nothing." What a shame! They missed the joy and adventure of being involved in the work of God in their day.

Paul had already explained this to the Corinthians in his first letter. There he spoke of laborers in God's field and of the rewards for fruitful labor (I Corinthians 3:6-15). He gives an illustration of two kinds of building materials, each having three degrees of worth. His emphasis is found in verse 13. "Each man's work will become evident; for the day will show it, because it is to be revealed by fire; and the fire itself will test **the quality** of each man's work."

The force of Paul's teaching lies not in how much work one does, but rather the *"quality of (one's) work."* How clearly has our Spirit motivated, Christ uplifting and God honoring acts of obedience characterized our labor? Useless works will be *"burned up"* (verse 15), which means — no reward for them. John tells us to *"watch"* ourselves. Lack of faithfulness can rob one of rewards previously attained (II John 8; Revelation 3:11). It would be profitable to take a moment and turn to Paul's advice to his young understudy found in II Timothy 2:20, 21. He speaks there of how to "... be a vessel for honor, sanctified, useful to the Master, prepared for every good work."

When is the *"judgment seat of Christ?"* We are not told the specific time of the *"judgment seat."* We know it is after we go to be with the Lord *"in the air,"* and before we come back to earth with Him. Let me speculate on a possible time of this "awarding bench" from something I've noticed. The *"elders"* are introduced to us in Revelation 4:1. They have *"golden crowns"* on their heads, meaning they have already been to *"the judgment seat of Christ."* Perhaps the *"judgment seat"* is one of our earliest appointments with the Lord, either by stepping through death's door into His presence, or when the Lord calls us to meet Him *"in the air."*

The Marriage Supper Of The Lamb

"The marriage supper of the Lamb" is introduced to us in Revelation 19:9, "Blessed are those who are invited to the marriage supper of the Lamb." In its context in this passage, *"the marriage supper"* seems to be just before the Lord returns to earth with, *"the armies which are in heaven,"* verse 14.

We are not advised as to the menu at the *"marriage supper,"* who will give the toast, or what the seating arrangements will be. If you are like me you are thinking, "Wow, it's enough just to be here." Be assured, the most gala event on earth crumbles to dust in light of a *"marriage supper"* like this.

At every marriage supper there is, of course, the Bride and the Groom. Jesus is the Groom, and the church is His bride. An interesting point to ponder is when this verse says, "Blessed are those who are invited to the marriage supper of the Lamb," Revelation 19:9. So who are the invited guests?

Well now! No bride sends herself an invitation. Since the church is the bride we're cannot the one's getting the invitation. Who is being invited? As far as we've been told there are only two kinds of created beings: angels and people. As soon as Michael and his warriors have kicked the dickens out of the devil and thrown his ragtag bunch of followers to the earth they could join us. So I imagine Michael and Company will be available, and what bride wouldn't want them at her *"marriage supper?"* The others, I cannot help but envision, are that heavenly body of Old Testament saints, also referred to in Scripture as the wife of Jehovah. Won't that be neat! So Israel and the holy angels will be our wedding guests. And you think you had a shindig of a wedding planned on this old ball of dirt we call Earth!

"The marriage supper of the Lamb" is a celebration of our eternal union with Christ Jesus our Lord, Savior and King.

The Bride And The Great Promise

Now, can you imagine this? The *"elders"* who, in Revelation 4:4, first came on the scene in Heaven are last mentioned in Revelation 19:4, still in Heaven. They are not seen again throughout the remainder of The Revelation. Someone else is though. Immediately in Revelation 19:7, 8 we hear glad rejoicing, for "the marriage of the Lamb has come and His **bride** has made herself ready. And it was given to her to clothe herself in fine linen, bright and clean; for the fine linen is the righteous acts of the saints."

The *"elders"* are gone and the *"bride has made herself ready."* When the *"church"* was visible on earth, there were no *"twenty four elders"* in Heaven. When the *"elders"* came on the scene in Heaven, the *"church"* was missing from earth, but no *"bride"* was seen in Heaven. When the *"elders"* disappear in Heaven, the *"bride"* appears. They cannot all three be visible at the same time. The three are one and are about to become four. She plays different roles at different times. And you thought life would be boring in Heaven.

She was the *"church"* on earth until she was called to meet the Lord *"in the air."* She then became the *"elders"* around the throne of God in Heaven and in the presence of the *"Lamb."* Those marvelous *"thrones around the throne of God"* will be the greatest graduate school you and I will have ever attended. We will learn more on those *"thrones"* in a moment than we've learned in all our years on earth, and we will have nearly seven years on those *"thrones."* But remember, once resurrected or translated to be with the Lord, *"thus we shall always be with the Lord,"* I Thessalonians 4:17. And our Lord has unfinished business to conclude.

First, of course, there is the *"marriage supper"* to attend. So you and I, *"the bride,"* now *"clothe ourselves in fine linen, bright and clean"* in preparation to be presented to the Groom, the Lord Jesus Christ. And you are prepared, for your *"fine linen is the righteous acts of the saints."* Stay with me a moment! You became a *"saint"* back on earth when you were washed in the blood of the Lamb. Your *"righteous acts,"* since coming to Christ become the *"fine linens"* of your wedding gown, the measure of God's glory given you that now radiates from your presence. Wow! Listen! This is important! Your wedding gown comes out of the treasures you have stored up in Heaven (Matthew 6:19-21). Store some up! Fill up your treasure chest now. Earth's trials and labors are the only "storing up" station at which your treasure chest can be filled. Fill it to overflowing! You'll sure wish then you had.

But that's not all. *"The marriage supper"* comes to a close. The honeymoon, however, will have to wait. The Groom has pressing business. Do you remember God's great promise? "And thus we shall always be with the Lord," I Thessalonians 4:17. Where the Lord goes, His bride goes. Observe! Here's a bride whose boots are going to do some walking.

Our magnificent Groom mounts a *"white horse,"* Revelation 19:11. His name is called *"Faithful and True."* We watch diligently as *"He judges and wages war." "His eyes are a flame of fire, and upon His head are many crowns."* He sports a secret *"name,"* no one else knows (verse 12). His *"robe is dipped in blood; and His name is called The Word of God,"* verse 13.

But hold on! Suddenly white horses stampede to position behind our Commander who lovingly bids us, "Mount up!" *"And the armies which are in heaven, clothed in fine linen, white and clean, were following Him on white horses,"* verse 14. Who are these *"armies,"* and from where have they come? The Scripture doesn't say?

Or, does it!

These *"armies"* are wearing *"fine linen, white and clean."* Those stated garments are only given to saints. So the saints of God are *"following the (Lord Jesus Christ) on white horses"* of their own. Since the word *"armies"* is plural, I can't help but imagine He has more than one. Let's see now, there is the bride. That would make one army. There are the Old Testament saints. Most of them already know how to use a sword. They are an army in themselves and have a vested interest as to what happens on Earth. So they would make a second army. Michael and the angels will be there, and they can dress anyway they want. They are holy, so I guess *"white"* will look good on them, too. They've already proven their battle worthiness. So they are perhaps a third army. Won't they be fun to fight along side! The devil and his bunch haven't a chance on earth or elsewhere. There's no place to hide. And here comes the Groom with His army of myriads upon myriads upon myriads.

So the *"church on earth"* becomes the *"elders in Heaven"* who becomes the *"bride"* at the *"marriage supper"* who becomes a part of the *"armies (from) Heaven."* Exciting! Thrilling! Fascinating! I haven't lost you, have I? And it is not just a story line. It is history future proclaimed and fast approaching that you and I, dear friend, will be never-before-so-alive participators in. You are a child of God, are you not? If not, settle that matter. The day rapidly approaches.

And some poor lost soul thinks Heaven will be mind numbing and tiresome and dull.

But wait! Attention is suddenly drawn back to our Groom for, "from His mouth comes a sharp sword." That sword, always representative of the Word of God, declares the measure by which He judges and wages war (John 5:22, 23; Acts 10:42; 17:31). He is ready to "tread the wine press of the fierce wrath of God, the Almighty," verse 15. As we speed through the air on our horses of glory, attention by all in Heaven and on Earth is drawn to our Groom's brightly shining banner. "And on His robe and on His thigh He has a name written, *'KING OF KINGS, AND LORD OF LORDS,'*" verse 16.

What a day!!! It's Armageddon for the world. It's deliverance for Israel! And, it's glory for the church!

Chapter Five

Revival Of The Roman Empire

"Yeah! Right! Harry Potter Wasn't Fictitious Either!"

Why Do The Heathen Rage?

Any close examination of The Revelation, as well as the Bible as a whole, clearly reveals it has as its overriding purpose the revelation of the Person and work of the Lord Jesus Christ. He is declared the creator, the originator, the sustainer and the ultimate answer to man and to this world's sin problem. He is known to be gracious and benevolent. But He is also, and understandable so, known to be severe with those playing loose with His Instruction Manual. So why do the heathen rage against Him? The answer to that question lies in the fact that man recoils at almost every authority — especially a divine and unavoidable authority. Yet, God was God in eternity past, He is now in time and He will be God in eternity future. He can therefore unequivocally and without braggadocio say, "I am the Great I Am." He will not and cannot budge on that forever role. So the heathen's rage in this sense is eternally senseless. (Whom else would you want in charge of all creation throughout eternity?) Man's raging is eternally senseless in that Jehovah God, were He an adversary, could not be a more benevolent adversary toward all who seek Him. Yet, if necessary, as the eternal God He also becomes the Judge of all defying Him — angels and mankind alike.

Jesus Christ is not an avowed adversary of the Father's crowning work of creation either, i.e. man and woman. The Holy Spirit who resides within us imparting God's life to us is certainly not our enemy either. However, God's Law does take up the role as our adversary. The Law, which can be summed up in the Ten Commandments, requires strict adherence to its demands. Without those Laws governing eternity future Heaven would eventually be Hell. And all of life would be pointless. The Law of God must reign. Should it not reign, how would a lawless eternity sound to you?

The problem of adherence to the Law is exacerbated by the fact that every man and woman has already broken every Commandment of the Law, either in thought or deed. I know this comes as unwelcome news to some. Notwithstanding, the righteous Law stands as a guard, a shield for a paradisal eternity. Break just one Law and justice requires due payment. Payment in this realm is eternal banishment from the presence of a perfectly holy and exalted God. The wages of sin is still death (Romans 6:23). Heaven cannot sustain even one person with just one unanswered and un-atoned for sin.

This is not fictitious. Harry Potter is! This is the real world.

Consider this: as with a child so it is with an adult. Tell him he cannot do something and self rises up on the balls of its feet gnarling its teeth. As King David found, "Behold, I was brought forth in iniquity, and in sin my mother conceived me," Psalms 51:5. He was speaking not of the sin of illegitimacy (yes, that's still sin), but of the sin-saturated nature with which he was born. David recognized the thoughts of his heart and the intents of his mind were evil continually. That is true of the whole human race. Just look at the U.S.

Congress! Its members are all adults — according to their driving licenses. But, here is an example closer to home. Do you have to train a child to behave or to misbehave? I need not say more. Their darkened little hearts are set on doing their own thing from the time they arrive. Yes, they are cute and helpless perhaps, but nevertheless sinful to the core. Maybe that's why they kick in their mother's womb. Just kidding! It's cramped in there, I'm sure. Memory fails me on that.

God confirmed Job to be a righteous man. Not perfect in his friends eyes, but perhaps the closest thing on earth to perfect in actuality. Yet, even Job recognized the sin problem separating him from God and cried out, "For He is not a man as I am that I may answer Him, that we may go to court together. There is no umpire between us, who may lay his hand upon us both (in reconciliation)," Job 9:32, 33. In that, Job was wrong. It's just the Umpire had not yet arrived upon the scene or revealed Himself.

That Umpire is Jesus Christ. He died in place of every man, woman, boy and girl. But He is not dead. He rose from the grave to place one hand on us and His other hand on God, reconciling us to the Father. Through faith in Him, that is turning from one's self and to the Lord Christ Jesus, sin is totally forgiven and forever removed. A new nature, God's nature, is at that point birthed within the believer declaring his or her sins to be PAID IN FULL and making that person ACCEPTABLE before God. The old sin nature still hangs around until the twice-born goes to be with the Lord, but sin's strength has been broken and its rule shattered. Victory over it is in reach of every child of God as he matures in Christ. See Romans 6:14 and 8:1, 2. As the law of aerodynamics overrules gravity, so God's nature overrules the sin nature in the child of God, or it's behind the woodshed time for the erring child in the family of God (Hebrews 12:7, 8). Oh yeah! He disciplines His own. See Hebrews 12:5-8.

Our Umpire Works Out The Game Plan

It used to be my coach's job to work out the game plan. So it is in the game of life. The Christian's Umpire not only mediates, He also calls the shots. This game of life is serious and can certainly be intriguing! Yet, in infinite wisdom God works it out for all coming to Him. Those rejecting His love and offer of salvation are left to fend for themselves in an eternity we'll not go into — yet!

Part of God's overall game plan is to allow sin, to a point, to run rampant in a world of sinners desiring to be free of all constraints and therefore free of the Law of God and of the Lamb of God. Some will turn from sin and to Christ Jesus — as many do. For them God has prepared the way of salvation. It is also true; many reject God's way. He will not force anyone to receive His Son. He *must*, however, enforce His Law. It is only right to mention again, there is a place prepared for the Lawless.

We've looked briefly at Israel, the special treasure of God, though an irritant and a dilemma to most others. You may have recognized she has many enemies in this world. Just look at the vast majority of the countries making up the United Nations. Israel has only a handful of friends. That will continue for a while, *though probably for only a short while*. And then it will come to an end. But, what brings it to that end? The answer to that question is more important and world shattering than most people today probably imagine. I said "probably" because a rapidly increasing number of people sense something big is coming down this world's pike. And it is! Israel will then be *almost* universally hated and forsaken by all but one group — the last group on earth she should trust. But she will!

For anyone to cross home base safely entails recognizing a number of events, nations and personalities. The mention of the first of these events has been and continues to be a

cause of derision among "think tanks, leftists and elitists."
We have already looked at that event, the rebirth of the
nation of Israel, God's infallible sign of Christ's soon return.
See again Matthew 24:32-35 for a quick refresher.

The second of these events is also already in place. You
can see it in the headlines of newspapers and magazines,
hear it on the monologs of radio talk show hosts, and read
it on the tickertapes of TV news programs from around the
world without even recognizing the significance. This, a
second major signpost of the Lord's coming, is the subject
of this chapter.

Rome Returns From The Grave

Headlines throughout the world's media describe what
the Bible says will happen just before the Lord Jesus' return
to this world. The world-ruling Rome of old, non-existent
since her last Emperor and Empire fell in A.D. 476, will
return to power in its second quest for world dominion. For
the Christian the fact of Rome's rise is neither wishful nor
unwise thinking. It is not a matter of pulling out of Scripture
an obscure passage of something that may or may not exist.
Rome's resurgence is a fact of Biblical prophecy. Rome's
global revival is revealed in a large number of passages
in Old and New Testaments alike. As evil as Rome was,
she will again be a kingpin in this world's coming history
— meaner, uglier and more evil than ever. From her will
arise the antithesis of Christ Jesus the Lord. Why the world
rejects Christ and receives Antichrist is beyond the thinking
of rational men. But then I suppose that answers the question
as to why. Whoever said most men are rational? Ask their
wives and you'll see!

Let's glimpse now at what the Bible says lies directly
ahead of us in the course of tomorrow's certain and already
foretold history. Oh heck! Let me just spill the beans, then

I'll go around and clean up the mess. You are about to see in a number of Old Testament passages, prophesied over 2,500 years ago, today's history in the making. Much of this has already been fulfilled concerning various nations and kingdoms, just as God said it would. Some of it has not been fulfilled, but will at its appropriate time, just as God said it would. You will then be led to even more revelation of this coming Roman Empire in the New Testament.

Now here is an important question every person *must* answer. If the prophecies of God's Word for nations of the past have been fulfilled just as the Word of God foretold they would be, is it not reasonable to believe the portions that have not been fulfilled will be fulfilled in their due time — just as God foretold them?

I hope you answered in the affirmative. If not, we've still a lot of convincing revelation to present, some of it unfortunately close to home. I don't want this dropped in your lap one day and you be unaware of it. But keep this in mind, God has never been wrong. Not once! He loves to divulge history before it takes place. He does so to further prove He is who He is, the great *I AM*. He is the ever-present One. He also does so to prove that future events and personages with Him are as sure as the past and present ones. He informs us of coming attractions to further reach out to this world of men and women for whom His Son died and rose to give life. He does so to instruct the simplest and confound the wisest of men that all may be blessed or held accountable. There is something about childlikeness that gains favor in His eyes. "Truly I say to you, unless you are converted (turned, repentance is in view) and become like children, you shall not enter the kingdom of heaven," Matthew 18:3. He does so because with Him the end is as clear as the beginning. And He does so because He does not wish for any person to perish but for all to come to repentance (II Peter 3:9). It's His way of reaching out.

We'll start in Daniel 2 and quickly run through several passages. Each of these passages is given to reveal the identity and the reality of the old Roman Empire springing to life and donning the gauntlet to regain its former position of world dominion. Only this time the Roman leader has help from a foreign god.

Nebuchadnezzar's Bothersome Dream

Daniel, as a young man, was a captive of war. Nebuchadnezzar king of Babylon conquered Jerusalem. In the spoils he took back to Babylon the precious vessels and instruments of the house of God and the best looking and wisest of the youth of Judah to serve in his court. Among them were Daniel, Shadrach, Meshach and Abed-nego. Daniel and his friends quickly proved themselves to be the wisest among their contemporaries, and eventually among all the wise men of the Babylonian Empire.

In the second year of his reign Nebuchadnezzar had a dream that troubled him greatly. He called for the wise men of Babylon to interpret his dream. For the purpose of ascertaining their veracity he demanded they relate to him both the dream and its interpretation. If they did not, horrifying things were on their horizon. They stealthily begged the dream be given them and they would interpret it. He begged to differ. Nebuchadnezzar wasn't stupid.

"The king answered and said, 'I know for certain that you are bargaining for time, inasmuch as you have seen that the command from me is firm, that if you do not make the dream known to me, there is only one decree for you. For you have agreed together to speak lying and corrupt words before me until the situation is changed; therefore tell me the dream, that I may know that you can declare to me its interpretation,'" Daniel 2:8, 9.

They could not, of course, relate the king's dream any more than Baal's prophets could call down fire from heaven. They were left with no wagon into which they could place either a true or false interpretation. The following day the king's command would be executed: "you will be torn limb from limb, and your houses will be made a rubbish heap," (verse 5).

Arioch, the king's commander, came for Daniel and his friends to execute them as well, who though young were already considered part of the wise men. Unaware of what had taken place Daniel through discretion and discernment convinced Arioch and the king to allow him and his friends to pray over the king's matter for that night. His request was granted.

That night God revealed to Daniel King Nebuchadnezzar's dream and its interpretation. The king's dream and its meaning has significance all the way down to us today, as well as for upcoming days. Here is the king's dream (Daniel 2:31-35): "You, O king, were looking and behold, there was a single great statue; that statue, which was large and of extraordinary splendor, was standing in front of you, and its appearance was awesome. The head of that statue was made of fine gold, its breast and its arms of silver, its belly and its thighs of bronze, its legs of iron, its feet partly of iron and partly of clay. You continued looking until a stone was cut out without hands, and it struck the statue on its feet of iron and clay, and crushed them. Then the iron, the clay, the bronze, the silver and the gold were crushed all at the same time, and became like chaff from the summer threshing floors; and the wind carried them away so that not a trace of them was found. But the stone that struck the statue became a great mountain and filled the whole earth."

That was the king's dream — one great statue made up of several materials diminishing in value from head to toes. Each of these kingdom's described by various materials are representative of empires that would rule the world from Nebuchadnezzar's day until a *"great mountain (fills) the whole earth."* As important as revealing the king's dream was to the wise men of Babylon, the interpretation has been and is far more important to nations, to us today and to many more in days just ahead. Here in brief is Daniel's interpretation and the now literally fulfilled details of the king's dream concerning four of the six world kingdoms from his day until the end of time. You can read Daniel's own words in Daniel 2:36-45. I'll summarize them here.

First, *"the head of that statue was made of fine gold,"* refers to Nebuchadnezzar and his kingdom, Babylon. "You, O king, are the king of kings, to whom the God of heaven has given the kingdom, the power, the strength, and the glory; and wherever the sons of men dwell, or the beasts of the field, or the birds of the sky, He has given them into your hand and has caused you to rule over them all. **You are the head of gold,**" verses 37, 38.

Indeed, Nebuchadnezzar, King of Babylon, was king of the whole world. The statues *"head... was made of fine gold."* No kingdom since the days of Daniel has ever attained to the glory and splendor of Nebuchadnezzar's Babylon. Many have tried to replicate it, but none has reached its pinnacle in military might, governance and glory. The Kingdom of Babylon was the crown of man's highest achievements. Its *"head... was made of fine gold."* So the first world domineering kingdom was Babylon. Even today in Iraq they are trying to restore Nebuchadnezzar's Babylon. Their efforts will never equal the original.

The second kingdom is pictured as having *"breast and arms of silver."* Eventually, Babylon was over run, conquered by the Medo-Persian Empire, which, as with all of these nations, ruled the entire earth. She is given the value of *"silver"* here. Silver is certainly valuable, but not as valuable as gold. The Medo-Persian era was mighty and wealthy, but her glory and prestige never reached the height of Babylon's splendor.

Concerning the third kingdom set before us we find, *"its belly and its thighs (were) of bronze."* Bronze is unquestionably valuable as well, yet its esteem cannot compare with the splendor and value of silver or gold. The same is true of this third world-ruling nation, the Grecian Empire. Thus, the continuing decline in symbolic value. Greek's power and wealth never attained the height of Babylon's or that of the Medo-Persian's.

The fourth great empire is depicted as having, *"legs of iron."* Again, less valuable than any of the previous kingdoms, nevertheless, this was perhaps one of the cruelest among the world-conquering empires. This is the Roman Empire that came into power in approximately B.C. 30 and ruled until A.D. 476. This is the Rome that was in control during the days of Christ as well as when Jerusalem was overrun in A.D. 70.

Among these first four world empires one was in existence when this dream was interpreted, the Babylonian Empire. Three were future when Daniel interpreted Nebuchadnezzar's dream, the Medo-Persian Empire, the Grecian Empire and the Roman Empire. Those three, though future when Daniel interpreted the dream, are now also past historical facts. They came into existence just as God promised they would, and just as His prophet openly declared.

If Daniel was right in interpreting the king's dream of world conquering nations that would arise, the probabilities are he was right about the remainder of his interpretation as well, that is, the governments that are yet to come.

The fifth kingdom has not yet come into world reigning power. She is, however, present among the nations of the world today and taking giant steps on the way to world dominion. This kingdom in the king's dream is shown as having, *"feet partly of iron and partly of clay."* The *"iron"* shows the strength of this fifth kingdom; and it will be strong. *"Clay,"* however, is not strong. It shatters easily. As everyone knows *"iron and clay"* do not mix. Yet, these all-important *"feet"* are made of both *"iron"* and *"clay."* This fifth kingdom will be partly strong, but it will also be partly weak. This fifth kingdom, as we will see on numerous occasions, is the revived Roman Empire.

From the same vicinity of the Roman Empire of old, this revived Roman Empire of the future will arise. It will have strength. In fact, no one will be able to stand against it for seven years, but it will also have ten kingdoms within it. And in that it will be weakened.

This prophesied revived Roman Empire is rising today out of that area of the world consisting of the old Roman Empire. She is growing strong in influence, power and wealth. She is known today as the European Union, also called the E.U., as I will often refer to her throughout the remainder of this book.

Daniel goes on and reminds the king of a *"stone (that was) cut out without hands."* It "struck the statue on its feet of iron and clay, and crushed them," verse 34. "Then the iron, the clay, the bronze, the silver and the gold were crushed all at the same time, and became like chaff... and the wind carried them away so that not a trace of them was found," verse 35. Nothing is left of the earlier kingdoms, but the *"stone that struck the statue became a great mountain and filled the whole earth."*

That *"stone"* is the Lord Jesus Christ whose sixth kingdom will rule the earth for one thousand years. After that, time will be no more. Eternity will be ushered in. But presently, we've still a lot of *proof* to examine. Can the Common Market of Europe, the E.U., be absolutely proven to be the revived Roman Empire declared so long ago? Hang onto that thought. We'll let Scripture decide.

Daniel's Dream Of Four Beasts

Daniel was given a vision of the four world domineering kingdoms of the earth he pinpointed earlier for King Nebuchadnezzar. Only now they were, "four great beasts coming up from the sea, different from one another," Daniel 7:3. The word *"sea"* in its symbolic form in Scripture represents the Gentile nations. It is out of these designated nations *"the beasts"* arise to worldwide power.

The first *"beast"* is pictured as *"a lion and had the wings of an eagle,"* (verse 4) and draws our attention back to Babylon. Her conquering the nations with ease and swiftness is seen in the *"wings of an eagle."* Those *"wings,"* however, *"were plucked,"* declaring its ability to soar was taken from it. This *"beast"* was *"made to stand on two feet like a man; a human mind (heart) was given to it,"* refers to Nebuchadnezzar humbly and finally recognizing the God of heaven.

The second *"beast"* resembled *"a bear"* (verse 5) and represents the Medo-Persian Empire. Strong and powerful she is seen with *"three ribs in its mouth between its teeth."* Indeed, the Medo-Persian Empire conquered three great world powers: the Babylonians, the Phoenicians and the Lydians. As prophesied she *devoured much meat!"*

The third *"beast"* represents the Grecian Empire and is described as *"a leopard."* On *"its back (were) four wings of a bird"* showing its swiftness and power in conquering. Yet, it also has *"four heads"* referring to the kingdom's division into four parts after the death of Alexander the Great. It became a divided kingdom under the rule of four of Alexander's generals.

The fourth *"beast"* is not given the identity of an animal. Rather this *"beast"* is indescribable, and as such has been dubbed, "the non-descript beast." She is too *"dreadful and terrifying and extremely strong"* to be described. This *"beast"* has *"large iron teeth. It devoured and crushed, and trampled down the remainder with its feet."* This refers us back to the Roman Empire we saw described by Daniel in Nebuchadnezzar's dream. Her destructive path is visually identified here.

One added description though is she is said to have *"ten horns."* Verse 24 tells us whom these *"ten horns"* represent. "As for the ten horns, out of this kingdom ten kings will arise." The Roman Empire pictured here encompasses not only the original Roman Empire we saw in Daniel 2, but also the revived Roman Empire of our day and the days immediately ahead. In this prophecy no gap between the two Roman Empires is shown. *"Ten kings"* will be given authority to rule over ten districts of this (later) Roman Empire, the revived Roman Empire.

"Another horn, a little one, came up among them." This *"little horn"* is Antichrist. "Three of the first horns (kings) were pulled out by the roots before it (the fourth beast)." Their insubordination cost them their lives and kingdoms. These *"ten kings"* are also mentioned in Daniel 7:20, 24 and Revelation 17:12, 13. We'll see more of them later. Our non-descript beast in Daniel's dream is primarily the revived Roman Empire and her *"dreadful and terrifying and extremely strong"* leader — Antichrist of the Tribulation period. Both Roman empires were extremely cruel, but the latter of the two will supersede and surpass every imaginable cruelty of the former.

Daniel's summarization of this *"beast"* is given us in Daniel 7:23: "Thus he said: 'The fourth beast will be a fourth kingdom on the earth, which will be different from all the other kingdoms, and it will devour the whole earth and tread it down and crush it." No one will desire to reside on Earth in these upcoming days!

The original Roman Empire is history gone by. This foretold revived Roman Empire is history in the making and on the earthly scene today in the countries composing the EU. Her place in history will be played out in full sway on Earth in a soon coming day. The leader of the E.U. will come to the surface when he confirms a seven-year covenant of peace for Israel. He will not, however, be recognized by the majority on earth until the midpoint of the Tribulation.

Daniel's Vision Of The Small Horn

Speaking again in Daniel 8:9 of *"the little horn,"* who is Antichrist, God gives us a glimpse of the sordid character of this world's coming false messiah. The following is Daniel 8:23-27.

"And in the latter period of their rule, when the transgressors have run their course, a king will arise, insolent and skilled in intrigue. And his power will be mighty, but not by his own power, and he will destroy to an extraordinary degree and prosper and perform his will; He will destroy mighty men and the holy people. And through his shrewdness He will cause deceit to succeed by his influence; and he will magnify himself in his heart, and he will destroy many while they are at ease. He will even oppose the Prince of princes, but he will be broken without human agency. And the vision of the evenings and mornings which has been told is true; but keep the vision secret, for it pertains to many days in the future."

This insolent one is Antichrist. His ability to kill and destroy will prove unmatched in all human history. Even those coming to a saving knowledge of Jesus Christ during these seven years of Tribulation are not immune to his murderous ambitions. Rather they are the primary target. Why shouldn't they be? He even opposes the Prince of princes, the Lord Jesus Christ. Surely he will vigorously oppose God's people. He can't win against Christ, so he'll just try to hurt as many of Christ's people as possible. That's the game plan.

But there is good news, too. *"He (Antichrist) will be broken without human agency."* This serious felon will be taken care of by God Himself. That we will see later as well. Daniel was told three times over, "this vision is not for you but for the end times," (Daniel 8:17, 19 and 26). Beloved, God reserved these truths for you and me.

The Prince Who Is To Come

For the second time Gabriel visits Daniel to share with him certain events related to the end times. Here Gabriel is sent to divulge the mystery of Daniel's Seventy Weeks. These weeks are recorded in Daniel 9:24-27. We covered this earlier in Chapter 3, so I'll refer you there for a more in-depth study of these important weeks of years leading up to the Lord Jesus' return. Presently, I simply want to point out Antichrist's part in these Seventy Weeks, which should actually be entitled Israel's Seventy Weeks. Remember, we are dealing here with a shrewd, deceitful and influential head of a brought back from the grave Roman Empire, the full-blown E.U.

These weeks refer to Israel's prophesied history from the decree of King Artaxerxes of Persia authorizing Jeremiah to return and rebuild Jerusalem, and then stretching on to the second coming of Jesus Christ. Israel was, of course, in exile when these seventy weeks were assigned to her as a nation. Three time periods reflect her future history until her rejected Lord returns to earth. The first time period was of 7 weeks (verse 25) representative of 49 years. The second time period was a span of 62 weeks (verse 25) representative of 434 years. The third time period is of 1 week (verse 27) representative of 7 years. The three together are a total of 490 years.

After the first two time periods totaling 483 years, "Messiah will be cut off and have nothing," verse 26a. That is exactly what happened. Israel at the end of the first 483 years would reject her Messiah and crucify Him. Upon His resurrection He ascended to the throne of His Father to await the Father's timing for His return. Meanwhile, verse 26 continues, "… and the people of the prince who is to come will destroy the city and the sanctuary."

Now, let's break this sentence down. It is not the *"prince who is to come"* who destroys the city and the sanctuary. It is *"the people of the prince who is to come (who) will destroy the city and the sanctuary."* The *"people"* who destroyed Jerusalem and the Temple were the Romans in A.D. 70. They were *"the people of the prince who is to come."* The *"prince"* is future. He has not yet come. He is Antichrist. He is the coming head of the European Union, the revived Roman Empire. He steps on the stage of human history when he miraculously *"confirms a covenant"* of peace for Israel with the Palestinians and in all likelihood some of the surrounding Arab/Muslim nations. He is not, however, at this time recognized for who he really is. His full unveiling will be when he commits the "abomination of desolation," (Daniel 8:11-13; 9:27; 12:11; Matthew 24:15; Mark 13:14). That will occur at the midpoint of the Tribulation.

The question often asked is, "Do you think he is alive in Europe today?" That question is not mine to answer. But, he very well may be. You'll see why as you continue traversing the pages of this book. The evidence of Antichrist and his place in the future of the E.U., the revived Roman Empire, is well documented in the Bible. And Europe is moving rapidly toward that infamous day.

Antichrist And Hell's Coming Warfare

Daniel 11:1-20, like much of prophecy, was spoken to nations concerning events that were history future when given, but are now history past. Since these prophecies were future to Daniel and King Darius of the Chaldans, they were history yet to come. They came in their time just as prophesied. Daniel's track record of accuracy can only be explained if he was God's spokesperson for that day. The literal fulfillment of remaining prophetic events not yet taken place cannot be explained away except by the wishful thinking of a heart as prickly as a porcupine, a mind made of mush, with eyes that cannot see and with ears that cannot hear.

Verses 21-39 speak of events that are yet to take place and will take place in the seventieth week of Daniel, the Tribulation period. Meanwhile verses 40-45 are a parenthesis. They don't fit in the running narrative without breaking the author's thought, but serve as a needful addendum to them. Verses 40-43 are future history and will occur between verses 21 and 22, while verses 44 and 45 and also future historically and will occur after verse 39.

The minute details and accuracy of Daniel's prophecies which were history future when given, but have been fulfilled, validate the accuracy and reliability of his prophecies that are still in the future. As we continue through the remaining chapters of this book, you may be surprised and perhaps greatly bothered by 2,500-year-old prophecies mirroring facts on the ground in our day. So get a glass of water, calm your nerves and read on. From this time on it is one bell-ringer after another.

In Daniel 11:21-39 we are given a running account of the coming Antichrist's warfare as if the events were being enacted before his eyes. I will list below Daniel's account of these days with only a few comments in parentheses to best illustrate the nature of this coming beast of a man.

"And in his place a despicable person will arise (Antichrist), on whom the honor of kingship has not been conferred, but he will come in a time of tranquility and seize the kingdom by intrigue. Verse 21.

"And the overflowing forces (enemy forces swept away) will be flooded away before him and shattered, and also the prince of the covenant. Verse 22.

"And after an alliance is made with him he will practice deception, and he will go up and gain power with a small force of people. Verse 23.

"In a time of tranquility he will enter the richest parts of the realm (the Egyptian realm), and he will accomplish what his fathers never did, nor his ancestors; he will distribute plunder, booty, and possessions among them, and he will devise his schemes against the strongholds (of Egypt), but only for a time. Verse 24.

"And he will stir up his strength and courage against the king of the South (Egypt) with a large army; so the king of the South will mobilize an extremely large and mighty army for war; but he will not stand, for schemes will be devised against him (the King of the South). Verse 25.

"And those who eat his choice food will destroy him (the King of the South)), and his army will overflow (be swept away), and many will fall down slain. Verse 26.

"As for both kings (Antichrist & Egypt), their hearts will be intent on evil, and they will speak lies to each other at the same table; but it will not succeed, for the end is still to come at the appointed time. Verse 27.

"Then he (Antichrist) will return to his land with much plunder; but his heart will be set against the holy covenant (God's chosen people), and he will take action (conspire against the Jews) and then return to his own land. Verse 28.

"At the appointed time (God's time) he will return and come into the South (another invasion of Egypt), but this last time it will not turn out the way it did before. Verse 29.

"For ships of Kittim (Cyprus) will come against him; therefore he will be disheartened, and will return and become enraged at the holy covenant and will take action; so he will come back and show regard for those who forsake the holy covenant. Verse 30.

"And forces from him (Antichrist) will arise, desecrate the sanctuary fortress (the Temple), and do away with the regular sacrifice. And they will set up the abomination of desolation (Antichrist's desecration of the Sanctuary, pronouncing himself as God). Verse 31.

"And by smooth words he will turn to godlessness those who act wickedly toward the covenant, but the people who know their God will display strength and take action. Verse 32.

"And those who have insight among the people will give understanding to the many; yet they will fall by sword and by flame, by captivity and by plunder, for many days. Verse 33.

"Now when they fall they will be granted a little help, and many will join with them in hypocrisy (these are those turning in others who accept Jesus Christ). Verse 34.

"And some of those who have insight will fall, in order to refine, purge, and make them pure, until the end time; because it is still to come at the appointed time. Verse 35.

"Then the king (Antichrist) will do as he pleases, and he will exalt and magnify himself above every god, and will speak monstrous things against the God of gods; and he will prosper until the indignation is finished, for that which is decreed will be done. Verse 36.

"And he will show no regard for the gods of his fathers, or for the desire of women, nor will he show regard for any other god; for he will magnify himself above them all. Verse 37.

"But instead he will honor a god of fortresses, a god whom his fathers did not know; he will honor him with gold, silver, costly stones, and treasures. Verse 38.

"And he will take action against the strongest of fortresses with the help of a foreign god (Satan); he will give great honor to those who acknowledge him, and he will cause them to rule over the many, and will parcel out land for a price." Verse 39.

This man of sin is the epitome of humanity apart from God. But again, what insight God gave Daniel over 2,500 years ago in communicating Antichrist's exact actions. Verses 40-43 in their historical context fit in between verses 21 and 22. This is the front-end period of the Tribulation, as we will see a little later. It is the First Battle of Gog and Magog and takes place very shortly after the head of the revived Roman Empire (Antichrist of the E.U.) inks an unconfirmed covenant of peace for Israel and the Palestinians. Could this covenant of peace be the infamous Road Map To Peace In The Middle East? Isn't some kind of a peace better than no peace whatsoever? Not if it is with the devil. You may well answer both questions yourself when we come to this battle. You will see the kings waging war and discover the results of it recorded in the Word of God.

Meanwhile, grasp the whole picture by inserting verse 40-43 after verse 21 above.

"And at the end time the king of the South will collide with him (Antichrist), and the king of the North (Russia and its confederacy) will storm against him with chariots, with horsemen, and with many ships; and he (Antichrist) will enter countries (the surrounding Muslim nations), overflow them (destroy them), and pass through. Verse 40.

"He will also enter the Beautiful Land (Palestine), and many countries will fall; but these will be rescued out of his hand: Edom, Moab and the foremost of the sons of Ammon. Verse 41.

"Then he will stretch out his hand against other countries, and the land of Egypt will not escape. Verse 42.

"But he will gain control over the hidden treasures of gold and silver, and over all the precious things of Egypt; and Libyans and Ethiopians will follow (fall) at his heels." Verse 43.

The next two verses, verses 44, 45 in their soon to be history context, belong after verse 39. This is the Battle of Armageddon so often spoken of. It occurs nearly seven years after the First Battle of Gog and Magog. This battle brings to an end the Tribulation period.

"But rumors from the East and from the North will disturb him (Antichrist), and he will go forth with great wrath to destroy and annihilate many. Verse 44.
"And he will pitch the tents of his royal pavilion between the seas and the beautiful Holy Mountain; yet he will come to his end, and no one will help him." Verse 45.

Daniel's tremendous book revealing so much that is going on in our day is brought to a close with these word, "Go your way, Daniel, for these words are concealed and sealed up *until* the end time," Daniel 12:9.
They are not "sealed up" any longer.

Antichrist In The Revelation

Antichrist is a man, a mortal man. As the Apostle John says in I John 2:18, "Children, it is the last hour; and just as you heard that antichrist is coming, even now many antichrists have arisen; from this we know that it is the last hour." The word "antichrist" is used in Scripture for an individual, the Antichrist. It is also used for a disposition or an attitude of Christ deniers.
What we are interested in here is the Antichrist. This individual is an actual man of flesh and bones. As a Christian can

be filled with the Holy Spirit, so also the coming Antichrist is a man filled with Satan. He will prove to be the world's most diabolical man. He sells himself fully to Satan. As a result, he evidences many unnatural abilities. No one will be able to stop him. For this God will step in, just in a nick of time.

His very name is the opposite of Christ. He is a fraud, a deceiver, a liar, a murderer and a pretender. Yet, he gets by with his many exploits due to his persuasive powers. This devilish rascal is believable, charming, intelligent and a leader among men. During the first half of the Tribulation he pulls the wool over most everyone's eyes. It is at the midpoint of the Tribulation when he commits the "abomination of desolation" that he is recognized for who he is. Yet, throughout the latter half of the seven-year Tribulation, he is still a demonic Pied Piper for most of the world.

Riding Onto The World's Scene

Antichrist is first seen in the Revelation in the beginning verses of chapter 6. "And I saw when the Lamb broke one of the seven seals, and I heard one of the four living creatures saying as with a voice of thunder, 'Come.' And I looked, and behold, a white horse, and he who sat on it had a bow; and a crown was given to him; and he went out conquering, and to conquer," verses 1, 2.

The little seven-sealed book seen here is the book of redemption. It is the title deed to this world. Remember, I told you. God created this world and He never signed over the title to it — to anyone. The Lamb of God now begins to open seal after seal revealing the rightful title to this planet. The word, "Come," is a word of permission to this first of four horsemen of the Tribulation to go forth with his treacherous deeds. Not even the devil can act without God's permission, let alone this his chief protégé, Antichrist. His name announces what he is, anti everything pertaining to Christ.

In this first portrait of him, we find he rides to authority on a *"white horse."* A *"horse"* in Scripture represents power. *"White"* stands for purity and righteousness. He comes quickly to power, for coupled with his persuasive abilities he deceitfully commandeers the traits of goodness and righteousness.

He has a bow in his hand, an implement of war. But no arrows are seen. He has the power to wage war, but his primary tactic lies in the art of statesmanship. He is extremely persuasive, and overnight becomes the world's darling. For some reason, a void has occurred leaving Israel without her long time American ally and protector. The E.U. strongman's initial victory is a peace proclamation he underwrites for the nation of Israel. But folks, don't be taken in. Do not forget! This is the devil's substitute Christ. He is Antichrist.

He also has a *"crown"* on his head. The *"crown"* here is the conqueror's *"crown"* — *"stephanos,"* a victor's crown. It is not the crown of proclaimed or acknowledged Deity. That crown is the "diadem," a kingly or imperial crown. The *"crown"* this white horse rider dons heralds a feigned peace by a fraudulent peacemaker. See Daniel 11:36, 37; II Corinthians 11:13-15; and II Thessalonians 2:8-10.

The *"white horse"* rider before us is Satan's Antichrist as he first appears on the world's scene. He is believed to be a man of peace and exercises demonstrative, unrestrained powers. He is deceitfully deceitful. Being more of a statesman in nature, he does, nevertheless, wield the power of military might. His wearing the victor's *"crown"* disguises the fact that nations will tumble. Watch out world! He does know how to wage war, as we will see.

Through a peace pact with Israel, Antichrist manifests himself as their protector. But careful Israel, look out Earth, a double-cross is in the making (Daniel 9:27). He declares "peace, peace," but there will be no peace apart from the Prince of Peace Himself, the Lord Jesus Christ. Yet, Christ's return is still nearly seven years in the future. Can the world survive until then? His introduction is just the beginning of seven years of deception, destruction and anarchy.

Revealing The Beast

Though we will not cover it here, there is a phenomenally pictorial view of Satan and his fallen hosts being cast down to earth in Revelation 12. It seems Michael and company outwitted them in combat. The devil knows the Good Book. Consequently, he knows he has only a short time left, and he's mad, folks. He's really mad! On earth it becomes difficult to differentiate between the actions of Satan and his right-hand man, Antichrist. Satan gives this devilish feign the powers he possesses. While Satan doubtlessly will be very active during this time, it seems most of his activities are directed through his man, Antichrist. So where one is you will generally find the other.

Revelation 13 then pictures Satan's right-hand stooge, Antichrist, from the midpoint of the Tribulation on. Let's see what the Lord revealed to John and what John reveals to us. The more we see of this every man's enemy, the more appalling and despicable we find him to be.

Satan has been cast to the earth and in the first verse of Revelation 13 we find him standing "on the sand of the seashore." From the waters before him rises a *"beast... out of the sea."* This *"beast"* is Antichrist in his last three and a half years on earth. The word *"sea"* symbolically stands for the Gentile nations, and this beast does come out of the Gentile nations, in particular the European Union.

He has *"ten horns."* This descriptive of Antichrist is explained in Revelation 17. As I mentioned earlier, *"horns"* in the Bible illustrate "power, authority." The *"ten horns"* are "ten kings, who have not yet received a kingdom, but will receive authority as kings with the beast for one hour," (17:12). These *"ten horns"* give us insight on how Antichrist rules over his divided kingdom. It has been wrongly thought by some that the area of the revived Roman Empire would be made up of ten nations. The European Union, as of the date of this writing, is already composed of 27 nations. Notice the language, is *"who have not yet received a kingdom."* Evidently, the E.U. will divide the nations or areas of the earth, most likely in the early stages of the Tribulation, into ten kingdoms, with a *"king"* over each. Each king is under Antichrist's direct authority.

John also notices the *"beast"* has *"seven heads."* Revelation 17:9 enlightens us as to the meaning of these *"seven heads."* "Here is the mind which has wisdom. The seven heads are seven mountains on which the woman sits." These *"seven mountains"* speaks of the city of Rome, built on seven mountains. The religious Babylon calls Rome home. But don't blame Catholicism alone for the diabolical world church of the end times. She most certainly will play a part, but she also will be united with many mainline protestant denominations. Add to them independent churches as well as other religions, all of which compromise Biblical doctrine for the sake of a false unity and peace.

Revelation 17:10 continues, "... and they are seven kings: five have fallen, one is, the other has not yet come..." The *"seven kings"* speak of the seven great kingdoms of the world. We saw only five in Nebuchadnezzar's and Daniel's dreams. Here seven are mentioned. In Daniel the great world-conquering dynasties were listed from the Babylon Empire and forward. Here the prophecy includes the other two world conquering kingdoms prior to Babylon, the Egyptian Empire and the Assyrian Empire. These seven are the complete list of world-conquering kingdoms. *"Five have fallen"* — these are the Egyptian, the Assyrian, the Babylonian, the Persian, and the Greek empires. All had passed off the scene of human history by John's day. *"One is,"* refers to the Roman Empire ruling at the time this was written. That totals six empires. *"The other (which) has not yet come,"* identifies the revived Roman Empire, the kingdom of Antichrist, the European Union of our day that makes up the landmass of the old Roman Empire.

"And on his horns were ten diadems." The *"diadems,"* worn by the *"kings,"* speak of the authority given them to rule. Antichrist's kingdom will be well organized. Great authority, power and fear will strictly enforce his reign. *"Ten"* is the number of completeness, and *"diadems"* speak of regal authority. These ten kings will have complete control of their kingdoms and of their subjects. No wonder Antichrist's bosom buddy, the false prophet, will be able to shut off food and provisions from all without the soon to be introduced mark of the beast.

"And on his heads were blasphemous names." We found in Revelation 17:9, 10 the *"seven heads"* identify Rome and the seven great kingdoms of the world. Here we find Blasphemy is written all over these *"seven heads."* Listen to Daniel's description of him and his authority in this coming day. "And he will speak out against the Most High and wear down the saints of the Highest One, and he will intend to make alterations in times and in laws, and they will be given into his hand for a time, times, and half a time," Daniel 7:25. *"Time, times, and half a time,"* refers to the Great Tribulation of Matthew 24:21. This is the last three and a half years of the Tribulation period.

Revelation 13:2 once again describes the four kingdoms of the Babylonian, Persian, Greek and Roman Empires by using the animals we have already seen: the lion, the bear and the leopard. The fourth of these kingdoms is once again pictured as a non-descript kingdom. Here, however, this kingdom's description includes all three of the previous empires to include their combined powers. That describes the coming revived Roman Empire. This fact will most especially be demonstrated in let blood and lost lives during the last half of the Tribulation. Horribly terrifying is all that can be said of this resurrected empire today.

This devil's henchman will be the most feared, yet revered man on earth. But remember, he is just a man — a Satan-filled, fueled and ignited man, but just the same, a man. The turning point of captivating nearly the entire earth will be around the time he commits the *"abomination of desolation,"* described in Matthew 24:15 and Daniel 9:27. That's a slap in the face of Israel. Most of the world won't care; they don't like Israel anyway. Yet, he desecrates the Temple. That's a slap in the face of God as well. It is at this time he declares himself to be God. About this time, or close on the heels of it, he will be *"slain"* (literally – *"smitten to death"*). Yet, he will rise from the dead counterfeiting the resurrection of Jesus Christ. He is referred to as the one who *"was (he was alive) and is not (he died) and will come (will come to life again) up out of the abyss,"* Revelation 17:8. Little wonder he deceives so many on planet Earth!

Can you imagine this? Let Christ rise from the grave, and it's "ho hum." Let Antichrist rise from the dead and the world follows and adores him. See Revelation 13:3, 4. Satan's resurrection of Antichrist will shock the world into a form of global satanic worship. The devil has forever wanted to be like God and to be worshiped as God. See Isaiah 14:14. He now gets his day in the limelight; well, make that pitch darkness. His time on center stage is not much in exchange for an eternity on the stones of the fiery pit. And to think, this being was once the wisest of all God's created beings.

Listen to the sad story. "And there was given to him a mouth speaking arrogant words and blasphemies; and authority to act for forty-two months was given him. And he opened his mouth in blasphemies against God to blaspheme

His name and His tabernacle, that is, those who dwell in heaven. And it was given to him to make war with the saints and to overcome them; and authority over every tribe and people and tongue and nation was given to him. And all who dwell on the earth will worship him, everyone whose name has not been written from the foundation of the world in the book of life of the Lamb who has been slain," Revelation 13:5-8.

Not much is left to the imagination here. It is either join Satan and his false Christ or be overcome by them. The souls of many of the faithful converts to Christ Jesus during the Tribulation are seen in the Revelation as being in Heaven and under the altar of God. They are safe now, eternally safe, but the loss of life and loved ones to get there is a story that will be told throughout eternity. I can imagine a conversation in heaven by a man whose life and that of his wife were brutally slain for the testimony of their conversion to Jesus Christ. "I was made to die last," the gentleman recalls. "Before my eyes my wife was cruelly and ruthlessly beaten. With ever sharpened knifes her skin was flayed from her body. While limp on the ground but still breathing a stake was driven through her heart as her head was severed by the murderer's sword. Oh look! Here she comes now. She's more gorgeous than ever." Victims of Islamic brutality can doubtlessly give that testimony in heaven today. Around the world Islamists are slaughtering these blood bought brothers and sisters in Christ in unimaginable numbers, in the millions — today. We'll see what the Scriptures say about the Muslim world shortly.

On earth, during the Tribulation, Antichrist will have and execute just such murderous authority. "And it was given to him to make war with the saints and to overcome them; and authority over every tribe and people and tongue and nation was given to him," Revelation 13:7. This is not fictional. This is tomorrow's reality. How many tomorrow's ahead no one knows. But it must come before Christ returns. And the stage is set!

What? Another Beast?

The remainder of Revelation 13 brings into focus another *"beast"* that is the compliment of the first *"beast."* This *"beast"* is the false prophet of the one-world church of the wicked dead. This universal church is married to the world and walks in lockstep with this world's Satan-possessed leader, Antichrist. The bad generally band in pairs, and that doesn't change here. If there is a false king there will be a false prophet. We have these two in King Antichrist and his counterfeit spiritual leader, the false prophet. People love religion. It gives them something to do and makes them feel good about themselves. Surely God, if there is a God, will take notice of our good works. So Antichrist for a while tolerates the willing self-subjugation of his loving and appreciative flock around the world. He will eventually, however, grow weary of all the religious pomp and pageantry. The thing about a spiraling false church is it becomes false to the core. Antichrist will eventually smell the rising stench of this church's rottenness, as will the nations and especially the *"ten kings."*

John tells us the "beast... had two horns like a lamb, and he spoke as a dragon," verse 11. *"Two"* is the symbolic number for testimony. *"Horns"* stand for power. Together they represent the testimony of this *"beast's"* power. And he does have power, phenomenal power.

This is the underling of the first *"beast."* This religious blowhard, "exercises all the authority of the first beast in his presence. And he makes the world and those who dwell in it to worship the first beast, whose fatal wound was healed," verse 12. He's has a full deck of cards with numerous extra Jokers and unlimited authority in promoting the *"first beast."*

After all, he is admired by the world. Is he not? He did rise from the dead. Did he not? He has exemplified a great ability to go forth, *"conquering, and to conquer,"* Revelation 6:2. Has he not? "No one has been able to stand before him," whispers the multitudes. "The persuasiveness of his oratory and the wisdom in his arguments have all gone unchallenged. This is just the man we need to lead the world to a reign of peace. Is he not? Oh, be assured. "Peace, peace" will be the chant, but there will be no peace.

"And he performs great signs, so that he even makes fire come down out of heaven to the earth in the presence of men." In his presence and due to his signs, men's mouths will drop, as does a child's at his first glimpse of a mighty sea. Revelation 13:14 states, "He deceives those who dwell on the earth because of the signs." So powerful does this second *"beast"* grow, he orders men to make an image of the first *"beast."* Amazingly, "there was given to him (the false prophet) to give breath to the image of the beast, that the image of the beast might even speak and cause as many as do not worship the image of the beast to be killed," verse 15. Who do you think gave the false prophet the ability to cause the *"image of the first beast"* to speak? God certainly didn't. But Satan has the ability to perform deluding signs. You can bet Satan gave this false prophet the abilities he exercises before men.

We are informed in verses 16 and 17 of even more despicable news. "And he causes all, the small and the great, and the rich and the poor, and the free men and the slaves, to be given a mark on their right hand, or on their forehead, and he provided that no one should be able to buy or to sell, except the one who has the mark, either the name of the beast or the number of his name."

Life will become insufferable for those without the mark of the beast, *"on their right hand, or on their forehead."* Can't buy! Can't sell! How will they escape starvation and nakedness? From this moment on, it is tough going for those coming to a saving knowledge of Christ Jesus. Run, hide, survive any way possible is the mantra of each day until Christ returns.

I would imagine all on this globe, with the exception of the smallest of children, have heard the numbers 666. This number is given us in the closing verse of Revelation 13. Many through the years have sought to give this number, 666, a more understandable meaning. It is the number of the *"beast."* But, is there a deeper meaning we are to discover? I don't know. Sometimes the simplest answer is the best. And I'm not going to throw out additional meanings to join the thousand floating around out there already. What we can know for certain is this; six is the number of man. Three of these sixes are mentioned, and three is the number of Divine perfection, or completeness. Perhaps God is telling us Antichrist is as complete as a man apart from God can be. Certainly, humanity is pitiful far from the Creator's design.

To me they are God's words of warning concerning Antichrist and his number: It's a man. It's a man. It's a man!"

A Woman On A Scarlet Beast

In Revelation 17, John writes of *"a woman sitting on a scarlet beast,"* verse 3. This *"woman"* John sees epito-mizes the Tribulation period's false church. She is described in Revelation 17:4-6 as, "… clothed in purple and scarlet," the colors of royalty and wealth. She "is adorned with gold and precious stones and pearls, having in her hand a gold cup full of abominations and of the unclean things of her immo-rality, and upon her forehead a name was written, a mystery, 'BABYLON THE GREAT, THE MOTHER OF HARLOTS AND OF THE ABOMINATIONS OF THE EARTH.'" A *"harlot"* in Scripture is a symbol of a wayward and adul-terous church or people. This one is *"the mother of harlots."*

Simply stated, God does not hold her in high esteem. To say the least! John continues: "And I saw the woman drunk with the blood of the saints, and with the blood of the witnesses of Jesus. And when I saw her, I wondered greatly."

"And the angel said to me, 'Why do you wonder? I shall tell you the mystery of the woman…. Here is the mind which has wisdom. The seven heads are seven mountains on which the woman sits. And the woman whom you saw is the great city, which reigns over the kings of the earth,'" Revelation 17:7, 9a, 18.

Let me break this down into some basic components. **First,** the *"woman"* is seen, *"sitting on a scarlet beast,"* verse 4. The *"beast"* is Antichrist, whom we'll see more of in a moment. Suffice it to say, this *"woman"* is in relationship with him and rides to worldwide power on the back of Antichrist and his kingdom, the *"scarlet beast."* God never endorses His kingdom being married to the world. In fact, He hates it. In such a relationship it constitutes the doctrine of the Nicolaitans: hated by the Ephesian church (Rev. 2:6), held to by the Pergamum church and domineered by the Thyatiran church. It is the doctrine of a class of clergy and religious leaders rising up to rule over the congregation. The power this *"woman"* has is phenomenal; but it is granted her for only a short span of time.

Second, she is described by all types of *"precious stones,"* verse 4. The word *"adorned"* is key; it infers she "has sought after and accepted" such wealth and luxury. The church of the Lord Jesus Christ, and Christians individually, like their Savior are to be humble and lowly in attitude and character. And YES, such godly attitudes can be firmly held while at the same time being rich in worldly things. Many have been the number of godly men and women whose means did not negate their manner of living a Christ-like life. But this woman is riding on the back of sought-after royalty. She is married to the world.

Third, she "having in her hand a gold cup of abominations and of the unclean things of her immorality," (verse 4) delights in them. The words, *"having in her hands,"* are critical. This world-church unashamedly holds to *"abominations,"* and relishes *"the unclean things of her immorality."* That language is used to describe her religious harlotries and abominations. She has led her people to be more in submission to the doctrines of demons and the *"unclean"* things of this world, rather than the teachings of God's Word.

Fourth, she is identified to the spiritually discerning by the name found written on her forehead: *"BABYLON THE GREAT, THE MOTHER OF HARLOTS AND OF THE ABOMINATIONS OF THE EARTH,"* verse 5.

Basically, she has degraded the Word of God to make herself the focal point of the world's religion. This movement progresses today at the speed of light. She is headed in an irreversible direction into spiritual oblivion for herself and for all her adherents.

Her full identity, and the hatred that goes with it, will not be fully recognized by the world until the latter days of the Tribulation. But, her movement toward the inevitable and despicable, *"Babylon the Great,"* designation, is in hyper-drive right now.

Who is this *"woman?"* There have always been false churches, from the early *"synagogue of Satan"* (Rev. 2:9), to cults and occults, to this most sinister of all churches — the counterfeit church, led by the false prophet and pictured here as *"a woman sitting on a scarlet beast."*

Yet, all with eyes to see and ears to hear rarely perceive her identity. For those without spiritual discernment, she remains cloaked in mystery.

There are two very distinguishable designations given us in this seventeenth chapter of The Revelation.

The first designation is in the ninth verse: "Here is the mind which has wisdom. The seven heads are seven mountains on which the woman sits."

Known for centuries throughout the world is the city that sits on *"seven mountains."* She is Rome, Italy. Rome is also the city that is host to the so-called "Holy Vatican," the seat of Roman Imperialism and Catholicism.

I want to refer you back to Revelation 2:18-29 where we discussed the letter to the Church of Thyatira. The Lord had a number of kind remarks and commendations concerning her. Yet, her name means a "continual sacrifice." The meaning of the word signals Thyatira's denial of the efficacy of Christ's death on the cross for the sins of the world. The church of the papacy offers a continual sacrifice on the altar of Rome to this day in atonement for sin. To Rome, Christ's death satisfied neither sin's judgment nor God's righteousness.

Review this church's teaching in Revelation 2:18-29. She eventually becomes the seat of the false prophet. The Lord's condemnation and judgment of her is more than a warning, it is a threat. And it is truly revealing. "Behold, I will cast her upon a bed of sickness, and those who commit adultery with her into great tribulation, unless they repent of her deeds," verse 22. There will be opportunity in the Tribulation for many to come to salvation. But, when the Lord gives the warning of being *"cast... into great tribulation,"* the day of repentance for this church is close to being over. Antichrist is fully revealed at the midpoint of the Tribulation. The church of the great harlot, *"and those who commit adultery with her,"* are on a swift moving wide river concealing a mighty current promising no return.

Is the false prophet, in this coming day, the Roman Catholic Pope? That will be revealed in the Tribulation! But I will offer you a can to kick down the road. Rome's present Pope, Benedict XVI, seeking to rush the sainthood of Pope John Paul II by a couple hundred years, will prove to be more evil in his doctrine than his predecessor. Pope John Paul II's life and testimony can only be measured by his beliefs, his actions and his words. To a highly Muslim crowd in Kazakhstan, he said (I kid you not, I am quoting this verbatim), "From this place, I invite both Christians and Muslims to raise an intense prayer to the One, Almighty God whose children we all are." He obviously knew neither the Bible nor the Koran. Again, in Kazakhstan he espoused, "It is a logic that can bring together Christians and Muslims and commit them to work together for the 'civilization of love.'" The Christian message is not logical to the world, John Paul. With such forerunners, it is easy to see how deceptive the False Prophet and Antichrist will be to the multitudes of unredeemed peoples around the world. Here is one more quote from John Paul II, "(It) is our dedication to build a more human world... to defeat the powers of evil and death." Sir, it is humanity that is the basis of the problem. Fallen humanity is not the resolution. Redemption from man's sinful nature is.

This may seem cruel to anyone steeped in religion, but consider this. The ring the Pope wears, passed down through the centuries, has on it a Latin inscription. Interpreted it reads: "The high priest of the heathen." The bowing of the knee and the head and the calling of any man Holy Father, or even "Father" in a spiritual sense is forbidden in Scripture, yet cleaved to, taught and practiced in Catholicism. The cult worship of a mother and child finds its way back to Babylon of old, and is still practiced in Roman Catholicism today. Most importantly, I didn't say it, the Lord did: *"The seven heads are seven mountains on which the woman sits,"*— Rome, Italy.

The second designation given in Revelation 17 of this *"woman"* is found in the 18th verse. "And the woman whom you saw is the great city, which reigns over the kings of the earth."

In Revelation 17:3, the false church rides to power on the back of Antichrist. In verse 4, we see her *"clothed"* in fine linens and precious jewels. In verse 6, she is found, *"drunk with the blood of the saints."* Now, in the verse before us, she is seen as, *"the great city, which reigns over the kings of the earth."* There have been few (if any) governments down through history that have soiled their garments with the blood of saints to the extent of the Roman Catholic Church. Not among the communists, or the Marxists, or the crusaders, no one has come close to the atrocities of Catholicism. (Well, Islam is seeking a prime spot in that race today.) It is hard to believe a church could be, *"drunk with the blood of the saints."* But, not if you have read Fox's Book of Martyrs and Haley's Bible Handbook, as it deals with *"The Inquisition."*

Let me balance this out, to the extent it can be balanced. Romanism is not the only religion represented in the world's coming counterfeit church. Under the false prophet's scepter will be many other so-called Christian groups. The Catholic Church for decades has been holding out an olive branch to all church groups and denominations: "Come back to the fold." Many are presently planning just such a strategic move. It would be disastrous if they were not already dead. Mainline Protestantism is at the head of the religious mob. These churches departed long ago from belief in the infallibility of the Word of God. Many have "united" with other failing branches of Christendom, forsaking Bible doctrine for the sake of unity. The rule of man is established in virtually all these former Christian groups and denominations. The three monkeys of old have been reduced to two: I see no evil and I hear no evil. And, there are many other groups from independent churches to charismatic churches reduced to let's just love one another churches, who will be marching under the banner of the new world church. In fact, just take the whole organization called The World Council of Churches, and dump them into Rome's lap. Fundamental Christianity, once the mainline protestant movement, is now scorned as "right wing extremists." The "radicalism" of this group is the tenet that God's Word is true, is to be believed, shared and lived in light of His coming.

Many will be the accommodations, the gives and takes, and the further dilutions of already diluted doctrine and practices to satisfy the demands and will of the assembling Roman groups. Watch them in the news! They will be steadily and openly conversing, forming and moving forward. While these united assemblies will be organizing, the ultimate pulling together will likely not fully transpire until the Tribulation begins, and the true church has been removed. The leader of this coming worldwide church will rapidly rise to the top. He will not, however, be fully engaged in power that is to be given him until the midpoint of the Tribulation.

God wants no one to be misled about the identity of this *"woman on the scarlet beast."* All need to stay clear of her, even today. She *"is the great city, which reigns over the kings of the earth."* She is Rome. Rome is the coming church of Antichrist and his False Prophet.

The Woman's Purpose

The ultimate purpose of this *"woman,"* the counterfeit church, is to bring under the yoke of Antichrist all those willingly submitted to him, and forcefully those who are not. This harlot has a world vision for which she desires to introduce a new paradigm — Satan rules, forever. Her way of going about it rivals organized crime. No, that's an understatement! No mobster has ever accomplished what Satan's False Prophet will accomplish through this world church.

Revelation 13:11-17 gave us some short but keen insight into the *"woman's"* purpose. There, she is referred to as *"the beast coming up out of the earth."* The earlier *"beast coming up out of the sea"* in chapter 13 is Antichrist. Everyone knows every good Antichrist needs a good False Prophet to herald him. And, this one is good! It is always best someone else shouts your praise. The world's false prophet does this exceptionally.

In verse 11, this "beast coming up out of the earth," is seen to have *"two horns like a lamb."* Now, I told you he is fraudulent. Satan and his own are counterfeiters. They mimic the things of God. Obviously, they have no imagination of their own. So it is no surprise the false prophet counterfeits the Lamb of God. The *"two horns like a lamb"* impression, however, is as far as the symbolism goes. He acts, walks, and talks (for a while) like the Lord Jesus Christ. Watch him closely, though. This verse goes on to say, *"and he spoke as a dragon."* A spawn of the dragon he is. However, his language, manner and voice will eventually give him away. In the beginning, He asks for submission. When it doesn't come, he demands it.

Verse 12 says, "He exercises all the authority of the first beast in his presence." We have two beasts here. But believe this, the *"first beast"* can and will out-manipulate the second *"beast."* As an underling of the *"first beast,"* this False Prophet performs in public with the authority of his superior. "He makes the earth and those who dwell in it to worship the first beast." His persuasive argument is drawn from the fact the *"fatal wound"* of the first *"beast"* was *"healed."* That will command some attention.

Verse 13 tells us, "… he performs great signs, so that he even makes fire come down out of heaven to the earth in the presence of men."

In verse 14 he takes his tricks a step further. He deceives everyone because of the signs. He then commands, "…those who dwell on the earth to make an image to the beast who had the wound of the sword and has come to life." This *"image to the beast"* is going to become a magnet for adulation and opposition.

Earth's False Prophet finds a way to squash most of the bickering. In verse 15, we find, "… there was given to him to give breath to the image of the beast, that the image of the beast might even speak and cause as many as do not worship the image of the beast to be killed." Many *"worship the image of the beast"* out of astonishment and acceptance. Others will *"worship"* it out of pure fear of the guillotines.

Here, in verses 16 and 17, is, perhaps, the most renowned of his infamous acts. "He causes all, the small and the great, and the rich and the poor, and the free men and the slaves, to be given a mark on their right hand, or on their forehead, and he provides that no one should be able to buy or to sell, except the one who has the mark, either the name of the beast or the number of his name."

Albeit, This Woman Is Dust

Many will be the atrocities of this *"BABYLON THE GREAT, THE MOTHER OF HARLOTS AND OF THE ABOMINATIONS OF THE EARTH."* I believe we can safely assume that the Scriptures purposely do not describe the vast majority of her ill-conceived atrocities.

No such creature as this *"harlot"* can survive long, not even in an evil world. The demise of the False Prophet's counterfeit church and power is revealed in Revelation 17:16, 17. Her undoing, doubtlessly, takes place in the home stretch of the Tribulation. Listen to her glorious collapse. "And the ten horns which you saw, and the beast, these will hate the harlot and will make her desolate and naked, and will eat her flesh and will burn her up with fire." The *"ten horns"* refer to ten kingdoms into which the revived Roman Empire will be divided for governmental control. These *"ten horns"* despise this religious harlot. Remember, *"harlot"* refers to the religious organization. Even evil men hate evil religions. Though the false prophet escapes harm, this church is dust, destroyed and will not be remembered. I would think her destruction fits perfectly with today's foolish philosophy of, "no God for me."

Listen to God's description of His destruction of this religious institution. "Behold, I will cast her upon a bed of sickness, and those who commit adultery (practice false religion) with her into great tribulation, unless they repent of her deeds. And I will kill her children with pestilence, and all the churches will know that I am He who searches the minds and hearts; and I will give to each one of you according to your deeds," Revelation 2:22, 23.

Just in case any of us missed the identity of this *"woman"* Revelation 17: 18 closes the chapter on her: "And the woman whom you saw is the great city, which reigns over the kings of the earth." No religion has ever *"reigned over the kings of the earth"* like the Roman Catholic Church.

Be it justifiably noted, the above verses communicate the False Prophet's church will seriously and permanently hit the skids. The False Prophet himself will survive the *"desolating,"* and the *"eating,"* and the *"burning up"* of his *"harlot"* kingdom. But, she will not escape the just reward for her every evil deed.

Back To Tomorrow

Having given us a better vision of the false prophet and his bogus religion, our attention is shifted once more to the *"first beast,"* Antichrist. Revelation 17:8 delivers a short statement concerning Antichrist's coming demise. "The beast that you saw was and is not, and is about to come up out of the abyss and to go to destruction." Brought to the front once again is Antichrist's death and resurrection in the terms: he *"was"* — he was alive. He *"is not"* — he's dead.

And he *"is about to come up out of the abyss"* — he comes back to life. He not only died and went to the *"abyss,"* but he came *"up out of the abyss."* That's quite a ride. But it seems the experience of the heat for that short time in the *"abyss"* didn't change his ways upon his return. In fact, he is now upon his resurrection more vicious and repulsive and sinister than ever before.

In several verses beginning in Revelation 17:9 we have a series of kings and kingdoms that help us better understand both Antichrist and his revived Roman Empire, the present day E.U. "Here is the mind which has wisdom. The seven heads (on the scarlet beast) are seven mountains on which the woman sits..." That is Rome. She rides to power on the back of Antichrist's political kingdom. Verse ten continues: "... and they are seven kings; five have fallen, one is, the other has not yet come; and when he comes, he must remain a little while. And the beast which was and is not, is himself also an eighth, and is one of the seven, and he goes to destruction."

Remember, the Revelation was given to John. In the days that he received it five of the seven great world-ruling empires had already passed from the scene. These five were the Egyptian Empire, the Assyrian Empire, the Babylon Empire, the Persian Empire and the Greek Empire. Those empires are the ones mentioned as *"five have fallen."* John was then told, *"one is."* The *"one"* ruling in John's day was the Roman Empire. That's six of the seven kings and their kingdoms.

The seventh kingdom is referred to as: *"the other has not yet come."* This empire will be as real life as the other six. The world's seventh empire has already been re-birthed. She is the European Union that sits on the landmass of the old Roman Empire. She is growing in prominence, influence and strength on a daily basis. We know this empire as the revived Roman Empire due to the language of Daniel 9:26.

In this passage of Daniel's seventieth week the history of Israel's future is laid out. Toward the end of the sixty-ninth

week, *"... the Messiah will be cut off and have nothing."*
That happened in the crucifixion of Jesus Christ. He paid
the price for sin, but He did not set up the kingdom of God
on earth. Forty years down the road the prophecy continues,
*"The people of the prince who is to come will destroy the
city and the sanctuary."* That too has happened exactly as
Daniel foretold. In A.D. 70 the Roman army overthrew
Jerusalem. The city and the Temple were destroyed and the
surviving Jews were carried off into captivity. Those who
destroyed Jerusalem were the *"**the people** of the prince who
is to come."* They were the people of the original Roman
Empire. The Prince *"who is to come"* is Antichrist who initi-
ates the last seven years of Daniel's prophecy by confirming
a covenant of peace for Israel. So we are looking at a resurrected Roman Empire, an empire situated where Rome previously sat. That, my friend, is today's coalition of nations, the
Common Market of Europe, the European Union.

From this seventh world-conquering empire Antichrist
will rise to power. When he does anyone with wisdom will
be able to recognize him. He inks an unconfirmed covenant of peace for Israel. There won't be too many men and
women with wisdom in that day, so his being recognized is
not all that likely. The end of verse 10 says, "... and when he
comes, he must remain a little while." That is, his reign will
be only for *"a little while."* Remember, this is Antichrist. He
is killed! And he comes back with a vengeance.

Watch Revelation 17:11: "And the beast which was and
is not, is himself also an eighth, and is one of the seven, and
he goes to destruction." He is an *"eighth"* who *"is one of the
seven,"* because he is the *"seven."* This is not too terribly
confusing. He was alive, he died and he comes back to life
again. The seventh world-conquering empire, the *revived*
Roman Empire, is a continuation of the sixth, the *original*
Roman Empire. Because Antichrist will rise from the dead

his kingdom becomes the eighth world-conquering empire, though he was part of the seven.

I like the last portion of the verse, *"and he goes to destruction."* That he will do! But not until he wreaks havoc on earth for another three and a half years, the last half of the Tribulation.

Bye-Bye Pretender and Harlot

You will remember *"the ten horns"* on the *"scarlet beast"* of this seventeenth chapter of Revelation. They are "ten kings who have not yet received a kingdom, but they receive authority as kings with the beast for one hour. These have one purpose and they give their power and authority to the beast," verses 12, 13. The world is evidently divided into ten kingdoms. Each of these *"kings"* receives power from Antichrist to reign over one of these divisions.

Suddenly in verse 14 we are thrust to the return of the Lord Jesus Christ at the end of the Tribulation period. "These (the ten kings) will wage war against the Lamb, and the Lamb will overcome them, because He is Lord of lords and King of kings, and those who are with Him are the called and chosen and faithful." They picked a fight with the wrong Sovereignty. Evil will always come to this dead end.

One of the actions of the *"ten kings,"* however, is noteworthy. Verses 16, 17: "And the ten horns which you saw, and the beast, these will hate the harlot and will make her desolate and naked, and will eat her flesh and will burn her up with fire. For God has put it in their hearts to execute His purpose by having a common purpose, and by giving their kingdom to the beast, until the words of God should be fulfilled." Even lost humanity of the vilest kind hates the duplicity of artificial and contrived religion. The false prophet evidently escapes the ravages of the *"beast"* and his ten subordinates. Only his devilish religious institution is ravaged.

A fitting end to this felonious duo of *"beast"* and *"false prophet"* is given us in Revelation 19:20. Their just desert concludes our duo's infamous reign of terror and occurs when the Lord Jesus returns to earth at the Battle of Armageddon. Here is how they go down. "And the beast was seized, and with him the false prophet who performed the signs in his presence... these two were thrown alive into the lake of fire which burns with brimstone."

And what about the devil? He's been behind all this the whole way. Well, he gets tied up in a thousand year knot. "And I (John) saw an angel coming down from heaven, having the key of the abyss and a great chain in his hand. And he laid hold of the dragon, the serpent of old, who is the devil and Satan, and bound him for a thousand years, and threw him into the abyss, and shut it and sealed it over him, so that he should not deceive the nations any longer, until the thousand years were completed; after these things he must be released for a short time."

A Quick Glance At Today's EU

The following information concerning the European Union has been taken from Wikipedia, the Free Encyclopedia. The full-blown development of the revived Roman Empire is written all over her existence.

The European Union (E.U.) was established in 1957 by the (get this) Treaty of Rome. She has seen tremendous and rapid growth since her inception with today's 27-nation membership. Her economy this year is $15 trillion U.S. dollars. The common currency, the euro, between the member states is in place. The populations of the member states are also members of the European Union. Passport controls and customs between most member states have been abolished. According to the E.U. she is the largest contributor of humanitarian aid in the world.

While member states are themselves responsible for their own territorial defense, the E.U. as a body adopted the Petersberg tasks of peacekeeping and humanitarian missions. The European Union's military mainly consists of the sovereign military of its member states. These militaries may be drawn on in case of national emergencies. The E.U. specific military includes a 60,000 member European Rapid Reaction Force and the E.U. Battle Groups of an additional 15,000 men. The E.U. member countries combined area of 1,707,642 miles is the seventh largest in the world.

Her economic strength and foreign trade are rapidly rising to the point of reviling the US. Her influence in world politics may be exceeding that of the U.S. right now. The European Union is well set for anything that may come her way. Unfortunately, it is what will come out of her that is a bother to Bible believing Christians and a threat to the world.

Chapter Six

From Russia & Friends With No Love

Strange Bedfellows And A War Of Hatred!

Who's Who In The Coming Tribulation

We have already begun looking into who's who in the coming seven years of Tribulation that will come close to destroying the planet. How close will man come to wiping out humanity? Here is the figure Scripture gives us. One out of every two people on the planet will be killed during a seven-year period. This is not a weatherman's forecast, a politician's guess or a military strategist's war room estimate. This is the inerrant Biblical fact on a coming horrendous loss of life, and I want to share with you the facts leading to that loss of life.

So far we've seen the rebirth of Israel and her reconstitution as a nation. And we just took a detailed look at the revived Roman Empire, the European Union of today, and the world's coming man of sin, Antichrist. We've also glanced briefly at the individual the Bible refers to by three descriptions: the *"beast out of the earth, the Mother of harlots, and* the *"false prophet,"* Revelation 13:11; 17:5 and 19:20. They are one in the same, the world's counterfeit religious leader.

Before jumping into Scripture's identification of Russia and friends, I want to set the stage for you by giving a little more Biblical insight into what brings about three more world wars, two of them within seven years of each other.

Israel, The Center Of The World

You've heard about the child, and probably an adult or two, who always had to be the center of attention. Well, Israel sort of asked for it as well. When God brought the Jewish people out of Egyptian captivity, they in essence said to their leader, "Moses, we are so thrilled over God's deliverance of us and our families, that we want you to tell Him that we desire to be His people and we want Him to be our God." (I paraphrased that, but you can find the story verbatim in Exodus 19 and 20.) In response God gave them the Ten Commandments saying, "Keep these and I will be your God and you will be My people." The people answered back, "All that the Lord has spoken we will do?" Sure they would! No one, apart from Jesus Christ, has ever been able to keep those commandments. Break one and you may as well have broken them all — which they did, over and over and over. But God made a covenant with them. Whether they would keep their covenant with Him made no difference. Their failures would cost them dearly over the years. But God always keeps His promises. Therefore, He started working with them and molding them into a people for His own possession. It was going to take awhile.

Meanwhile, on the backside of some dark planet, Satan got his chief lieutenants together to map out a strategy for defeating God's purpose. You see God had told Abraham (who was before Moses — for you Baptists) that through him all the nations of the world would be blessed. Satan's strategy, therefore, was to keep God from blessing Israel, which would make Him a liar, or at least imperfect in His foresight. Since then it has been quite a back and forth battle and it's still going on. If God would break His covenant with Israel, how could He, being imperfect, punish Satan for also having failed in an area or two — to say the least.

There is a saying in Islam, "The enemy of my enemy is my friend." Satan's thought had a different twist to it; "The friend of my enemy is my enemy." Therefore, his battle against the nation of Israel, and especially her offspring, Jesus, continues to this day.

The reality of spiritual warfare will be found nowhere more pronounced than in the people and in the history of Israel. From her calling out as a nation she has been God's *"special treasure."* But, let's allow Scripture to speak for itself. To Israel, upon her exodus from Egypt, God declared, "Now then, if you will indeed obey My voice and keep My covenants, then you shall be My *special treasure* among all the peoples, for all the earth is Mine," Exodus 19:5.

Moses, on many occasions, reminded Israel of her special place in the heart of God. "For you are a holy people to the Lord your God; the Lord your God has chosen you to be a people for His *special treasure* out of all the peoples who are on the face of the earth," Deuteronomy 7:6.

This same statement in its exact words was used again by Moses in Deuteronomy 14:2. In Psalm 135:4 the psalmist wrote, "For the Lord has chosen Jacob for Himself, Israel for His *special treasure*." The Old Testament also concludes with these same words, even in a day of apostasy, "'And they will be Mine,' says the Lord of hosts, 'on the day that I prepare My *special treasure*, and I will spare them as a man spares his own son who serves him,'" Malachi 3:17. This same thought and quote is echoed again in the New Testament.

In Matthew 13 the Lord Jesus declares in parabolic form His future intention for the nation of Israel. "The kingdom of heaven is like a *treasure* hidden in the field, which a man found and hid; and from joy over it he goes and sells all that he has, and buys that field," verse 44. In this parable salvation is procured for the nation of Israel as the *"man... goes and sells all that he has, and buys that field."* The *"man,"* of course, is the Lord Jesus Christ. The *"field"* is the world. He *"found and hid"* again the *"treasure"* within it. Purchasing the *"field"* through the giving of His life on the cross, the Lord Jesus assured the *"treasure in the field"* would be His at the time of His choosing.

That *"treasure"* is Israel, God's *"special treasure"* throughout the Old Testament. The time as to when He will reveal this *"special treasure"* forever will occur during the Tribulation as Israel recognizes Him as Messiah and Lord.

Paul, teaching on Israel's present spiritual condition, informs us of this very thing. "For I do not want you, brethren, to be uninformed of this mystery, lest you be wise in your own estimation, that a partial hardening has happened to Israel until the fullness of the Gentiles has come in; and thus all Israel will be saved," Romans 11:25, 26a.

Of course, God has an archenemy. Should a people or a nation be His *"special treasure,"* rest assured fire from the dragon will be directed toward that group. This, too, is seen throughout the Bible and in modern day history. Addressing their situation in Egypt, from which Israel received God's deliverance, Moses reminded them, "But the Lord has taken you and brought you out of the iron furnace, from Egypt, to be a people for His own possession, as today," Deuteronomy 4:20. The fierce pressure Israel faced, would often face, and still faces is described as an *"iron furnace"* on numerous occasions. Satan is alive and well and savagely contesting God's purpose in Heaven and on Earth. Prayer, faith and steadfastness are the chief weapons of the people of God, be they Jewish or Gentile. But never forget, while this war is fought in Heaven, Satan's battles are directed on earth toward the people belonging to God and walking closest to the Lord. Are you set for battle? Prayer, faith and steadfastness are the keys to heaven's victory.

This truth has never escaped the minds of God's people. Listen to Solomon's dedicatory prayer over the Temple of God. In reference to Israel he prays, "... for they are Thy people and Thine inheritance which Thou has brought forth from Egypt, from the midst of the iron furnace," I Kings 8:51. Later Jeremiah would refer to Israel's deliverance from Egypt when God told him to speak to the men of Judah and Jerusalem, "Thus, says the Lord, the God of Israel, 'Cursed is the man who does not heed the words of this covenant which I commanded your forefathers in the day that I brought them out of the land of Egypt, from the iron furnace, saying, "Listen to My voice, and do according to all which I command you; so you shall be My people, and I will be your God,""" Jeremiah 11:3, 4.

Satan's strongest assaults are against those God desires to bless and use. Because of that God told Abraham and his descendants, "I will bless those who bless you, and the one who curses you I will curse," Genesis 12:3. It can be costly being on God's side — then and now. Nevertheless, accept it by faith; coming rewards are worth the price of victory won through diligence. Again, if God gives the promise of a blessing, understand Satan has other designs. Against no one has this been more real than Israel, the *"special treasure"* of God. From the start God's intention has been to use Israel to bring salvation to the world. It was through Israel that Messiah the Lord and Deliverer would come. With God's love and purpose for Israel, however, expect the dragon's fury toward her. Israel has incontestably paid the price, and it is a price that has been wrung from her generation after generation.

Daniel's Seventieth Week, the Tribulation period, will be Satan's all out attack on Israel. He must thwart the purpose of God, and the ethnic cleansing of Israel is his strategy. Following are the nations and their roles Satan purposes to use in his attempt to dash God's plan for the ages.

The White Horse Rider

We've covered this, so I won't dally here, just long enough to remind you who this *"white horse"* rider is. Revelation 6 sets into motion the events of the Tribulation period. The Lamb of God has taken the seven-sealed book, the book of redemption, and begins to open its seals. Each seal describes horrors coming upon mankind. Yet, they are only the beginning of sorrows. As the Lamb broke the first of the seven seals, "one of the four living creatures with a voice of thunder (said), 'Come,'" verse 1. The word *"come"* is not spoken to John, but to the white horse rider. It is his command to *"go" or "proceed,"* freeing the rider to initial his infamous place in history.

The *"white horse"* rider is Antichrist, the new head of the revived Roman Empire, today's European Union. He comes on the scene at the opportune time to save war from breaking out in the Middle East. Something has happened. America no longer can or will support her long time friend of many years, Israel. Israel, probably in desperation, turns to the #1 guy in the world not to turn to. Antichrist through craftiness and deception inks a covenant of peace for her. Neither Antichrist nor his superior, fallen Lucifer, has any love for Israel. But poor Israel! She and her people are so battle worn and fatigued today any attempt at peace is like a ray of sunshine. But just as foolish as giving away land for peace today, this *"covenant"* is even more so a door to mayhem and destruction. For a very short while it seems things just might work out between Israel and her neighbors.

Peace, however, is not in the Arab/Muslim mindset. Nor is it in Russia's vocabulary.

We covered this extensively in the previous chapter. But take note. The White Horse Rider is the first of four horse riders. The following three come on the scene of world history swiftly and with extreme, indefensible power.

The Red Horse Rider

No sooner than the peace pretender confirms a covenant with Israel, the next horse rider stampedes the Middle East. Israel had no more than a brief respite, and possibly no good night's sleep. "And when He broke the second seal, I heard the second living creature saying, 'Come.' And another, a red horse, went out; and to him who sat on it, it was granted to take peace from the earth, and that men should slay one another; and a great sword was given to him," Revelation 6:3, 4.

As soon as peace is declared, war is determined. Without warning the *"second seal"* is opened and the world is thrown into anarchy. War, like no war before it, engulfs the nations.

"Red" stands for blood. And this *"red horse"* rider baths the world in that precious and crimson fluid. War quickly follows on the heels of the world's deceptive leader and his covenant with Israel. No surprise here! Scripture warns all with ears to hear: "While they are saying, 'Peace and safety!' then destruction will come upon them suddenly like birth pangs upon a woman with child; and they shall not escape," I Thessalonians 5:3.

The *"great sword"* in Revelation 6:4 speaks of the extensiveness and destructiveness of this coming war. No war to date has been so ferociously fought, nor has any war brought such devastating results. The *"sword"* mentioned here is the Greek word for "dagger," not the long sword we are prone to imagine. This *"sword"* is small enough to be hidden under a coat. Together these two words give us a double meaning. First, *"great"* imparts the image of awesome, extensive. Second, the type of *"sword"* pictures a surprise attack. This attack on Israel, though massive, is by stealth. It is a clandestine attack on God's special treasure. *"Peace and safety"* has been but hollow warble. Antichrist, of course, steps into the fray. Nevertheless, from this moment until the Lord's return war rages.

There will be great divisions as to who this peace-affirming savior of Israel is. Such differences of opinion will lead brother to fight against brother, family against family, and nation against nation. Classes and races of people will be pitted one against another.

The Black and Ashen Horse Riders

The third and fourth horse riders follow quickly as their *"seals"* are broken. The third horse is a *"black horse"* whose rider has *"a pair of scales in his hands."* He represents famine and pestilence as the daily needs of one person is the portion of an entire family.

The fourth horse is an *"ashen horse."* *"Ashen"* is pale gray, the color of death. "And he who sat on it had the name Death; and Hades was following with him. And authority was given to them over a fourth of the earth, to kill with sword and with famine and with pestilence and by the wild beasts of the earth," verse 8. The language is exceedingly descriptive. *"Death"* holds one's body in the grave. *"Hades"* holds the soul of the deceased without Christ. This *"fourth horse"* rider whose name is *"Death"* slays with the "sword and with famine and with pestilence and by the wild beast of the earth." The slain in this early Tribulation battle will be swallowed by *"Hades"* to await the final judgment.

Early in The Revelation the Lord Jesus spoke sweet relief to His own, *"I have the keys of death and hades,"*

Revelation 1:18. *"Death"* is the grave and holds the bodies of those who have died, good and bad. *"Hades,"* also translated *"hell,"* holds the souls of all who have died without the Lord Jesus Christ. *"Hades,"* of course, cannot touch those who are secure in the hands of Jesus. For the dead in Christ, "… to be absent from the body, is to be at home with the Lord," II Corinthians 5:8. Quite a change of scenery Heaven is from Hades!

The war that introduces the world to the reality of hell on earth begins shortly after Antichrist confirms a *"covenant"* of peace for Israel. "And I looked, and behold, an ashen horse; and he who sat on it had the name Death; and Hades was following with him. And authority was given to them over a fourth of the earth, to kill with sword and with famine and with pestilence and by the wild beasts of the earth," Revelation 6:8. One-fourth the population of the planet dies during this opening war of the Tribulation. One out of every four people is dead. Greater than one and a half billion men, women and children's lives snuffed out in a short, vicious period. Is there a more explicit picture of the depravity of human nature than man's lack of value for human life?

The Bible identifies those bringing this unimaginable war to all who dwell on the surface of the earth. This is not the often-mentioned Battle of Armageddon. Armageddon is still seven years down a long, harsh and hard road. This war is fought at the Tribulation's beginning. It has been appropriately named, The First Battle of Gog and Magog. Yes, another battle of Gog and Magog is down the road a ways, the last battle to ever be fought. Between these two battles of Gog and Magog is the well known, at least in name, Battle of Armageddon.

The First Battle of Gog and Magog

Identifying the nations involved in this battle is not difficult. The Bible tells us who the participants are. Only a brief
study is needful to attach the names of those involved. To
set the stage let's go to Daniel 9:27: "And he (Antichrist)
will make a firm covenant with the many for one week...."
The *"confirmed covenant"* is Antichrist's protection agreement for Israel. With this *"covenant"* in place the *"red
horse"* rider becomes uneasy and dares not delay an attack
any longer. The Middle East is too strategic for survival to
ignore. Besides, the EU is ill prepared and far outnumbered
to defend Israel on such short notice. She hasn't the army to
facedown such a formidable foe of nation after nation in this
confederacy. Yes, she confirmed the covenant for Israel. But
who would have believed Israel would be in the crosshairs
of nations so very, very quickly?

In Daniel 11, after describing Antichrist's power in
verses 36-39, verse 40 mentions the trouble that follows
the *"covenant"* between the EU and Israel. "And at the end
time the king of the South (Egypt) will collide with him
(Antichrist)...." That may or may not mean a battle roars
between these two. I doubt that it does. But it certainly does
mean there is going to be some head-butting politically and
in all likelihood some minor military action between these
two. It will be enough to enrage Antichrist against Egypt for
verse 42 informs us that after he takes care of the "northern"
problem, *"Egypt will not escape"* his wrath. The war to beat
all wars to date is about to take place, and no one anticipates
the dramatic and surprising results.

Verse 40 continues: "... and the king of the North will
storm against him (Antichrist)...." That definitely spells war.
Who is this King of the North *"storming"* into the Middle
East setting off The First Battle of Gog and Magog? Who
is this roughshod nation bringing the world to a collective

gasp? A hint: over the last several decades she has been preparing for this battle.

Deciphering The Participants

The rider of the *"red horse"* of Revelation 6 is detailed for us in Ezekiel 38:2: "Son of man, set your face toward Gog of the land of Magog, the prince of Rosh, Meshech, and Tubal, and prophesy against him...."

"Gog" interpreted means, "end time ruler," and simply refers to the commander of this invading nation.

"Magog" was a son of Japheth, the grandson of Noah. Genesis 10 gives the account of the descendants of Noah while history lists the areas they settled after the flood. A comparison of the two identifies the nation instigating this attack. *"Magog"* has been identified by numerous writings dating all the way back to Flavius Josephus. The historian Josephus lived in the days of the Apostle Paul and wrote a history of the Jews, *The Antiquities Of The Jews.* In *The Antiquities,* Josephus identified *"Magog"* over 1900 years ago in this manner: "Magog fathered those that from him are called Magogites, but who are by the Greeks called Scythians," (pages 30, 31).

The Scythians settled the southern and southwestern areas of the country known today as the southern portions of Russia. Jewish scholars down through the centuries have identified the Magogites as nomads, a very barbaric people who roamed the Caucasus Mountains between the Caspian and Black Seas. These are the very areas identified as the south and southwestern portions of modern day Russia and many of her former Soviet block nations.

Highly respected Christian scholarship also identifies *"Magog"* as the southern regions of Russia: Dr. R. Young in *Young's Analytical Concordance of the Holy Bible*; also *Eerdman's Handbook to the Bible; and Dr. William Jenks.*

Dr. Jenks gave this identification of *"Magog:"* "The Jews of his day thought 'Magog to be the Scythian nations, vast and innumerable, who are beyond Mount Caucasus and the Palus Maeotis, and near the Caspian Sea, stretching even to the Indies.'" That description portrays the southern regions of Russia. Numerous other notable scholars such as Drs. John Gill, Dwight Pentecost, G. Rawlinson and one of the most scholarly books ever written on the exegesis of Scripture, *"Genesius' Hebrew and Chaldee Lexicon,"* all agree *"Magog"* is Russia. This is not, however, the only description Ezekiel gives us of this invading last days' *"red horse"* rider.

"The prince of Rosh" needs little interpretation. Russia has not always been called Russia. Prior to the eighteen century her name was *"Rosh."* Even today the short popular form of Russia refers to her pedigree, "Rossiya."

"Meshech" is another grandson of Noah and son of Japheth (Genesis 10:2). History records it that Meshech migrated directly north after the flood and settled the capitol city of Russia, situated on the western side of Russia and named after him, "Moscow."

"Tubal," is still another grandson of Noah and son of Japheth (Genesis 10:2). History once again reveals the open secret of this nation's identity. *"Tubal"* with his family traveled to the northeast and settled on the eastern side of Russia founding a major city named after him, Tobolsk, often called the eastern capitol of Russia.

In Ezekiel 38:3 God directly addresses the descendants of Noah whose names outline the end time nation of Russia: "Thus says the Lord God, 'Behold, I am against you, O Gog (end time ruler who is the) prince of Rosh (Russia), Meshech (Moscow), and Tubal (Tobolsk).'" That description outlines the entire nation of Russia. Scripture cannot be any more obvious than that.

Russia's Partners: Many other nations will be in alignment with Russia in her attack on Israel and the EU's

Antichrist. Ezekiel 38:7 details Russia's marching orders: "Be prepared, and prepare yourself, you and all your companies that are assembled about you, and be a guard (commander) for them." Russia is to lead a multitude of nations against the small nation of Israel. The list of names of these *"assembled"* nations is like reading today's front-page headlines. Ezekiel 38:5, 6 provide the names on the short list of Russia's Muslim Confederacy. These named more or less are dominant Muslim nations. Yes, you read correctly! It is a Russian/ Muslim Confederacy. Some bedfellows, huh?

The first name you see is that of *"**Persia**."* Persia changed her name in 1935 to **Iran**. Even today Iranians like to be called Persians. There is no doubt as to the allegiance of this nation that lies to the east of Israel. She enjoys a strategic alliance with Russia and China, the latest in Russian and French military equipment and her armies are Russian trained. Her present leaders, religious and political, have taken Iran back centuries to being today a high-pitched mouthpiece for the twelfth Imam, Islam's resurrected deliverer.

*"**Ethiopia**"* has never changed her name. We can just spit it out with ease — **Ethiopia**. She is to the south of Israel, is referenced in Daniel 11:40 and shares in an alignment with *"the king of the South."* She, too, is and will continue to be under Russian command, training and armament. We now have a northern (Russia), an eastern (Iran) and a southern (Ethiopia) pronged attack poised on Israel.

*"**Put**"* is the son of Ham, the grandson of Noah (Genesis 10:6). History tells us that after the flood Put resettled his family in the area known today as **Libya**. As with the other nations in this list of Russian cohorts, Libya's hatred of Israel is superseded only by Iran's. She has been and likely is a military fortress of Russian equipment, technology, training and leadership. Libya is located to the southwest of Israel giving the Russian juggernaut a north, east, south and westerly approach in their extermination attempt on God's

chosen people. Egypt may well give safe passage for Libya's attack on Israel. Libya could also spring her attack from the Mediterranean Sea. I'd bet on the latter. But with Egypt's obvious involvement she would certainly allow Libya passage.

Take your map of the world and look at Gog's four-sided attack on Israel. No sane person could help but say, "Israel is dust!" Her chance of survivability — zero. Zilch! Non-existent! But these are not the only nations involved in this attack on Israel.

"Gomer" should be of no surprise to anyone. Gomer, too, was a son of Japheth, the grandson of Noah (Genesis 10:2). He and his offspring traveled some distance and settled in a country well known for raising infamous leaders, **East Germany**. Anti-Semitism is as strong in East Germany today as anytime in her sordid history, and matches that of any Muslim nation.

"Beth-togarmah" means "the house (Beth) of Togarmah." Togarmah was a son of Gomer, the grandson of Japheth, the great grandson of Noah (Genesis 10:3). Togarmah and his household settled the area named after him, **Turkey**. Turkey, while seeking semi-cordial relations with the West, never gets too far from Russian obeisance. Her troops are trained and often commanded by Russian officers. An important nation to American interest in the Middle East, she has acquired American technology as well. Her equipment for the most part, however, is Russian made and maintained; with the exception of armaments willingly provided by America for favors rendered. Turkey is to the north of Israel bordering Syria.

"...many peoples with you" refers to *"many"* other nations included in this confederacy. It would be within reason to say the Muslim nations that composed the former Soviet Union, until it's fall in November 1989, will add manpower to the assault on Israel. Nations such as Kazakhstan, Uzbekistan,

and Kyrgyzstan will be involved. In addition to the above nations expect any or all of the following to add to those *"many people with you"*: the Sudan, Lebanon, Syria, Jordan, Iraq, Saudi Arabia, the Gulf Emirates, Yemen, Algeria, and most every other Arab and Muslim nation (there are twenty-six of them) to unite against God's chosen people, Israel. Some will be in support and logistics. *"Many"* will be militarily involved. There will be *"many peoples with"* Russia. Yet, all of them combined are not enough to fight God over His *"special treasure."*

The Russian Muslim Confederacy and their attack on Israel will most certainly be thwarted. Most scholars believe God directly intervenes in Israel's defense. He certainly has in times past. And I believe He will here, too. Yet, on the human side, I am also convinced He uses Antichrist and the E.U. army of the revived Roman Empire in His squashing of Russia and her alignment of nations. Remember, the devilish feign of the E.U. promised Israel protection. He cuts through the Russian confederacy like a juggernaut. Through stunning victory, or at least claiming it for himself early in the Tribulation, Antichrist consolidates his strength, prestige and authority upon other world powers. But don't take God out of the equation. He is the One who actually destroys Russia's Arab/Muslim confederacy. Antichrist just gets or takes the credit. Read the entire passage of Ezekiel 38 and 39 for all the startling details of Russia's dinosauric defeat.

Directions In The Bible

Let's go back to Daniel 11:40 and the words, *"the king of the North will storm against him."* In God's sight Israel is the center of the world. He tells us so in Ezekiel 38:12. Speaking of Israel in this battle, He refers to her as those, "who live at the center of the world." The word *"center"* is the Greek word for *"navel."* All events center on her.

Directions in the Bible are given in reference to her. Take a map of the Middle East and lay a ruler running north and south though the center of Jerusalem. Go directly north and you will run slap dab through Russia's capital city, Moscow. Russia is also referred to as *"the remote parts of the north"* in verse 15, meaning her location is to the north of Turkey. Russia is graphically and geographically pinpointed as commander of this confederacy of Arab/Muslim nations in this the dawning battle of the Tribulation period, The First Battle of Gog and Magog.

The Result of Russia's Attack

What is the result of Russia's attack on Israel? Enormous, to say the least! Space prohibits printing it all here, but look up and carefully read the self-explanatory verses of Ezekiel 38:14 – 39:24. Here is a sampling of what you will find. And it is only a descriptive sampling.

"Therefore, prophecy, son of man, and say to Gog, 'Thus says the Lord God, "On that day when My people Israel are living securely, will you not know it? And you will come from your place out of the remote parts of the north, you and many peoples with you, all of them riding on horses, a great assembly and a mighty army; and you will come up against My people Israel like a cloud to cover the land. It will come about in the last days that I shall bring you against My land, in order that the nations may know Me when I shall be sanctified through you before their eyes, O Gog,"'" Ezekiel 38:14-16.

"And it will come about on that day, when Gog comes against the land of Israel," declares the Lord God, "That My fury will mount up in My anger. And in My zeal and in My blazing wrath I declare that on that day there will surely be a great earthquake in the land of Israel. And the fish of the sea, the birds of the heavens, the beasts of the field, all the creeping things that creep on the earth, and all the men who are on the face of the earth will shake at My presence; the mountains also will be thrown down, the steep pathways will collapse, and every wall will fall to the ground. And I shall call for a sword against him on all My mountains," declares the Lord God. "Every man's sword will be against his brother. And with pestilence and with blood I shall enter into judgment with him; and I shall rain on him, and on his troops, and on the many peoples who are with him, a torrential rain, with hailstones, fire, and brimstone," Ezekiel 38:18-22.

"And I shall strike your bow from your left hand, and dash down your arrows from your right hand. You shall fall on the mountains of Israel, you and all your troops, and the peoples who are with you; I shall give you as food to every kind of predatory bird and beast of the field; for it is I who have spoken," declares the Lord God. "And I shall send fire upon Magog (the land of Russia) and those who inhabit the coastlands in safety (Russian and Muslim nations); and they will know that I am the Lord," Ezekiel 39:3-6.

The armies of Russia and her confederate nations will *"fall on the mountains of Israel."* With no breath in them! No one could have imagined what God had in mind for this enemy of Christ Jesus and murderer of the people of God for so many hundreds of years. And it is not just Russia's demise. Write off the vast majority of Islam's fighting men as non-existent as well. Poor Mohammad, your dream of world dominion is flushed down the toilet of inevitability. Israel will be burying the dead of the Russian army and her Arab/ Muslim cohorts for seven months (39:11-16). Additionally, portions of Russia's homeland and some of the coastal cities of her confederate nations will also be destroyed (39:6). God says, "And I shall send fire upon Magog and those who inhabit the coastlands in safety; and they will know that I am the Lord," (39:6). Do yourself a great favor. Go back now and read these two chapters, Ezekiel 38, 39, in their entirety.

They will now paint quite a picture for you. The destruction of the enemy of God and man at the hands of God is pictorially amazing.

The Timing Of Russia's Attack

The specific time of Russia's attack on Israel is not given. There is, however, a phrase in Ezekiel 38:10, 11 that offers a possible timeline of her attack. "Thus says the Lord God, 'It will come about on that day, that thoughts will come into your mind, and you will devise an evil plan, and you will say, "I will go up against the land of unwalled villages. I will go against those who are at rest, that live securely, all of them living without walls, and having no bars or gates."'"

When Antichrist inks the covenant of peace for Israel it will likely involve the removal of the defensive walls Israel has been building. That won't take long. The signing of the covenant begins the Tribulation period. We cannot be certain of the date of that signing. Yet, with all lights seemingly turning green for the Lord's return, a hard look at the infamous "Roadmap To Peace In The Middle East" needs to be made. The United States, the European Union, Russia and the United Nations contrived this "roadmap" for a "peaceful" existence of a Palestinian state living alongside the nation of Israel. U.S. President George W. Bush presented the outline of the Roadmap in a speech on June 24, 2002. Since then there have been many bumps in the working out of details and in a peaceful willingness by both groups, Israel and the Palestinians. That's understandable! The so-called Palestinians will never live in peace with Israel. Their leaders have one purpose and that is to drive Israel into the sea. And Israel will never cease targeting those who are ceaselessly trying to kill her people. That's understandable!

The Roadmap's full implementation is already three years behind. The general specifics for successful execution of the Roadmap are laid out in three timetables.

One. An end must be made to Palestinian violence. Palestinians must begin political reform. Israel must withdraw from disputed areas and halt further expansion. And the Palestinians are to arrange free elections.

Two. An International Conference to support Palestinian economic recovery and a process leading to Palestinian statehood must be held. The Palestinians and Israel are to establish provisional borders, resolve regional water issues, economic development, refugee status and arms control.

Three. There is to be a second international conference establishing a permanent status agreement, an end to conflict, an agreement on final borders, the fate of Jerusalem refugees and the settlements. Finally the Arab state is to agree to peace deals with Israel.

As of the writing of this book US Secretary of State Condoleezza Rice and Britain's former Prime Minister Tony Blair are expending all energies and resources to get the Roadmap back on fast tract. It is, as they suppose, the best chance for peace in the Middle East. This agreement, however, in Biblical reality is a Roadmap To Destruction For Israel. It requires forcing her to give to the Palestinians more and more land for peace — a peace that will never be honored by the Arab/Muslim nations. Among the audacities required of Israel is the giving up of half of Jerusalem and the disastrous right-of-return to homes owned by the families of all pre-1952 Palestinian refugees. That means Israel will no longer be an Israeli state in that such a flood of Palestinians will outnumber Israel's Jewish residents. The blind-sighted problem Israel has is she is so battle weary she may accept most any arrangement that has even a faint chance of succeeding. But poor Israel, until Jesus comes, no other solution will work.

At the moment of this writing newly installed Israeli President Shimon Peres has crafted and turned over a peace initiative to Israeli Prime Minister Ehud Olmert, Palestinian Authority President Mahmoud Abbas, the E.U. and the U.S. Peres went quite a bit outside his authority in doing so. But this just shows how desperate many Israelites are to find a workable peace. According to WorldNewsDaily.com, "Peres' plan calls for Israel to hand 97-percent of the West Bank over to Abbas, with Israel retaining a small number of the territory's Jewish communities. In exchange for Israel keeping some land, the Jewish state will give the PA control of Arab Israeli cities north of Tel Aviv which, together with the evacuated West Bank territory, would amount to the equivalent of 100 percent of the West Bank." Top European Union diplomats have told the media they want a US sponsored international conference scheduled for this November to lead to negotiations on a final agreement with the Palestinians.

Israel's leaders have quickly forgotten the nightmarish quagmire turning over the Gaza Strip has created. Gaza is today a black hole for illegal arms smuggling, arms that will be used to massacre Israeli civilians. And rockets from Gaza have not ceased being fired into Israel since turning that area over to Hamas, so necessary to Israel's defense.

Toward this fall's international conference the Bush administration is expected to pull out all stops to establish in the near future negotiations leading to a Palestinian state. Meanwhile, President Bush and Secretary of State Condoleezza Rice are urging Abbas and Olmert to establish a framework that will lead to a breakthrough at this November's meeting. Many other concessions have already been made by Olmert granting increased Palestinian control of the West Bank, another territory necessary to Israel's defense, the removal of security fences, roadblocks, checkpoints and the release of hundreds of gunmen belonging to Al Aqsa Martyrs Brigades.

Why would the dovish Israelite government do this? They do so because of their hope for peace without their long awaited Prince of Peace. They do so because of their battle-weariness. And they do so because they cannot comprehend the Arab mindset of allowable treachery, lies and further murdering that is the makeup of Islamic doctrine.

Here is the real kicker. Scripture states, "For thus says the Lord of hosts, 'After glory He has sent me against the nations which plunder you, for he who touches you, touches the apple (pupil) of His eye," Zechariah 2:8. God made a covenant with Abraham and his descendents through Isaac that He would bless those that bless her and curse those that curse her (Genesis 12:3; 22:18; 24:36; 26:3, 3; 27:29; 28:14; Numbers 24:9; Acts 3:25; Galatians 3:8). Woes belong to the nations that *"plunder"* her. Isn't it amazing that Russia is a member of the Quartet drawing up the Middle East Roadmap to oblivion? Yet, simultaneously she is the King of the North sitting around a topographical layout of the Middle East planning Israel's annihilation? It will not be surprising if we find out that around that topographical map with Russian commanders are also the Islamic fascists mentioned in Ezekiel 38. Who on this earth cannot figure out that Russia is a dangerous nation and incapable of trust? Oh yes! U.S. politicians with their payouts of political vouchers for votes and Israel's land for legacies — that's who!

What about other nations requiring Israel to submit to indefensible borders? Causing her to give up land necessary for her protection is well in the range of *"plundering"* her. Those doing so will suffer the greatest judgments of God. We have already seen God's judgment of Russia and the Muslim nations. And we know what lies ahead for the revived Roman Empire, the E.U., although we have not looked at her actual destruction yet. What about America? And where is China in all this? Just thoughts to ponder! We'll let Scripture answer these questions in due time.

Presently, let's get back to Russia and her Arab/Muslim confederacy's defeat. Ezekiel 39:9, 10 mentions that, "those who inhabit the cities of Israel... will not take wood from the field or gather firewood from the forest...." They will not need to cut firewood! Here is the reason: "... for seven years they will make fires of them (the weapons of Russia and her fallen confederacy)." Her weapons may be as hard as steel but they will burn like wood in the ovens of Israel. This *"seven year"* period points to Russia's attack coming directly on the heels of Antichrist's confirmed *"covenant"* with Israel. The signing of that *"covenant"* began the Bible's long touted Tribulation period. Therefore, the *"seven years (of) making fires (with the weapons)"* comes hot on the heels of the Tribulation's beginning and runs to the end of that period.

When will this battle of Gog and Magog take place? It is not at the end of the Tribulation this battle takes place. It is not in the middle of the Tribulation this battle occurs. It is in the early days of the Tribulation this battle roars across the planet for a short period of time. But don't minimize this space of time. The First Battle of Gog and Magog claimed the lives of one-quarter of earth's population (Revelation 6:8). That would total 1,522,727,272 people. Again, God delivers the deathblow to this fiendish and wretched group. The Russian and Arab/Muslim confederacy will lay dead on the mountains of Israel. Antichrist relishes getting the credit for the victory. And he does! Though he probably has little to do with it, he uses it to elevate himself to new heights. The Tribulation has just begun in full earnest.

A Banquet For The Birds And The Beasts

The *"beasts"* in these verses is not Antichrist or his pompous and despicable reprobate religious leader, the false prophet. Instead, this is a sacrifice God is putting on for *"every kind of bird and to every beast of the field,"* Ezekiel 39:17.

Russians and Muslims are the main course. That's right! I did not come up with this. I'm just reporting it. They are food for the desert's dining table.

The First Battle of Gog and Magog has ended. To this Russian/Muslim confederacy God promised, "I shall strike your bow from your left hand, and dash down your arrows from your right hand. You shall fall on the mountains of Israel, you and all your troops, and the peoples who are with you; I shall give you as food to every kind of predatory bird and beast of the field. You will fall on the open field; for it is I who have spoken, declares the Lord God," Ezekiel 39:3-5.

The great shame is Russia's rejection of the Word of God. That Word would have warned her of the destruction of going her own way. Russia is not alone in that category.

For all my life men have asked, "How will Russia be kept from her goal of ruling the world?" That same question has been asked concerning the resurgence of Islam. Islam's unholy book, the Koran, requires conversion of the world to its faith, subjugation to servanthood those who will not convert, and death to those who refuse to serve Muslims. God has different plans. It is He who steps in to deliver His people when the Russian/Muslim confederacy attacks. And by His feast, God assures no bone goes un-picked. Listen, it is the Lord's command. He has messengers to clean up the mess Gog leaves behind.

"And as for you, son of man, thus says the Lord God, 'Speak to every kind of bird and to every beast of the field, "Assemble and come, gather from every side to My sacrifice which I am going to sacrifice for you, as a great sacrifice on the mountains of Israel, that you may eat flesh and drink blood. You shall eat the flesh of mighty men, and drink the blood of the princes of the earth, as though they were rams, lambs, goats and bulls, all of them fatlings of Bashan. So you will eat fat until you are glutted, and drink blood until you are drunk, from My sacrifice which I have sacrificed for you. And you will be glutted at My table with horses and charioteers, with mighty men and all the men of war,"' declares the Lord God," Ezekiel 39:17-20.

No army is safe when their Maker turns on them. But it is only the beginning of a red river that is rising.

Chapter Seven

Living Through The Tribulation
Dodging Bullets And Dancing With The Devil!

The Tribulation Pictured

We are now fully engaged in the first half of the Tribulation. I don't mean to belittle anything those on the planet will experience over the following seven years, but I want to give you as true a picture as possible of how progressively horrible life will become on earth for all her inhabitants. If you think what you are about to read is bad, consider the first three and a half years to be a day in the park compared to the final three and a half years of the Great Tribulation. And by no means can any description of this time do justice to the reality of the suffering Earth and her inhabitants are about to endure. Only those without Christ enter the Tribulation. The forever family of God has been *"caught up"* to meet the Lord in the air.

Here are the brutal facts for those entering the seven years of Tribulation. One's chance of making it through the Tribulation is 1 in 2. This will be a time of unparalleled testing, reducing Earth to no more than fifty percent of her pre-Tribulation population. There will be opportunity to come to know Christ during these seven years. Doing so, however, will lessen one's chance of making it through. But during this time, that may be desirable! Death for Christ's sake is simply a door of escaping this world's torment. Those accepting Christ as Lord and Savior and survive the Tribulation have a special treat in store. You will inherit the Millennial Kingdom of Christ on earth and will live another one thousand years. You will age during this time, but you will not die. Don't be concerned over your appearance by that time. The Lord's got some good wrinkle cream that will be handed out as you enter eternity's pearly gates. It will be your joy to inhabit the kingdom and repopulate the earth. You can join us immortals after the thousand years are up. But, teach your kids well and regularly during the Millennial reign. They've their own Battle with Gog and Magog to face later on. Be sure they are on the right side.

Please, allow me one last word on this for all entering the Tribulation. Log this in your mind. I mentioned above this is a test. Every person entering into these troubled waters will make a decision for or against Christ Jesus. You will either bow to Him, or you will harden your heart toward Him. Bow!

The Lord Jesus in answer to a question from His disciples gave a short version of the times of the end, especially as concerns the Jews. If you plan to be on the planet at that time, read on. It will affect you as well. His brief explanation is found in Matthew 24. First of all, He tells them to watch what they hear and see. "See to it that no one misleads you. For many will come in My name, saying, 'I am the Christ,' and will mislead many. And you will be hearing of wars and rumors of wars; see that you are not frightened, for those things must take place, but that is not yet the end. For nation will rise against nation, and kingdom against kingdom, and in various places there will be famines and earthquakes. But all these thing are merely the beginning of birth pangs." The above is pretty much self-explanatory and can be confirmed by any rational person today, especially those in the fields of security. By rational I am including you. Rational people are the only ones who will read this book through.

The Lord then takes them a step into the last *"week"* of Daniel's Seventy Weeks, which if you remember is God's timetable of Israel's history until Messiah's coming. This same span of seven years is also the Tribulation period for all left on the planet. The *real church* by now has been removed. And the Holy Spirit's restraining power on sin has been removed as well (II Thessalonians 2:7-12). By *real church*, I refer to the universal church, not the local church. These are those who actually know Christ Jesus, not those who profess to know Him, but will find themselves left behind. The physical plant of many churches will continue cranking out the program. These will be drawn to join the world church, the false prophet's baby, if they are not already members. Others, coming to a saving knowledge of Christ during the Tribulation will doubtless have to go underground for fellowship, teaching and for protection.

The Lord's narrative in Matthew 24 continues in verses 9-13. "Then they will deliver you to tribulation, and will kill you, and you will be hated by all nations on account of My name." He is speaking here primarily to the Jews. The Christians were raptured and other Gentiles have not converted yet. So you are not going to be hated so much if you are a Gentile. Become a Christian and you will be hated as well, and eliminated as soon as possible. Jews are Jews and are hated and killed simply because they are Jews. Let them become Christians and they will be doubly hated.

"Cut! Stop the narrative a moment. Israel is already *"hated"* by almost all the nations," you say. Yet, when the Tribulation begins that hatred will be multiplied worldwide. Remarks such as, "If it had not been for you Jews and your stubbornness, none of this would have ever happened," will be mild language in comparison to that days' reality. Jews individually will immediately be sought after and *"killed"* around the world. Antichrist promised national safety, not personal safety. Okay, restart the narrative.

"And at that time many will fall away and will deliver up one another and hate one another. And many false prophets will arise, and will mislead many. And because lawlessness is increased, most people's love will grow cold. But the one who endures to the end, he shall be saved." Those who *"fall away and deliver up one another,"* is in reference to relationships. It speaks to the fact that many individuals, including professing but false Christians, will betray and turn in one another. No one will know who can be trusted. These difficult times will be more difficult that most of us can imagine. Food, clean water and other necessities of life rapidly grow scarce. Depraved instincts during such times lead to *"hatred,"* the mother of murderers. With a breakdown of law and order *"love grows cold,"* becoming harder than tempered steel. People will turn inward for self-preservation. Many will become robots for Antichrist's whelms.

The midpoint of the Tribulation has now been reached in the Lord's narrative. Matthew 24:14-22 says of this time, "And this gospel of the kingdom shall be preached in the whole world for a witness to all the nations, and then the end shall come. Therefore when you see the abomination of desolation which was spoken of through Daniel the prophet, standing in the holy place (let the reader understand), then let those who are in Judea flee to the mountains; let him who is on the housetop not go down to get the things out that are in his house; and let him who is in the field not turn back to get his cloak. But woe to those who are with child and to those who nurse babes in those days! But pray that your flight may not be in the winter, or on a Sabbath; for then there will be a great tribulation, such as has not occurred since the beginning of the world until now, nor ever shall. And unless those days had been cut short, no life would have been saved; but for the sake of the elect those days shall be cut short."

The gospel's message being preached worldwide will be a reality in the last three and a half years of Israel's Travail, called the Great Tribulation. We'll see how and by whom *"the gospel will be preached"* just shortly. The *"abomination of desolation"* is in reference to Antichrist's defiling the temple of God. The Jewish Temple will in all likelihood be rebuilt during the first half of the Tribulation, if not immediately before (which I doubt). [This is a likely scenario. Antichrist, having confirmed a peace agreement for Israel, and having defeated the Russian/Muslim confederacy allows Israel to rebuild her Temple. Whether the Temple will be on or away from its original setting Scripture does not say. But the European Union's strong man is now in charge. Along with Russia a great number of the Islamic nations were destroyed they when came to wipe out Israel. There is not much the vestiges of Islam could do, if anything, to stop Israel from tearing down the Dome of the Rock.] Whether that transpires or not, this devil inspired leader of the free world will eventually offer profane sacrifices on the rebuilt Temple's altar. He will then declare himself to be God. That moment begins the second half of Daniel's Seventy Weeks, the Great Tribulation.

The majority of the verses in the above passage deal with the Jewish people's necessity of *"fleeing"* Antichrist's wrath. They must escape and they must do it quickly and expeditiously. Thus, the warning to *"pray (their) flight may not be in winter"* or with *"babes."* They will flee to a place God has prepared for them, possibly Petra in the Jordanian dessert. God has already begun preparing Petra and other locations today through mission efforts organized for that very purpose. There is a phrase in the above passage in verse 21, which states, *"... for then there will be a great tribulation, such as has not occurred since the beginning of the world until now, nor ever shall."* The Great Tribulation will be a time of unimaginable misery, hardship and suffering. It will be much like a woman with birth pangs, and is referred to as such in the title, *The Time of Israel's Travail*. War will be ongoing, but the above-italicized phrase indicates that this particular event will be so tumultuous that only God's original creation of the world can compare to it. Call it big bang or boom, it will be unlike anything before it all the way back to creation. I'd rather be on another planet at that time, thank you. Actually, I doubt it will affect the clouds, and that's where I'll be.

The Lord summed up these various events of Matthew 24 with His main teaching point in reference to His return. He gave us the parable of the fig tree in verses 32-36. "Now learn the parable from the fig tree: when its branch has already become tender, and puts forth its leaves, you know that summer is near; even so you too, when you see all these things, recognize that He is near, right at the door. Truly I say to you, this generation will not pass away until all these things take place. Heaven and earth will pass away, but My words shall not pass away. But of that day and hour no one knows, not even the angels of heaven, nor the Son, but the Father alone."

Israel is the fig tree. Her *"branch"* became *"tender, and put forth its leaves"* decades ago. The *"generation"* seeing Israel's re-birth, as a nation will also see *"all these things take place."* God declares, *"This generation will not pass away until all these things take place."* I didn't say that, Jesus did! According to this passage and others in the New Testament, no one knows the *"day and hour"* of the Lord's return. There have been enough false religions prove that point on mountaintops already. But, we absolutely with clarity are to know the general timing of His return.

The word *"generation"* has been a point of contention for many. Some say a *"generation"* is 40 years, some say

60 years, and some say as much as 100 years. I think 100 years is a little long and indefensible. It is certainly possible for us to know the general vicinity of the Lord's return and not know how many years makes a *"generation."* Forty years has already passed, and sixty years is almost over. Personally, I believe a *"generation"* is a general life span, which is considered by most to be 70 years. Knowing Israel became a nation on May 14, 1948, you can do the math. Personally, I would not get caught up in narrowing the years down to months or weeks. There are too many good things in which to be involved in reference to Christ's return and to the Christian life in general to tie oneself down to anything that could hinder one's greatest usefulness. Who knows if the sentence, *"its branch has already become tender, and puts forth its leaves,"* refers to May 14, 1948 or to a time shortly after that date? His coming is near and we need to be about His work, looking up only from time to time. Remember, His coming for His own is not visionary, but auditory: *"For the Lord Himself will descend from heaven with a shout, with the voice of the archangel, and with the trumpet of God."* We don't have to see Him to hear him.

Remember, it's watch and work and play occasionally. Someone else said it best. "Live as if His coming is today; plan and work as if it is one hundred years away."

Antichrist's Rage

Antichrist's victory, or his perceived victory, over Russia and her Arab/Muslim confederacy, adds to his already inflated bravado and ambition. He becomes a man filled with unmeasured pride, disdain and arrogance. Of course, being the world's kingpin he has much housekeeping and organizing to see to. Yet, he does not forget the nations whose armies attacked him. Some of those along the coastlines and a portion of Russia have already been hit hard by none other than God Himself. Here are God's words concerning their just punishment. "And I shall send fire upon Magog and those who inhabit the coastlands in safety; and they will know that I am the Lord," Ezekiel 39:6. *"Magog,"* of course, is southern Russia. Imagine that! Russia thinks she is a god unto herself. (Good grief, so does America.) In reality, if one is a true atheist she cannot be her own god, for then there would be a god. I don't think Mr. Putin has ever been informed of that! The *"coastlands"* identification makes the geography far more wide spread. The term could refer to Russia's coastlands and/or those of many of her confederacy; which is probably the case. We'll just have to wait and occasionally look down on this war from above. In Israel Antichrist keeps his word concerning the *"covenant"* of peace, at least for the first half of his seven-year promise. Besides, Israel didn't challenge him, the Russian/Muslim confederacy stuck out its tongue at him. Israel can wait; these others are in for a broad-swiping military lashing.

Daniel 11:20-30, once again, lists the exploits of Antichrist between the signing of Israel's infamous peace covenant until the timing of the abomination of desolation at the mid point of the Tribulation. We covered that in the previous chapter. So I'll not belabor the point here. It is enough to realize Antichrist will be as desirous of conquering the world, as were the Islamic fascists before him.

Two Witnesses

In the midst of the darkest days of humanity, God gives a ray of Son-light. Well, that is determined by whose side one is on. In every generation God has provided a witness as to His love and provision of salvation. No decision *for* Christ is mandatory. But to make no decision is to decide against Him. One's sin is then on his or her back forever. Whisk it away at the foot of the cross while it is today.

Even during the Tribulation's days of uncertainty, fear and depravation, God makes available salvation's message. In the first three and a half years, two witnesses are in the streets of Jerusalem preaching, arguing and inviting Jews primarily to accept Jehovah's Son as Israel's long ago rejected Messiah. These two witnesses are, "the two olive trees and the two lampstands that stand before the Lord of the earth," Revelation 11:4. Never in these wishy-washy days of converting people to a religion and to a church have you ever heard such messages as these two bring. God, on the other hand, is pretty pleased with these two. Hear of the authority He gives them.

"And I will grant authority to My two witnesses, and they will prophesy for twelve hundred and sixty days, clothed in sackcloth," Revelation 11:3.

"Twelve hundred and sixty days" is three and a half years. The first half of the Tribulation is designated for the ministries of these two servants of God. The English word "witness" derives from the Greek word *"martyr."* And these two *"witnesses"* are, as their designation implies and as you will see, *"martyrs"* for God's sake. They are prophets of God sent to deliver a message of salvation or judgment to a perishing generation. Prophets *"prophesy."* That is, their mission is to call God's people, in this case Israel, to repentance and to a walking relationship with Him through Christ Jesus the Lord. That is what *"prophets"* do! *"Sackcloth"* is the dress of grief, sorrow and humility. These two are *"granted authority"* from God. And He has been pleased to bestow it. As such nothing touches them until their purpose is fulfilled. And that's twelve hundred and sixty days down the road.

"These are the two olive trees and the two lampstands that stand before the Lord of the earth." Zechariah 4:3 mentions these *"two olive trees."* It does not tell us who they are, but verse 14 of this chapter does give us their status. "These (two olive trees) are the two anointed ones, who are standing by the Lord of the whole earth." Our *"two witnesses"* are God's *"anointed ones"* who have a special task to perform during the first half of the Tribulation. In so doing they are *"standing by the Lord of the whole earth."* Complete His will without wavering and the same things can be said about you. Wouldn't that be a joy!

That's not a bad standing, now or in eternity. The great problem is many who want to fellowship with Christ in eternity don't seem to care much about walking with Him in time. Jesus' company can be embarrassing at times. "He might command an ongoing reformation in me." Yes, such could even cause people to talk. Might cost us a friend or two; could even cost you job. "And, what is it with this tithe thing? I need what I've earned for my family, the future, a new car, clothes, vacation, etc...." We are so spiritually poor! God's two witnesses to Israel are calling her to repentance and faith in Jesus Christ at a time when it will cost them their lives. Millions have been there before. Millions are there now! And we are worried about ten percent of our income? Eighty percent of today's churchgoers sit around trying to figure out how to minimize and excuse ten cents out of a dollar. "Let's see, can't I deduct taxes, lunches and gas from the gross and then figure from the net? There are little Johnny's braces, too. God forbid he grows up looking like that." What kind of martyrs will they be? The Lord's two *"anointed ones were standing before the Lord of the whole earth."* So are we with God's enabling!

"Lampstand" is another depiction of these *"two anointed ones."* As is the reference to the church in Revelation 1:20, these *"lampstands"* are not the light, but "bearers of the light." These two witnesses have one all-consuming purpose for twelve hundred and sixty days. Their purpose is to provide a faithful witness of the Lord Jesus Christ. And, I take it they knew when and how they would die for their testimony.

Their constant message is broadcast around the world. Jews and Gentiles alike hate what they hear and see in these two. "Religious bigots! Who do they think they are talking to us that way? What right do they have to criticize our government when we are all just trying to get along? Pigs!" And few, if any, accept what they hear, see or say. But our witnesses' constant drumming messages are captured in the minds of men and will, during the last one thousand two hundred and sixty days, have a God-ordained impact on the hearts of many.

Some have indignantly questioned, "What? 'If anyone desires to harm them, fire proceeds out of their mouth and devours their enemies; and if anyone would desire to harm them, in this manner he must be killed,' Revelation 11:5. What kind of a God is it that would send these two to kill us simply because we object to what they stand for? Can't you just let love reign? Pig!" I have a better question. "What sort of God would He be were He not to do that?" God is a God of love, mercy and grace. But so many human hearts have hardened to the point of no return. Why would a loving God not severely judge anyone seeking to silence His last days' witnesses to those who might sooner or later desire Him? That's called preaching the whole story. It would not be a loving God to allow sin to reign indefinitely. But, let me go one step further. God's primary attribute is not love or mercy or grace. His primary attribute is holiness. All other attributes stem from His ever-present holiness. Therefore, the judgments of God must separate those who deny Him from those who will acknowledge Him in repentance and faith. God is always righteous and just in His actions.

Scripture identifies only one of these *"two witnesses"* in Malachi 4:5: "Behold, I am going to send you Elijah the prophet before the coming of the great and terrible day of the Lord." The ministry of these two will be during the first three and a half years of the Tribulation. The Lord Himself confirmed that Elijah is one of these *"two witnesses"* who would come before that great day in Matthew 11:14. Look it up! The other *"witness"* is thought to be Moses. Perhaps that is why God hid Moses' body. These two were seen with the Lord Jesus on the Mount of Transfiguration. The following description of these *"witnesses"* and their works during the Tribulation matches that of Elijah and Moses' previous ministries. Nevertheless, we will have to wait and see if Moses is the second *"witness."* It has also been proposed that instead of Moses, the second witness might be Enoch. That's possible as well. Like Elijah, Enoch is the only other human who did not see death (Genesis 5:24). No point in arguing the point, we shall see from grandstands high over the earth. And whatever we decide is not going to decide who this second witness is anyway.

Malachi also records God speaking of these two important witnesses, *"Behold, I am going to send My messenger, and he will clear the way before Me,"* verse 3:1. Matthew 11:10 records the Lord's validation of Malachi's message. When the things of the Messiah didn't seem to be adding up to the imprisoned John the Baptist, he sent a messenger to ask Jesus, "Are You the Expected One, or shall we look for someone else?" Earlier a group of Jewish priests and Levites came to John the Baptist and asked, "Who are you? Are you Elijah?" And he said, "I am not," John 1:19-21. Now listen to what the Lord had to say about John. To a multitude of Israelites He said, "If you care to accept it, he himself (John the Baptist) is Elijah, who is to come," verse 11:14. Had Israel accepted the Lord Jesus Christ as their Messiah, then John the Baptist would have been Elijah, *"who is to come."* They did not receive Him; they rejected Him and the Lord Jesus knew they would. So the offer was never really on the table. Elijah is still to come.

Is your Bible handy? Turn to Revelation 11:3-13 and discover the power invested upon these *"two witnesses,"* their ministry, death, resurrection and ascension. God's two witnesses are eventually killed by Antichrist who "comes up out of the abyss (to) make war with them, and overcome them and kill them," verse 7. That does not happen, however, until "they have finished their testimony," verse 7. And an effectively delivered testimony it was.

The world, however, thinks differently. So delighted are earth's inhabitants over God's witnesses deaths, they leave the *"witnesses'"* dead and decaying bodies in the open street for three and a half days. Gifts among the unredeemed are exchanged with one another. Hell's Christmas has arrived. The world rejoices over their apparent demise. Our day is the more a day of easy salvation rather than regenerate transformation. In a day of determining a tree by fruit it bears, a man's ministry could well be judged not by the size of it, but by the anger it generates.

These *"two witnesses"* are not the church being raptured at the Tribulation's midpoint as some have wrongly suggested. They are God's *"two witnesses"* prophesied of so long ago. Their ministry completed, they are called to give up their lives. In camera shot of the whole world and after three and a half days dead God causes these men to, *"stand on their feet."* The result: *"Great fear fell upon those who were beholding them,"* Revelation 11:11. I'll bet! I wonder if they took their presents back for a refund? Watch this! "And they (those who saw them) heard a loud voice from heaven saying to them, 'Come up here.' And they went up into heaven in the cloud, and their enemies beheld them," verse 12. The sad thing here is that the call to *"come up here"* could not be offered to the onlookers, but only to His two faithful witnesses. The world rejoices when these two meet death. But it will be a short-lived holiday. The celebration ends abruptly! Was their ministry at the cost of their lives ineffective? Not at all! Their ministry is confirmed by

God through their resurrection and is used by God to quickly initiate Israel's redemption.

The Seven-Sealed Book

Revelation 5 contains one of the most spectacular sights in all God's Word. This is a parenthetical chapter. Such chapters, and The Revelation has many of them, momentarily stop the flow of the chronological events of the Book. Important persons or events necessary to understand or carry out the message of The Revelation can then be explained. And we have a very important one here.

In verse 1, John sees in the hand of God the Father "a book written inside and on the back, sealed up with seven seals." This seven-sealed book is the Book of Redemption of this world and all of us who abide in it. The question is then asked, "Who is worthy to open the book and to break its seals?" No one in heaven or earth was found worthy to open it. To do so would require worthiness beyond the ability of sinful man, or even holy angels.

Finally, in answer to John's emotional outburst, an elder points him to, "the Lion that is from the tribe of Judah, the Root of David," explaining, "(He) has overcome so as to open the book and its seven seals." That *"Lion,"* of course, is Jesus the Savior. He is then seen to be *"a Lamb standing, as if slain."* That is some victorious Lamb! That is also what makes Him so very worthy. Without sin, He substituted His pure and spotless life for mine — yes, yours too. He is now seen walking up to His Father and taking the Book, *"out of the right hand of Him who sat on the throne,"* verse 7. The *"right hand"* is the hand of acceptance. Jesus *"standing as if slain"* is the reason the beautiful song is sung with such emotion, "Worthy Is The Lamb."

In Revelation 6 the Lord Jesus begins breaking the seals of the Book. With the breaking of each seal an event occurs, one after another, taking us through the first half of the Tribulation. You'll recognize some of these below that we've already mentioned.

The *"first seal"* is broken (verses 1, 2) and out comes a *"white horse,"* whose rider is the world's false messiah deceiving and seeking to spiritually bankrupt the world and those that dwell in it.

The *"second seal"* is broken (verses 3, 4) and out of it came forth the *"red horse"* rider. Here the Russian/Muslim confederacy is seen attacking Israel.

The *"third seal"* is broken (5, 6) and out of it comes forth a *"black horse"* rider representative of famine around the world. Perhaps part of the famine is due to America's corn going to make fuel rather than food. Hummm!

The *"fourth seal"* is broken (verses 7, 8) and out of it comes forth an *"ashen horse,"* whose name is *"Death and Hades."* It is here at the beginning of the Tribulation we see one fourth of the population of earth perishing on the grinding stones of war.

The *"fifth seal"* is broken (verses 9-11) and *"the souls of those who had been slain"* are seen under the altar of God in heaven. These are those men and women who forfeited their lives by testifying of a saving knowledge of the Lord Jesus Christ. This they unashamedly did in the midst of the Tribulation period. It is a cruel and foolish world indeed.

The *"sixth seal"* is broken (verses 12-17) and *"a great earthquake"* turns the sun black, "the whole moon became like blood; and the stars of the sky fell to the earth... and the sky was split apart like a scroll... and every mountain and island were moved out of their places." So fearful was the breaking of this seal that "kings... great men... commanders... the rich... the strong... and every slave and free man, hid themselves in the caves and among the rocks of the mountains; and they said to the mountains and to the rocks, 'Fall on us and hide us from the presence of the Lamb;

for the great day of His wrath has come; and who is able to stand.'"

The *"seventh seal"* is broken (Revelation 8:1, 2) and *"and there was silence in heaven for about half an hour."* Someone cruelly, and I mean brutally, once said this verse proves there will be no women in heaven. They cannot keep silent that long. It was not I for I know the real meaning of the verse. Out of the *"seventh seal"* comes forth the seven trumpet judgments of God upon man's world. These *"trumpets"* begin to blow after the abomination of desolation triggers the second half of the Tribulation. Scripture refers to this time as the Great Tribulation. The reason *"there was silence in heaven for about half an hour,"* is the fearful awesomeness of these trumpet judgments that are coming upon the earth. Such insight caused heaven to gasp. No one could speak for *"about half an hour."*

It is with the removing of the *"seventh seal"* from the book of redemption that Antichrist is assassinated. Who kills him and by what means we are not told. His assassination could be the result of his committing the abomination of desolation: defiling the altar and pronouncing himself as God. Orthodox Jews would not take kindly to the altar's defamation. Whoever it was played into the hands of Satan. Since Jesus was killed and rose again, Antichrist should be slain and rise also. The fact of Antichrist's death is pronounced in several Old and New Testament passages. We've covered these passages previously, so I'll only mention the New Testament verses now.

Revelation 13:3 references, "... a beast coming up out of the sea," verse 1. The *"beast,"* as we have seen is Antichrist. The *"sea"* in Scripture, used in its symbolic form, refers to "Gentile nations." Scripture further points, as you will remember, to *"the prince who is to come"* being the leader of the revived Roman Empire, the former Common Market of Europe, today's European Union, the E.U. This third verse says, "And I saw one of his heads as if it had been slain, and his fatal wound was healed. And the whole earth was amazed and followed after the beast." The word *"slain"* means, "smitten to death." That's about as dead as one can be. Verse 12 of this same chapter once again mentions his fatal wound: "And he (the false prophet) makes the earth and those who dwell in it to worship the first beast, whose fatal wound was healed." Finally, Revelation 17:8 connects this *"beast"* with the one spoken of in the Old Testament in this manner: "The beast that you saw was and is not, and is about to come up out of the abyss...."

So Antichrist is going to be killed at the midpoint of the Tribulation. He won't stay dead though. Evil is always sticking up its awful head. He'll come back to life more enraged than ever. Perhaps it was the accommodations during his brief stay with death in *"the abyss"* that has him up in arms. What do you think?

Antichrist More Enraged Than Ever

Antichrist is more enraged than ever and turns his fury fully on Israel. He makes a slight-of-hand move directly against her by proceeding to the Temple to commit Daniel's prophesied *"abomination of desolation"* (Daniel 9:27; 11:31; Matthew 24:15). He thus breaks the covenant of peace he signed with Israel three and a half years earlier.

It is around this time Antichrist receives *"a fatal wound;"* yet, he is miraculously *"healed"* (13:3). Well, of course, the devil's son has to die and rise again. Matthew records the Lord Jesus' teaching on this infamous day. The record in his Gospel shows the gravity of the moment. Read the whole passage to get all the seriousness and significance that God intends (Matthew 24:15-27). Revelation 12:6, 14 also references this event: "And the woman fled into the wilderness where she had a place prepared by God, so that there she might be nourished for one thousand two hundred and sixty days," (three and a half years). "And the two wings of the great eagle were given to the woman (Israel), in order that she might fly into the wilderness to her place, where she was nourished for a time and times and half a time from the presence of the serpent," verse 14. The Jews that are able to make it to God's hideout will be protected and taken care of by Him for these last three and a half years. The midpoint of the Tribulation has been reached and Earth has become the most dangerous speck of dust in the universe.

(Note: The Bible passage concerning Israel being given *"the two wings of the great eagle… that she might fly into the wilderness to her place"* has often been attributed to being that of the United States, that is, her Air Force, since our national emblem is the eagle. I hope that is so. However, I don't believe it speaks so much of the manner of her delivery from Satan's grip, as to the swiftness and power of her deliverance. This same picture is drawn for us of Israel's long-ago deliverance from Egypt. "You yourselves have seen what I did to the Egyptians, and how I bore on eagles' wings, and brought you to Myself," Exodus 19:4. That speaks of the power and swiftness of God's delivery of His people. We'll watch from above to see if the U.S. has anything to do with it! Let's pray so!)

That which has been impossible to date, is now in Antichrist's power. He kills God's *"two witnesses"* (Revelation 11:3-14) who faithfully testified and pronounced God's judgment on the streets of Jerusalem for the previous three and a half years.

Upon Antichrist's resurrection the Tribulation's false prophet requires a statue be made in honor of his revived boss. See Revelation 13:14-18. This religious apostate even has the power to give the statue of Antichrist the ability to breathe and speak. Antichrist's irreligious friend, this *"beast from the earth,"* then requires the mark of the beast without which no one can buy or sell. The infamous mark is required on the hand or on the forehead of every human alive — at the risk of not staying alive. The situation on earth continues to go from bad to worse until Israel's rejected Messiah, the Gentile's Savior returns.

By the way, the *"mark of the beast"* is *"on"* the hand or *"on"* the forehead. The Greek word used for *"on"* is *"epi."* *"Epi"* infers *"upon."* Had it been a mark *"within,"* where it could not be visually seen, the Greek word *"en"* would have been used. This mark is visibly seen *"on"* the hand or *"on"* the forehead of the one receiving it. It is a public, unashamed association with Antichrist and kin. I covered that because some ladies don't really want a mark openly showing. Sorry about that, my friends. Worse still, the mark also assures a permanent destination, a ticket to Hell. Satan will get them any way he can.

Up to this point, for reasons known to God alone, Satan has been allowed to pop in and out of heaven, seemingly at will. At this point of the Tribulation the dragon of old is cast down to earth. He, too, is greatly enraged, *"knowing that he has only a short time,"* Revelation 12:12. Isn't that amazing! This serpent believes the Bible but refuses to accept the obvious. What a mind-boggler Satan on this day will be to the many on earth having denied his existence. The serpent imparts to Antichrist his *"power, throne and great authority,"* Revelation 13:1-6. Many throughout the world are then required to worship this devilish *"beast"* (13:4). Where's the ACLU when a real need arises? Pun intended!

(There is a reason the world's false messiah is called Antichrist. Satan's time is spent in duplicating the things of God. He is like a kid in an evil Toy Land, but he is no kid. He himself plays the netherworld's role of godfather. Who could have guessed? What could possibly make him feel good after all this time longing to, yet still facing the inevitable inability to, "make himself like the Most High?" See

Isaiah 14:13, 14. Antichrist is the presumed god the son. And the false prophet is Satan's god the unholy spirit.)

Antichrist, unable to destroy Israel due to her protection by God, turns on those coming to and confessing Christ as Lord during the Tribulation. His attention is also full-throttle toward subjugating or completely destroying the surrounding nations not in compliance with his governmental demands. He attacks them with the fierceness of a lion robbed of her cubs and with the power of a dragon. Daniel 11 outlines Antichrist's military exploits during this period. Verse 40f says, "... and he will enter countries, overflow them, and pass through." That's not good!

At will Antichrist enters these countries that refuse to dance with him and *"overflows"* them. That is to say, he "overpowers" them; he devastates them. Verse 41 adds, "He will also enter the Beautiful Land, and many will fall...." *"The Beautiful Land"* is a term in Scripture for Palestine (Psalms 48:2; Daniel 8:9; 11:16). Unable to do anything about Israel's fleeing *"to her place"* in the wilderness (possibly Petra), the E.U.'s strongman turns on any and every person and nation that does not bend the knee before him. That would include the so-called Palestinians. They are Arabs and mostly Muslim. Antichrist's hatred of them is due in part to their brothers being a lion's share of the Russian contingency, and because their religion does not point to him as head. Well, indirectly to be sure!

"Then he will stretch out his hand against other countries, and the land of Egypt will not escape," Daniel 11:42. Remember, I told you so. This world's coming ruler will not forget any nation that rebelled or fought against him. Total submission is officially demanded. Nothing less will suffice. "He will gain control over the hidden treasurers of gold and silver, and over all the precious things of Egypt; and Libyans and Ethiopians will follow at his heels," (vs. 43). That is, they too will "fall in his wake." Most countries in these areas are Muslim in make-up. Not many go unscathed, as *"he will enter countries."* I would imagine that statement means most of the North African countries will succumb early on, or be subdued by him later. Over a three and a half year period his army will do a lot of walking, and it seems they visit and pound this area three times.

So raw and empowered is Antichrist, he makes sport of conquering nations. Read again Daniel 11:36-39 and Scripture's depiction of the arrogance, disdain, gall, greed and limitless power of this Satan-driven man. He does not go unchallenged; yet he is proven to be unstoppable. Nonetheless, his free ride is only for a limited time.

The Sealed 144,000

Allow me to set the stage for the events under this title: The Sealed 144,000.

The second half of the Tribulation has begun. Antichrist has been raised from the dead and is now indwelled and energized by Satan himself. Both are mad. That's a mild way of saying it. They are furious, angry and uncontrol-lable throughout the coming twelve hundred and sixty days. Antichrist wants Jewish blood on his hands, but God in His secret place is protecting most of the Israelites. That adds to the European's strongman's fury. So he turns to others worldwide, Jews and Gentiles alike, who are turning in faith to Jesus Christ. Guillotines are established everywhere as the least costly and most effective way of cleansing the world of these maddening, menacing and world unsettling interlopers.

So God ups the ante with a little drier, hotter and still-air heat. Chapter 7 of The Revelation is a parenthetical chapter. The flow of information concerning the chronological order of events during the Tribulation is temporarily halted. It's like a TV station's flashing attention getter. NEWS ALERT!

NEWS ALERT! NEWS ALERT! Accept here we really do have a news alert, a good news alert. First, there is an event. Second, there is a warning. And third, there is a good news revelation.

First, there is an event. And a hot event it is. Four angels are pictured in verse 1 as "holding back the four winds of the earth, so that no wind should blow on the earth or on the sea or on any tree." The season of the year is not given us. But I know God, and He does nothing that will not yield the desired effect. Believe me, it's summer time; without doubt it is August. And no wind is going to blow, not even a breeze. The temperature is 105° and rising. Humidity is 100%. Yes, you can squeeze water from a rock. And no leaf moves on any tree on earth. Why? Maybe it is just to aggravate the tree-huggers. I don't know why. He doesn't tell us. But, He can do as He pleases because this is His earth and these are His judgments. Man seems to have forgotten, there is a Creator, and as Creator it is His planet to do with as He pleases.

Second, there is a warning in verses 2, 3, "And I saw another angel ascending from the rising of the sun, having the seal of the living God; and he cried out with a loud voice to the four angels to whom it was granted to harm the earth and the sea, saying, 'Do not harm the earth or the sea or the trees, until we have sealed the bond-servants of our God on their foreheads.'" Such words herald more news than a hurricane's warning. The earth, the sea and the trees are about to be harmed. Get ready!

Third, there is a good news revelation! This is the really important message conveyed in this chapter. The revelation in this passage is in answer to the many questions as to, "Will anyone be saved during the Tribulation?" And, "How will they be saved if there is no preacher?" So God gives us this special passage to bring sweet relief concerning what will eventually be the means of salvation for millions upon millions, even in earth's darkest days.

We saw during the first half of the Tribulation that God gave the world two mighty preachers called the *"two witnesses."* Their preaching was not in vain. We don't know how many people came to Christ as a result of their preaching. They were a not so pretty rag-tag couple of men. Maybe people didn't like them, or were afraid of them. If their hearts weren't right they had good reason to be. These were insightful prophets. More importantly, they were God's men with God's message. In Revelation 6:9 John "saw underneath the altar (of God) the souls of those who had been slain because of the Word of God, and because of the testimony which they had maintained." Many had already come to faith in Christ Jesus, and many of those became the first Tribulation saints to give their lives in testimony of God's love, mercy, grace and forgiveness. The slaying of "these rebel prophets who just can't get along with others" occurred before we came to Revelation 7. And now the *"two witnesses"* are gone. Who will pick up their mantle?

Here's the answer. Nothing else on earth can happen until the "angel... (with) the seal of the living God... sealed the bondservants of our God on their foreheads. And I (John) heard the number of those who were sealed, one hundred and forty-four thousand sealed from every tribe of the sons of Israel," verses 2-4. In verses 5-8 the tribes of the sons of Israel are listed with the numerical figure by each of their tribes designating *"twelve thousand"* men from that tribe were sealed. All total 144,000 Jewish men from the twelve tribes of Israel are sealed. I think God took so much pain in designating the tribes and number from each tribe just so no one apart from one selected group of Jewish men would ever claim to be the 144,000. What do you think? Yeah, yeah, I know what you are thinking.

What is the purpose of these 144,000 Jewish evangelists? These stamped, sealed and delivered Jews are sent to the four corners of earth to preach the Gospel to every nation, tribe, tongue and people on the face of the planet. The result of their ministry is detailed in Revelation 7:9-17. But, pay attention to verse 9 in particular. "After these things I looked, and behold a great multitude, which no one could count, from every nation and all tribes and peoples and tongues, standing before the throne and before the Lamb, clothed in white robes, and palm branches were in their hands."

Who are these multitudes? That question is asked for us in verse 13. Verse 14 gives us the answer: "These are the ones who come out of the great tribulation, and they have washed their robes and made them white in the blood of the Lamb." These are those who either heard one of the 144,000 Jewish evangelists, or heard indirectly their message from another, and placed their faith in the Lord Jesus Christ. A great multitude, which no one could count, is brought to a saving knowledge of the Savior.

These Jewish evangelists are like 144,000 Billy Graham's with a three and a half year mission: "That every ear may hear." That has been the goal many fine Christian denominations have sought to fulfill and have laid the groundwork for. It is during the ministry of the 144,000 Jewish evangelists, however, that this God-ordained mission is completed. And, they did a mighty fine job of it.

But it was not without problems. Remember, these 144,000 had *"the seal of God on their foreheads."* That *"seal"* is the stamp of God whereby neither Satan, nor his Antichrist, nor his false prophet, nor any of their lackeys can touch a hair on one of their heads. This satanic trio tries in every way possible though, they hunt them down daily, they lay traps, they try to blow them up, they poison them, and they gun them down, but the seal of God protects them every step of the way. In fact, when the Lord Jesus returns to earth at Mount Zion, guess who is with Him? "And I (John) looked, and behold, the Lamb was standing on Mount Zion, and with Him one hundred and forty-four thousand, having

His name and the name of His Father written on their fore-heads," Revelation 14:1.

Mission accomplished! Millions saved out of the Great Tribulation. God sealed them. Satan tried to destroy them. God wins. Game over! These men will doubtlessly be inter-viewed about their exploits and talked about for quite a while in eternity to come. Their evangelistic, super thriller lives have been a cross between Billy Graham and a redeemed James Bond. These 144,000 have been dodging bullets and dancing the side step with the devil. May God bless them!

God's Judgments During The Great Tribulation

With every *"seal"* removed the *"seven sealed book"* required judgment upon man and on the world. These judg-ments all came about during first half of the Tribulation. A *seal* in the Bible certifies ownership. Make no mistake about it, this world still belongs to it original Owner and Creator (Psalm 24:1, 2). The *"seal"* judgments consummate as the "seventh seal" is broken bringing forth even greater judg-ments, the *"seven trumpet"* judgments. These judgments will occur on earth during the Great Tribulation, the last three and a half years of Jacob's trouble. Here in brief are the *"seven trumpet"* judgments. I highly recommend you turn in your Bible to Revelation 8 and read the entire narrative. You will find these judgments are only one to three verses in length, and though horrific, they are rich in revealing all that is coming upon the earth. For anyone not on your way to heaven, you may find this information helpful, hopefully sooner rather than later.

These *"trumpet sounds"* seem to blend in with one another at times, and indeed they do. These judgments coming upon man and earth follow one another in rapid succession. Some of these judgments last for a period of time while others come and then go and still others overlap them. So read the full narrative as to "these things (that) are coming upon the earth."

The first *"trumpet sounds"* and hail and fire, mixed with blood, are thrown to the earth. The result: a third of the earth and trees were burned up (Revelation 8:7), and all the green grass was burned up, Revelation 8:7. We've all seen, at least on TV, the horrible result of fires burning the forest and fields and homes in various areas of our nation and in other parts of the world. With the coming of this judgment there will be no "getting a handle" on these fires. Can you imagine it? A third of the earth is *"burned up and all the green grass."*

The second angel sounded and something like a great mountain burning with fire was thrown into the sea. The result: a third of the sea became blood; a third of the creatures in it died; and a third of the ships were destroyed (Revelation 8:8, 9).

The third angel sounded, and a great burning star fell from heaven, and it fell on a third of the rivers and on the springs of water. Its name is Wormwood and it poisoned a third of the water. Many men died from the poisoned waters (Revelation 8:10, 11). This is unfortunately reminiscent of the old saying, "Water, water everywhere, but not a drop to drink," (from Coleridge's "Rhyme of the Ancient Mariner"). The water from one's tap may indeed be good. But can't you just imagine the hesitation with every glass, "I wonder if anything has broken into our water supply?"

The fourth angel sounded with the result that a third of the sun, moon and stars were struck. A third of their light was darkened during the day and night (Revelation 8:12).

Suddenly, in Revelation 8:13, as if out of nowhere three *"woes"* are mentioned as coming upon the earth. These *"woes"* are connected with the last three trumpet judgments. Their purpose in part is to stress the grievousness of the remaining judgments. They will be far more severe than the preceding ones.

As the fifth angel sounded a star fell from heaven and the key to the bottomless pit was given him (Revelation 9:1-12). This *"star,"* if not Satan, is a leading General in Satan's band of fallen misfits. He opens the bottomless pit where the meanest and most unimaginable fallen angels have been imprisoned, sparing the world up to this point. These were too horrifying to let loose on earth. They are now released. Out of the smoke of this pit came locusts with the power of scorpions. They have permission to torment mankind for five months. Men will not die from their stings, but they may well wish for death. They have a king over them. This is definitely Satan. His names are *"Abaddon"* in Hebrew and *"Apollyon"* in Greek. Interpreted these names mean Destruction and Destroyer. The first *"woe"* is past.

When the sixth angel sounded his trumpet, the four angels who are bound at the Euphrates River were released (Revelation 9:13 -10:7). These are the four angels that ignite the Battle of Armageddon killing a third of mankind. They drum up an army of two hundred million men for battle.

Think on this. Seven years earlier the earth was populated with well over six billion people. As of August 21, 2007 there were more than 6,700,000,000 people on earth and 9 on the space station. We can't forget them. One fourth of the world died in the First Battle of Gog and Magog, that's 1,675,000,002 who perished in the opening battle of Daniel's Seventieth Week. Less those taken up in the rapture. That leaves planet earth with 5,025,000,007 people still kicking and breathing, I'm sure with a sigh of relief. Now we are seeing another one third of Earth's remaining population will die at Armageddon. That leaves a planetary population of only 3,502,272,730 or thereabouts alive on Earth. One half Earth's population dies in less than seven years. One out of every two people on Earth will have perished. And those seven years could begin at any time. If there is a silver lining to this it has to be found in the mortuary business.

Additionally, *"seven peals of thunder"* described themselves to John (Revelation 10:3, 4). However, John was told not to write down the things the *"peals of thunder"* spoke. We'll find out soon enough, I'm sure. The second *"woe"* is past.

Then the seventh angel sounds and the great dragon is cast down to the earth (Revelation 11:15 – 12:12). The great dragon, the serpent of old, the devil and Satan are all names of Heaven's infamous Lucifer of long ago. Satan, knowing his time is short, stampedes with a vengeance after Israel. God, however, will not allow her to be caught. Next, Satan the blunderer turns on the rest of her offspring, who keep the commandments of God and hold to the testimony of Jesus. These are those who come to a saving knowledge of Christ during the Tribulation period. Many during this time will cash in their lives and hold on to their testimony. That explains the many who are martyred during this time. The third *"woe"* is past.

We might ask, "Could anyone endure any more than all that has come upon mankind?" The answer is, "Yes!" More is on the way.

Revelation 15:1 introduces us to "seven angels who have seven plagues, which are the last, because in them the wrath of God is finished." Chapter 16 gives us a vivid picture of these seven bowls of the wrath of God. Here they are in rapid order.

"The first angel went and poured out his bowl into the earth; and *it became a loathsome and malignant sore* upon the men who had the mark of the beast and who worshiped his image," verse 2. Evidently those having received Christ are graciously spared this disease.

"And the second angel poured out his bowl into the sea, and it became blood like that of a dead man; and *every living thing in the sea died*," verse 3.

"And the fourth angel poured out his bowl upon the sun; and it was given to it to *scorch men with fire*," verse 8.

"And the fifth angel poured out his bowl upon the throne of the beast; and his kingdom became darkened; and they gnawed their tongues because of pain, and they blasphemed the God of heaven because of their pains and their sores; and they did not repent of their deeds," verses 10, 11.

"And the sixth angel poured out his bowl upon the great river, the Euphrates; and its water was dried up, that the way might be prepared for the kings from the east," verse 12. The kings from the east are in reference to China and her fellow Asian nations. This is the prophesied army of 200,000,000 men. They will be able to walk across the great river Euphrates to their death in a red river rising in blood. In a 1969 TV documentary entitled, *The Voice of the Dragon,"* Chairman Mao boasted of China's ability to field an army of 200,000,000 men. Is it coincidental that China's number of her fielded army matches that of Scripture's projection many, many years ago?

"And the seventh angel poured out his bowl upon the air; and a loud voice came out of the temple from the throne, saying, 'It is done.' And there were flashes of lightning and sounds and peals of thunder; and there was a great earthquake, such as there had not been since man came to be upon the earth, so great an earthquake was it, and so mighty. And the great city (Jerusalem) was split into three parts, and the cities of the nations fell. And Babylon the great was remembered before God, to give her the cup of the wine of His fierce wrath. And every island fled away, and the mountains were not found. And huge hailstones, about one hundred pounds each, came down from heaven upon men; and men blasphemed God because of the plague of the hail, because its plague was extremely severe," verses 17-21.

Major Events Of The Great Tribulation

Other than the seal, trumpet and bowl judgments, we want to look into the major events of the last half of the Tribulation, the Great Tribulation. The length of this time period will be cut a little short of the projected three and a half years in Daniel's seventieth week. The Lord divulged to His disciples that this period would be like nothing, "Since the beginning of the world until now, nor ever shall. And unless those days had been cut short, no life would have been saved; but for the sake of the elect those days shall be cut short," Matthew 24:21, 22.

I need to pick up here where we left off in the above section entitled, Antichrist More Enraged Than Ever. The abomination of desolation began the Great Tribulation. Israel, at that time, recognizes her forefathers rejected their promised Messiah nearly two thousand years ago, and every generation has continued to do so until now. Do past errors always have to be repeated? At this moment of profanity in the Temple, Israel acknowledges Jesus Christ as her Lord and Messiah.

Instantly, Satan, Antichrist and the false prophet seek to turn the table on Israel. They are determined on her complete destruction. She runs for her life. Revelation 12:1-6 draws a graphic picture of this fascinating event.

"And a great sign appeared in heaven: a woman clothed with the sun, and the moon under her feet, and on her head a crown of twelve stars," verse one. In the Greek language the words translated *"a great sign,"* mean *"a marvelous signpost."* And that is exactly what it is. And what a word of testimony it is. This *"signpost"* is straight from the Jewish Scriptures. The Scriptures we call the Old Testament. The *"woman"* pictures Israel. The *"sun, the moon and the stars"* all point back to Joseph's dream recorded in Genesis 37:9-11. The *"sun"* = Joseph's father; the *"moon* = Joseph's mother; and the *"stars"* = Joseph's eleven brothers, Joseph himself being the twelfth. Together they represent the nation of Israel, a nation of perpetual promise in the design and plan of God.

"And she was with child; and she cried out, being in labor and in pain to give birth," verse two. This is why the Great Tribulation is called, "The Time of Israel's Travail."

"And another sign appeared in heaven: and behold, a great red dragon having seven heads and ten horns, and on his heads were seven diadems," verse three. The *"red dragon,"* of course, pictures the fiery dragon whose name is Satan. Seven is the number of perfection; while a head is the emblem of intelligence. Combine them and you have a picture of Satan's diabolical wisdom. *"Ten"* is the Biblical number of completeness, while *"horns"* represent power. Together they picture the completeness of Satan's diabolical power. *"Seven diadems"* depict the perfection of Satan's consummate authority, regal power and reign of terror. For these reasons, Paul referred to him as *"the prince of the power of the air,"* in Ephesians 2:2.

I sincerely hope you are starting to get a real picture of your enemy and mine. The first rule of war is, "know your enemy."

"And his tail swept away a third of the stars of heaven, and threw them to the earth. And the dragon stood before the woman who was about to give birth, so that when she gave birth he might devour her child," verse four. The *"stars of heaven"* speak of the angels who followed Satan in His rebellion against God prior to man's appearance on earth. He and they are thrown to the earth at the beginning of the Great Tribulation (Revelation 12:7-9). The great serpent has always sought to destroy the lineage of the Lord Jesus Christ. That is the continuing storyline here.

"And she gave birth to a son, a male child, who is to rule all the nations with a rod of iron; and her child was caught up to God and to His throne," verse five. That *"child,"* of course, is the Lord Jesus. The *"rod of iron"* speaks of authority. We'll see more of that in our final chapter, "A Place Prepared." *"Her child (being) caught up"* pictures Christ's ascension after His resurrection. We don't have time here for a full explanation, but the Lord was *"caught up"* in order for the church to "come in." The church age by all signs is nearing its end, at which time the One *"caught up"* will "come down" again.

"And the woman fled into the wilderness where she had a place prepared by God, so that there she might be nourished for one thousand two hundred and sixty days," verse six. When Israel comes to a saving knowledge of Christ Jesus at the midpoint of the Tribulation, this verse will be discovered and will put the pieces of the puzzle together for her. Presently it is necessary that she flee. In as few as 1,260 days she knows it will be over. Thankfully, those days for the sake of Israel and for the entire surviving world will be cut a little short. That in itself is a show of God's mercy!

Uncanny rage can only qualify Antichrist's thrawarted, exasperated and wrathful disposition after his inability to lay hands on the people of Israel, God's special treasure. Therefore, he goes after anyone he can, people of all ages and nations of all descriptions. I've referred you to Daniel 11 before. I do so again. This passage gives an insight into the mind and character of this fiend of God and man. In all reality it appears impossible for us to understand him without being a 5-star-studded psychopath.

I am going to quote three passages with very little comment. What is important is that you see the despicable character and utter vulgarity of this world's kingpin, the E.U.'s coming strongman. This is the man with whom all caught unaware when Jesus sounds His trumpet (I Thessalonians 4:16) will have to contend, though they find themselves defenseless against this beast. Watch these verses carefully.

The passages are Daniel 11:31-39, Revelation 13:5-8 and Daniel 11:40-45. A good reference Bible will lead you to all Antichrist's exploits during these days.

Daniel 11:31-39:

"And forces from him will arise, desecrate the sanctuary fortress; and do away with the regular sacrifice. And they will set up the abomination of desolation." This is the moment that identifies the midpoint of the seven-year Tribulation period.

"And by smooth words he will turn to godlessness those who act wickedly toward the covenant, but the people who know their God will display strength and take action.

"And those who have insight among the people will give understanding to the many; yet they will fall by sword and by flame, by captivity and by plunder, for many days.

"Now when they fall they will be granted a little help, and many will join with them in hypocrisy." That means false believers will infiltrate the true believers' gatherings as spies for Antichrist.

"And some of those who have insight will fall, in order to refine, purge, and make them pure, until the end time; because it is still to come at the appointed time.

"Then the king will do as he pleases, and he will exalt and magnify himself above every god, and will speak monstrous things against the God of gods; and he will prosper until the indignation is finished, for that which is decreed will be done.

"And he will show no regard for the gods of his fathers or for the desire of women, nor will he show regard for any other god; for he will magnify himself above them all.

"But instead he will honor a god of fortresses, a god whom his fathers did not know; he will honor him with gold, silver, costly stones, and treasures.

"And he will take action against the strongest of fortresses with the help of a foreign god; he will give great honor to those who acknowledge him, and he will cause them to rule over the many, and will parcel out land for a price."

Revelation 13:5-8:

"And there was given to him a mouth speaking arrogant words and blasphemies; and authority to act for forty-two months was given to him.

"And he opened his mouth in blasphemies against God, to blaspheme his name and His tabernacle, that is, those who dwell in heaven.

"And it was given to him to make war with the saints and to overcome them; and authority over every tribe and people and tongue and nation was given to him.

"And all who dwell on the earth will worship him, everyone whose name has not been written from the foundation of the world in the book of life of the Lamb who has been slain."

Daniel 11:40-45:

This passage, while a continuation of the above, summarizes the beginning of the Tribulation and the First Battle of Gog and Magog (verse 40), then moves forward into Antichrist's military exploits during both halves the Tribulation (verses 41-43), and then ahead to the Battle of Armageddon (verses 44-45).

"And at the end time the king of the South will collide with him, and the king of the North will storm against him with chariots, with horsemen, and with many ships; and he will enter countries, overflow them, and pass through." This is the First Battle of Gog and Magog where Russia and her confederate Arab/Muslim armies are defeated (verse 40).

"He will also enter the Beautiful Land, and many countries will fall; but these will be rescued out of his hand: Edom, Moab and the foremost of the sons of Ammon (verse 41).

"Then he will stretch out his hand against other countries, and the land of Egypt will not escape (verse 42).

"But he will gain control over the hidden treasures of gold and silver, and over all the precious things of Egypt; and Libyans and Ethiopians will follow at his heels (verse 43)." Other passages show he enters and plunders *"many countries."* However, trouble is now brewing in the *"Beautiful Land."* The Battle of Armageddon is rising just over the horizon.

"But rumors from the East and from the North will disturb him, and he will go forth with great wrath to destroy and annihilate many. And he will pitch the tents of his royal pavilion between the seas and the beautiful Holy Mountain; yet he will come to his end, and no one will help him (verses 44-45)."

Antichrist, like all men before and after him, will run his course. Armageddon will prove to be his undoing, although he is not killed. We'll see his just reward shortly.

Meanwhile, let's see who these kings of the east and the north are. And why did rumors of them disturb Antichrist.

From The East

Revelation 9:13-21 sheds further light on the number of the army from the East and a description of the carnage of the world's most horrible war, Armageddon. The end result of Armageddon is one third of the earth's population will be killed (verses 15, 18).

The rumor that bothered Antichrist concerning the kings of the East was, *"the number of the armies of the horsemen was two hundred million,"* verse 16. That gives reason to bother even a hardened apostate like the devil's child. Who would believe such a number? John figured that out, too. So for added emphasis and to authenticate the magnitude of the number, John says emphatically, *"I heard the number of them."* This number has been ridiculed and scorned for centuries: "No one can field such an army as this," man has often and disagreeably argued. Yet, not only does China boast of being able to field such a mammoth army, but the CIA also reports China's current ability in fielding such a military. Remember, it is not just China's army. Just as Russia led a group of armies, so will China. They could easily and probably will include India, Thailand, North and South Korea, Japan and other far eastern nations.

Do you remember my mentioning that God sees Israel as the center of the earth, and all directions in the Bible are from Jerusalem? Take your map once again. Lay a ruler running East and West through Jerusalem. Directly to the Far East is the world's largest nation, The People's Republic of China. Do not believe for a moment China will allow anyone to capture the oil of the vital Middle East, or blow it apart while she keeps her powder dry.

"The sixth angel who had the trumpet" (Revelation 9:14) was told to, "Release the four angels who are bound at the great river Euphrates." These *"four angels"* will gather the armies of the East together, all 200,000,000 of them for battle.

Another angel, the *"sixth angel"* with the bowl of God's wrath, is the one with the authority to dry up the Euphrates River (Revelation 16:12) making way for the Kings of the East to compete for this valuable land. It will be interesting to see how the *"sixth angel"* does it. To the astonishment of all nations gathering together, they themselves are the wine, the appetizer, the salad, the three portions of the main course and don't forget the dessert: "And I saw an angel standing in the sun; and he cried out with a loud voice, saying to all the birds which fly in midheaven, 'Come, assemble for the great supper of God; in order that you may eat the flesh of kings and the flesh of commanders and the flesh of mighty men and the flesh of horses and of those who sit on them and the flesh of all men, both free men and slaves, and small and great,'" Revelation 19:17, 18.

Seven years prior God gave a sacrifice to the beasts of the field and the birds of the air. Seemed a fitting way to clean up the mess of The First Battle of Gog and Magog. Now He offers the carnage of Armageddon as a *"great supper"* to the birds of midheaven. No invitations were declined.

From The North

The armies of the European Union, lead by Antichrist, along with the armies from the East are joined by additional armies from the North. Russia is in the *"remote North"* (Ezekiel 38:15), but as we saw less than seven years earlier she was vastly defeated and major portions of her nation were destroyed (see Ezekiel 39:3-6). I doubt this is she. So who are these armies *"from the North?"* Some remnants of Russia's defeated and now rag-tag army may be included. In this instance, however, the northern group is not called, *"the remote North;"* just, *"the North."*

This nation could well be a reconstituted Turkey army to the north of Israel. She could well pick up fallen Russia's lead. Syria, Bulgaria, Romania and perhaps breakaway states of the former USSR would want to join in and not sit idly by while all the nations of the world are invading these valuable lands. With most of these states it is not the Muslim factor that would force them to risk everything, but the oil. This battle, in the minds of the nations involved, will determine the haves and the have-nots. Believe it, it is oil that moves the world. This battle is genuinely the mother of all wars. Any army that can be fielded around the world will join in.

The stakes are too high for any nation to sit out the world's most devastating conflict, Armageddon.

There are many other nations involved that are not mentioned on this end-time marquee of Scripture. But, don't believe for a moment they were slighted. They, too, will be there. All the nations will be involved. Isn't it amazing? As much talk as there is about Armageddon, when the real Armageddon comes to town, no one recognizes it until it is too late to escape the slaughter. And a slaughter it is.

Armageddon

Antichrist's army along with the armies of the East and North are gathered in the Valley of Megiddo. Revelation 16:13-16 and 19:19 makes certain we understand; there are many more armies enjoined in this battle. "And I saw coming out of the mouth of the dragon and out of the mouth of the beast and out of the mouth of the false prophet, three unclean spirits like frogs; for they are spirits of demons, performing signs, *which go out to the kings of the whole world,* to gather them together for the war of the great day of God, the Almighty," Revelation 16:13, 14.

Zechariah was given insight into this gathering as well, "Behold, I am going to make Jerusalem a cup that causes reeling to all the peoples around; and when the siege is against Jerusalem, it will also be against Judah. And it will come about in that day that I will make Jerusalem a heavy stone for all the peoples; all who lift it will be severely injured. *And all the nations of the earth will be gathered against it,"* Zechariah 12:1, 2. Zechariah continues: "For *I will gather all the nations against Jerusalem to battle,* and the city will be captured, the houses plundered, the women ravished, and half of the city exiled, but the rest of the people will not be cut off from the city. Then the Lord will go forth and fight against those nations, as when He fights on a day of battle," Zechariah 14:2, 3. The battle of the ages is engaged.

With the collapse of the economic Babylon and lawlessness running rampant around the globe, no nation on earth can stay home and twiddle their thumbs and fiddle while hoping to ride out this wave. Every man's sword is against one another. A picturesque passage of the carnage of this war is given us in the closing verses of Revelation 14. Here is where you find the depth and length of the river of flowing crimson blood.

Man's rebellion and hatred bringing the world to this point is in fact rebellion against God and against His Son Jesus Christ. Armageddon is the result of God allowing man and his sin to take him where he begs to go — anywhere but under the authority of God the Father and the Lord Jesus Christ.

"Another angel came out of the temple which is in heaven, and he also had a sharp sickle. And another angel, the one who has power over fire (fire represents judgment), came out from the altar; and he called with a loud voice to him who had the sharp sickle, saying, 'Put in your sharp sickle, and gather the clusters from the vine of the earth, because her grapes are ripe.' And the angel swung his sickle to the earth, and gathered the clusters from the vine of the earth, and threw them into the great wine press of the wrath of God. And the wine press was trodden outside the city, and blood came out from the wine press, up to the horses' bridles, for a distance of two hundred miles," Revelation 14:14-17.

God, after repeated efforts and offers of mercy and grace, allows man to go his desired way. Rushing toward Armageddon, as in the days of Noah, man's sin runs its course. When it does judgment invariably follows. *The wages of sin is (still) death,"* Romans 6:23. And more death than the world has ever imagined is now played out on the battlefield of human depravity. A river of blood from men and beasts is poured out in the Valley of Jezreel from the city of Megiddo in the north to the Negev in the south. Armageddon's river of blood is from four to five feet high (*"up to the horses' bridles"*). This red river rises quickly. The measurement of its width varies with the contour of the valley from ten to thirty miles wide, *"for a distance of two hundred miles,"* Revelation 14:20.

A battle of such proportions is unimaginable. Yet, this is the result of man's rebellion against his Creator. "But God could have stopped it! He didn't have to allow it to happen," someone may say. It was not God's choice; it was man's choice. God does not force anyone's obedience. He does, though, give ample warning as to the consequences of sin and rebellion. Don't bring the blame game to God's throne. It is never His will that any should perish (II Peter 3:9). The decision is in man's hands alone, always has been, always will be — until it comes to the day of accountability. Then it's God's way.

The King And The Armies Of Heaven

The Tribulation is now almost over. Armageddon has brought the world to the edge of self-extermination. In fact, the Lord declared about these rapidly approaching days, "Unless those days had been cut short, no life would have been saved; but for the sake of the elect those days shall be cut short," Matthew 24:22. The battle does not slacken, however, until the Lord Jesus places His feet *"on the Mount of Olives."* Zechariah 14: 3 tells us, "Then the Lord will go forth and fight against those nations, as when He fights on a day of battle."

This is the historical account of Jesus Christ's return to earth. Historical because God wrote tomorrow's history in eternity past.

The Apostle John in speaking of this day wrote: "And I saw heaven opened; and behold, a white horse, and He who sat upon it is called Faithful and True; and in righteousness He judges and wages war. And His eyes are a flame of fire, and upon his head are many diadems; and He has a name written upon Him which no one knows except Himself. And He is clothed with a robe dipped in blood; and His name is called The Word of God. And the armies which are in heaven, clothed in fine linen, white and clean, were following Him on white horses. And from His mouth comes a sharp sword, so that with it He may smite the nations; and he will rule them with a rod of iron; and He treads the wine press of the fierce wrath of God, the Almighty. And on His robe and on His thigh He has a name written, 'King of Kings, and Lord of Lords," Revelation 19:14-16.

Get over it Satan. You soon become flaming fodder.

The armies of the world crumble at His appearing. He said He would be back, and He is back to stay. Coupled with the Lord's return is a spiritual forget-me-not that empowers and encourages His own to live in light of these prophetic times: "When Christ, who is our life, is revealed, then you also will be revealed with Him in glory," Colossians 3:4. The reality of Christ in you and you in Christ will be publicly and universally declared on this great day. "And on that day His feet will stand on the Mount of Olives, which is in front of Jerusalem on the east..," Zechariah 14:4.

Revelation 19:19 - 20:3 gives us plenty of reasons to praise the Lord's return in this victory of the ages. I can hear the chatter and buzz now. What are we going to do about all these slain? Remember, the Battle of Armageddon claims the lives of one-third the population of the world, that's another 1,675,000,000 slain. Half the world tragically perishes in less than seven years. John the seer used to have a lot of questions. Now he's giving the answers. "And I saw an angel standing in the sun; and he cried out with a loud voice, saying to all the birds which fly in midheaven, 'Come, assemble for the great supper of God; in order that you may eat the flesh of kings and the flesh of commanders and the flesh of mighty men and the flesh of horses and of those who sit on them and the flesh of all men, both free men and slaves, and small and great,'" verses 17, 21. Well, I guess that settles that.

The birds in the world will without a doubt be glutted for quite some time. Here is an amazing thing. Just after the birds of the air clean up the carnage of Armageddon, the animals of the world under the new leadership of Jesus Christ will be non-carnivorous. Think maybe they got their fill. Perhaps the birds, like the children of Israel after eating quail for thirty days, will say, "Please, no more for at least a 1,000 years."

Let's see! We've still got a little cleaning up to do. Where's that *"beast,"* and where did that false prophet go? They weren't killed. They're probably toothless about now. Ah, but John had an eye on them as well. "And I saw the beast and the kings of the earth and their armies, assembled to make war against Him who sat upon the horse, and against His army. And the beast was seized, and with him the false prophet who performed the signs in his presence, by which he deceived those who had received the mark of the beast and those who worshiped his image; these two were thrown alive into the lake of fire which burns with brimstone," verses 19, 20.

I wonder if being thrown "alive" into the fiery lake is worse than being thrown in some other way? Must be! Sure sounds like it!

The beast and the false prophet are unsettled in for eternity and are out of the picture forever. What about all those folks that followed them? Must we still contend with them?

Certainly not! "And the rest were killed with the sword which came from the mouth of Him who sat upon the horse, and all the birds were filled with their flesh," verse 21.

Well, there's still Satan. Where the devil is he? "And I saw an angel coming down from heaven, having the key of the abyss and a great chain in his hand. And he laid hold of the dragon, the serpent of old, who is the devil and Satan, and bound him for a thousand years, and threw him into the abyss, and shut it and sealed it over him, so that he should not deceive the nations any longer."

Malachi has a good word for us too: "'For behold, the day is coming, burning like a furnace; and all the arrogant and every evildoer will be chaff; and the day that is coming will set them ablaze,' says the Lord of hosts, 'so that it will leave them neither root nor branch. But for you who fear My name the sun of righteousness will arise with healing in its wings; and you will go forth and skip about like calves from the stall. And you will tread down the wicked, for they shall be ashes under the soles of your feet on the day which I am preparing,' says the Lord of hosts," Malachi 4:1-3.

Wow! Well, what about God's own? Did they all make it out?

Certainly! God never fails nor allows to slip through His fingers one child. Christ has always assured the safe passage and deliverance of His own. And He has the power to fulfill every promise. In Revelation 14:14-16 His *"sickle"* figuratively speaks of a similar truth the Israelites experienced in Egypt. There the protective hand of God passed over the homes of the Israelites protecting them from the death angel. That same night the grim reaper took the firstborn in every home unprotected by the blood of the Lamb on their doorposts. God gives His own this picture during the time of Armageddon. They have nothing to fear.

"And I looked, and behold, a white cloud, and sitting on the cloud was one like a son of man, having a golden crown on His head, and a sharp sickle in His hand. And another angel came out of the temple, crying out with a loud voice to Him who sat on the cloud, 'Put in your sickle and reap, because the hour to reap has come, because the harvest of the earth is ripe.' And He who sat on the cloud swung His sickle over the earth; and the earth was reaped."

Christ Jesus is the One on that cloud overseeing the safety of His own. Not one goes unnoticed, nor will one ever slip through the safety of His hands. That is such a powerful and liberating truth for God's own. He never fails. Consider now His promise to those outside heaven's imparted righteousness. For them it is, "into the great wine press of the wrath of God," Revelation 14:19. It is from that very *"wine press"* at Armageddon the red river rose.

But oh, there is more, much, much more.

Chapter Eight

What About America?

*"What? Me Worry! I'm Counting On
The Rapture!"*

Revealing End Time Truths

The question asked above concerning America is not only a sound one, but also one that should be asked with increased regularity — What About America? It is one thing to sit back in our easy chairs, study the Bible and scripturally point a finger measuring, judging and condemning other nations and peoples, their beliefs, their actions and their appointed place in prophecy. But what is in store for America? The almost universal refusal to examine the above vital question has for us a double antidotal comparison. It is a seeking to remove a splinter from another's eye while overlooking the beam in one's own eye by the proverbial ostrich that has its head buried deeply in the sand. If that sounds awkward as a sentence, it should. But it is nowhere near as awkward as demonstrated in its present day reality. In truth, it is even deplorable. Yet the living reality of it is replicated daily by Bible students, pastors and prophesy teachers throughout the land. Most prophecy teachers will not even deal with these passages refusing to acknowledge

their very existence and the many descriptives given to identify the unnamed nation in question. I, on the other hand, like
stirring the waters. Someone has got to, especially when the
subject matter is so vitally important to all Americans.

So, allow me to press home the question once again. What
about America? Is it possible to identify her in the Bible?

In asking this question, I must cover all the bases,
including one or two we've already mentioned. I'll try not to
bore you by keeping these comments short. Here's one.

There is a verse referring to Israel's miraculous escape
from the dragon at the midpoint of the Tribulation: "And
the two wings of the great eagle were given to the woman,
in order that she might fly into the wilderness to her place,"
Revelation 12:14. "See," many suggest, "America's emblem
is the eagle. That must be America airlifting Israel out of
harm's way." That is a nice thought, and I would like to think
it is true. I will even go so far as to say, "I hope it is true!"
But that hope is, at best, a stretch. A similar description is
used earlier in Scripture in reference to God's deliverance
of Israel from Egypt: "You yourself have seen what I did
to the Egyptians, and how I bore you on eagles' wings, and
brought you to Myself," Exodus 19:4. Israel will doubtlessly
experience a miraculous deliverance from Satan's wrath
at the midpoint of the Tribulation. However, to identify
America as the *"eagle"* of Revelation 12:14 is to, at best,
"hopefully" attach our identity. But, *we can pray* that God
might give us that great privilege. And who knows but what
our aircraft in the Middle East are not the means of Israel's
transportation?

As prophetic Scriptures are examined there are passages
where the one to whom a prophecy is given is told to, "seal
(it) up until the end time." Daniel was told that on at least
three occasions: 8:26, and 12:4, 9. Over the past half-century
many olden prophetic passages have come alive. For instance,
after her great and prolonged dispersion, few people more

than sixty years ago have believed Israel would ever be a nation again. I said, "few," because there have been, down through the past two millenniums, some insightful students of Scripture that simply took God at His Word and accepted Biblical truths that others sought to explain away. Israel's re-nationalization is one of those instances. With such a great dispersion lasting well over nineteen hundred years, the theory came about by some that the church had replaced Israel as the descendents of Abraham. Spiritually, if we are men and women of a like faith as Abraham's, then we are his descendents. However, nowhere through acceptable methods of interpreting Scripture can it be said replacement theology is factual. Truth is quite the contrary, dear Watson. However, one hundred years ago some (by not studying all related Scriptures) might have thought Israel had passed forever off the horizons of history. That was hardly the case; although back then it was easier to teach theory rather than argue a future unseen fact. Nevertheless, it was a failure in believing God's Word.

Over the years others have taught varying ideas concerning the return of Christ. One of those theories is Amillennialism, which teaches that through religious agencies and denominations the Gospel message would convert the world until (basically) the Lord could accept it and come back. World wars since the early 20th century sort of contradicted that thought with man's ability to kill by the millions. Such a theory as "the world is getting better" is also contradicted by a large number of passages in Scripture.

There are today no Scripture passages that remain veiled to those that seek truth before God. That is why the closing and crowning book of the Bible has leapt to life over the past half century. Additionally, many have come to realize the Revelation was written "for the churches," Revelation 22:16. (They must have peeked at this last forbidden book of the Bible when no one was looking.) Therefore, it begins and ends with a blessing on "those who read and those who hear the words of the prophecy, and heed the things which are written in it, for the time is near," Revelation 1:3 and 22:7.

That, my friend, is why so many end time truths, Old and New Testaments alike, have literally leaped from the pages of Scripture in our lifetime. What a privilege has been given to us to live in this day.

So let me ask the question again, "What About America? Never named, is America described in Scripture?

Is It Possible To Identify America In Prophecy?

From the outset, let me say this in underlined, bold letters. <u>**The Bible never mentions America by name**</u> as it does the many nations we have already studied. Those nations in the near, middle and far east are located in areas known during the more than 1,500 years of the Bible's writing, and are identified by name or Scriptural references and recorded history.

Having said that, a legitimate question must be asked. Is the U.S.A. *described* in the Bible? That question brings us to this study. The answer is yours to decide. But, let me just muddle your mind for a moment and suggest the passages we are about to study *do not describe America*. That would bring to the surface other questions. If these are the last days for the church, how can America, the world's only (as we boast) superpower, not be mentioned as a major player on the world scene? She *is* the economic center of the world. She *is* the world's single greatest military power. So, where is she in the days leading up to Christ's return? Does something remove her from the economic and military position she presently holds? If America is not described, these questions become impossible to answer.

The U.S.A.'s absence, from being a power player on the world's scene, would certainly open the door for the

European Union's strongman to *"confirm a covenant"* with a defenseless Israel. Scripturally, from the beginning of the Tribulation America *is nowhere in the picture*. With the European Union inking a covenant of peace for Israel, America is nowhere to be found on the world scene. She is absent as a defender of Israel. She is absent in political affairs. She is absent in monetary might. She is absent in military power. The greatest most blessed nation since the earth's founding is simply absent, missing from the world stage. A.W.O.L.

That leaves only *guesses* as to what might have happened to her. In over thirty years of studying this, I can only *imagine* two solutions if America *is not* described in Scripture. And I must have been taught this, for it is the same excuses that most Bible and prophecy teachers give today when asked this question.

One, America without a whimper quietly succumbs to being an out-of-the-picture subordinate of the European Union. We become a lackey in league with Antichrist. I shutter over that thought.

Two, by an act of God, America is defeated to the point of being incapable of having a political, monetary or military impact on world affairs. She is instantly reduced to a second or third world country, or no country at all. If I had to choose, I would cast my ballot for the latter over the former. What that means is our sins have caught up with us. We probably *"cursed"* Israel and brought down the judgment of God on this nation.

But why *guess*, when Scripture is so revealing.

There are three chapters in the Bible devoted to describing an end time and unnamed economic center of the world. The Scriptures tell of God's judgment of her — why she is judged, by whom the judgment comes and the timing of her judgment. The descriptives are numerous of this financial powerhouse found in **Revelation 18** and **Jeremiah**

50 and 51. Three things concerning this end time city and nation need to be mentioned in order to proceed on a solid foundation.

First, whoever this end time player in world events mentioned in the above three chapters is, while called *"Babylon"* and *"the daughter of Babylon,"* she is described as a city and a nation. Most prophecy teachers identify her as Babylon in Iraq. I strongly disagree with that suggestion for the following reasons. While never referred to by name, there are many descriptives in these three chapters identifying this end-time nation. It is not permissible by any measure of Scriptural interpretation to pick among the descriptives choosing some and disregarding others. One cannot claim some descriptives fit a particular nation and ignore the many that do not. All descriptives, *like pieces of a puzzle*, must identify the city and nation described to say, "This is she."

Every time I ask why *this is* the rebuilt Babylon of old, the answer is always the same. "She is called *"Babylon the Great"* in Revelation 18. It has to be Babylon in Iraq." Now that presents a number of problems. I will only briefly mention three.

Problem number one, the religious Babylon of Revelation 17 is also called *"Babylon the Great,"* a city situated on *"seven mountains."* Most all Bible scholars agree this Babylon is Rome, and it doubtlessly is. Now, if the end time religious Babylon is not in Babylon, why must the end time economic Babylon be in Babylon?

Problem number two, this city and nation is also said to be the *"daughter of Babylon"* — that means she is a descendant, "in the spirit or likeness of Babylon," not necessarily the setting of Babylon, as is true of the religious Babylon as well.

Problem number three, in the three chapters describing this end time Babylon, few if any of the descriptives fit

Babylon in Iraq. Additionally, with her background they can never fit Babylon, Iraq in the future.

(There is a heinous problem among us today in the pulpits and in the pews. I think I've already mentioned this, but it is too important not to bring it back to your attention at this time. I say this humbly and un-accusingly and as guilty as anyone. I too fell into this trap many years ago. I do love learning from my mistakes. The problem can be stated as simply as this. Most of us know more of what we have been taught than what we have studied. A favorite friend, teacher, preacher, pastor or professor states something to be true. It sounds plausible, so we accept it as Gospel without checking Scripture to see if these things are true. In this we need to be more like the Bereans who daily examined the Scriptures to see if the things Paul was teaching them were true (Acts 17:11). Unlike the Bereans, many of our opinions are formulated by what we hear or have been taught. That's not good! In fact, that's bad. Worse than that, it's very bad. For instance, someone may say, "Cleanliness is next to godliness." That sounds good. Cleanliness is necessary for healthiness, so that should be godly. You'd be surprised how many people believe that saying is in the Bible. It is not. Around the world are precious people in the sight of God who know Him but know little about sanitation. The quote, while well intended, is false, no matter how well intended it is. What I am saying is this, "You should check out what I say." And that goes for what everyone else says. The matter before us is too important not to be examined carefully. The days of, "Trust me," ended with Jimmy Carter's Presidency.)

Second, we cannot say, upon looking at these descriptives, this is definitely the United States of America, even if every descriptive fits. The reason we cannot is because we do not know the timing of the Lord's return *"in the air"* for His own. If His coming is within months, years, or even a couple or three decades, it may well be America. I know of no other country today that qualifies under every descriptive in these three chapters. But that decision is yours to make. If the Lord's coming is many decades away, another country, through a variety of causes, could displace America in the status quo she now enjoys and has held for quite some time.

Third, my main point is valid whether or not this is America. If we understand God's judgment on this described city and nation, and see that as a nation we also are well described, what sort of people should we be in seeking God's mercy, forgiveness and grace? How should we order our lives in accordance with the revealed will of God so as to avoid such a devastating judgment as is found concerning another city and nation whom we mirror in every aspect?

The chapters we are about to study are called "companion chapters." They describe the same events, the same city and the same nation, complimenting one another while each adds additional detail. I recommend you read these chapters from the Bible several times over, highlighting each descriptive that identifies this city and nation. The following is divided into six sections: **Descriptives Of The Economic Babylon, Why God Judges Her, Who Attacks Her, How Her Attack Occurs, When Her Attack Occurs, and Why Such A Devastating Judgment?**

Descriptives Of The Economic Babylon

Revelation 18

1. The whole of all three chapters we will study, Revelation 18 and Jeremiah 50 & 51, describes this end time nation as the economic center of the world. This is a **telltale sign** of who this nation is. As the power money broker, she is able to pull the political, economic and military strings of nations around the globe. She is described as a nation unparalleled in wealth, power and might.

2. In verse 2, because of permissiveness and tolerance leading to acceptance, she is said to have "become a dwelling place of demons, a prison (haunt) of every unclean spirit, and a prison (haunt) of every unclean and hateful bird."

Such language is used throughout the Bible in reference to false religions, professors and practices. What nation has been so tolerant and politically correct it has become a *haunt* of every imaginable religion, cult and occult?

Recently a Catholic priest stated that Christians in an outreach of respect and love for Muslims should refer to God as Allah to show our brotherhood with Islam. "Beside," he said, "both of our religions can be traced back to Abraham." How absurd can lost humanity be? Can you imagine God calling down from heaven saying, "Elijah, don't be such a hard-headed numskull? You should treat Baal's four hundred and fifty prophets as brothers instead of calling down fire from heaven to embarrass them. My sake, Elijah! You don't plan on killing them, do you? Come on now Elijah, apologize to them. In fact, to show the brotherhood of all humanity, let Baal's priests know that from now on you will also call Me Baal." Yeah! Count on it! Had Elijah suggested such a thing, there would have been 451 dead that day. While many in Catholicism have criticized this priest for his statement, he is pretty much in line with comments from the last two Catholic popes.

3. Verse 3 states that, "All nations have drunk of the wine of the passion of her immorality."

This end time economic Babylon has polluted the world with addiction to her pornography, rebellion, alcohol, films, videos, idolatry, adultery, homosexuality, cults and occults, etc.

4. Verse 3 says, "Kings of the earth have committed acts of immorality with her."

Pacts and agreements have been signed. She has gone to bed with other nations for economic, military and political gain.

5. Verse 3 is a **telltale sign**; "the merchants of the earth have become rich by the wealth (power) of her sensuality (luxury)."

This nation purchases more goods than any other. She keeps the money coffers of the *"the merchants of the earth"* well stocked. Enough is never enough to satisfy her desire for *"luxury."* What other nation runs the trade deficient of the United States? What other nation could run the trade deficient of the United States?

6. Verse 7 claims she has *"glorified herself."*

She lifts herself and her desires above all others. In her lofty position she is able to politically or militarily dictate demands around the world.

7. Verse 7 is a **telltale sign** reiterating she has *"lived sensuously (luxuriously)."*

Compared to the rest of the world her people live luxuriously. Her poor are among the richest people on earth.

8. Verse 7 is a **telltale sign** listing her boasts, "I sit as a queen and I am not a widow, and will never see mourning."

She believes her position, power, and greatness defends her.

9. Verses 9, 10 has, "the kings of the earth weeping and lamenting over her" saying, 'Woe, woe, the great city, Babylon, the strong city! For in one hour your judgment has come.'"

With the destruction of this nation, kings *"weep and lament"* because of their economic loss, but "stand at a distance because of the fear of her torment." That is, they are distraught because of what they will no longer receive. Yet, they *"stand at a distance for fear"* of what has happened to her. Radiation is no fun.

10. Verse 11 declares, "The merchants of the earth weep and mourn over her, because no one buys their cargoes any more."

Here is another **telltale sign**. Why do no other nations buy the merchants' cargoes? No other country can afford the merchandise *"the merchants of the earth"* regularly sold to this end-time economic *"Babylon."* The *"merchants"* livelihoods go up in the smoke of her destruction. It is one thing to have people weep at one's funeral, but the reason for weeping here is *"because no one buys their cargoes any more."* Just goes to show, money purchases only point-of-sale friends.

11. Verse 16, a **telltale sign**, finds the merchants crying, "Woe, woe, the great city, she who was clothed in fine linen and purple and scarlet, and adorned with gold and precious stones and pearls; for in one hour such great wealth has been laid waste!"

The list of items in this verse shows the vast abundance of her pleasures. She has sought fineries due to her high and lofty position. Her purchases are mainly desires, luxuries that enriched the merchants. These items are constantly beyond the needs of everyday life. Once again, the merchants' *"woes"* are centered on one thing, *"for in one hour such great wealth has been laid waste."* Few citizens in most countries of the world are able to own, much less display such wealth.

12. Verses 17-19, a **telltale sign**, show some of the other numerous areas of life affected by this city and nation's demise. "And every shipmaster and every passenger and sailor, and as many as make their living by the seas, stood at a distance, and were crying out as they saw the smoke of her burning, saying, 'What city is like the great city?' '... Woe, woe, the great city, in which all who had ships at sea became rich by her wealth, for in one hour she has been laid waste!'"

You know, you have to look hard and long through these passages to find concern for this city and nation. Instead, the mourning is all for the losses kings, merchants and travelers will now experience. Employees, pleasure and business travelers of the world *"cry out"* as all aspects of life and livelihood are affected by this nation's passing. How often during the news coverage of 9/11/01 were commentators heard saying in anguish and disbelief, "Oh, New York, New York, the great city!" Notice the repetition of the phrase *"one hour,"* referring to the suddenness, the swiftness and the rapidity of her destruction. Her fall will be fast, furious, decisive and final.

13. In verse 23 a strong angel says, "Your merchants were the great men of the earth, because all the nations were deceived by your sorcery."

"Sorcery" means witchcraft as well as charms and spells. Babylon's *"merchants were the great men of the earth because"* of the spells cast by the allurements of her wealth.

Jeremiah 50

14. In verse 11 the Lord says of Babylon, "Because you are glad, because you are jubilant, O you who pillage My heritage (Israel)."

To *"pillage"* is to steal, to take away. The reference to God's *"heritage"* refers to Israel, but would certainly also include those things that would affect her defenses and her safety. A major power of influence making demands that would render her vulnerable or defenseless, such as, giving up her protective fence, the Gaza Strip, the West Bank, the Golan Heights and certainly half of Jerusalem, "the apple of God's eye," would count as *"pillaging (God's) heritage."* God's criticism here is of the nation possessing the power to dictate to Israel such demands.

15. In the same verse God says, "Because you skip about like a threshing heifer and neigh like stallions."

A *"threshing heifer"* is one who has "grown fat in the grass." It speaks of economic prosperity to the point of gluttony. The neighing *"stallions"* picture unbridled pride, loftiness, dominance and self-confidence. Such haughtiness and power might result in requiring Israel to submit to demands, such as dividing Jerusalem, removing defensive barriers, giving up land for peace, putting her national sovereignty at risk, or forcing her to live side-by-side with those determined on her destruction — all for a "peace pact" cementing a presidential legacy. *"Skipping about"* shows lack of moral decisiveness; checking the wind; for you today, against you tomorrow.

16. Verse 12 mentions this Babylon's mother. "Your mother will be greatly ashamed, she who gave birth to you will be humiliated."

Most nations do not have a *"mother."* Some, like America, do — England. Babylon's *"mother (being) greatly ashamed... humiliated,"* could speak of England's embarrassment as Babylon's closest and only staunch ally in the European Union.

17. In verse 21, a **telltale sign**, the Lord says, "Against the land of Merathaim, go up against it, and against the inhabitants of Pekod."

"Merathaim" means "double rebellion." This nation characterizes herself: "No one tells me what to do. I am in charge of my own destiny. I am the greatest military power and economic center the world has ever seen. No one can defeat us. I will do as I please." *"Pekod"* means "the land of punishment;" that is, she is a land devoted to punishment.

18. Verse 23 is another of our **telltale signs**. "How the hammer of the whole earth has been cut off and broken."

This nation has hammered home it's will and way across the continents of the world. Economic and military strength has a tendency to do that.

19. In verse 29 we have God's complaint against this end time Babylon. "For she has become arrogant against the Lord, against the Holy One of Israel."

Mark the mention of *"Israel."* Babylon's turning against Israel adds up to her *"arrogance against the Lord... of Israel."* Yet, from olden days God warns of the consequences. See Genesis 12:3; 27:29; Numbers 24:9; Romans 1:21-32.

20. Verse 37 is another **telltale sign** of this economic Babylon of the last days. "Against all the foreigners who are in the midst of her."

The word *"foreigners"* interpreted is "mixed multitude." This land is inhabited by a hodgepodge of the many nationalities of the world. She is "a melting pot" of the world.

21. Verse 42 refers to this nation as the "daughter of Babylon."

She is a nation "in the spirit of Babylon of old." She is like the original in thoughts and actions. She is a descendent in attitude and character. As a *"daughter,"* she is one of the same mind and disposition.

Jeremiah 51

22. In verse 1 the Lord calls these end time Babylonians, "the inhabitants of Leb-kamai."

"Leb-kamai" means, *"the heart of those who rise up against Me."* This is a reference to the root problem of this nation who has forsaken God. Once with Him, she has rebelled against Him and against His authority.

23. Verse 3, "Let not him who bends his bow bend it, nor let him rise up in his scale-armor."

This is an obvious reference to this nation's armies and her air force. Her attack will be pronounced and conclusive. There will be no opportunity or heart for a counterattack, as is referenced in *"not bend his bow."*

24. Verse 7 makes an amazing statement. "Babylon has been a golden cup in the hand of the Lord, intoxicating all the earth. The nations have drunk of her wine; therefore the nations are going mad."

Take the first statement alone and it might seem this nation has been a blessing to the Lord. But we are never allowed to take a sentence out of its context. Babylon has been the means of *"... intoxicating all the earth."* God often uses His enemies to bring about His purpose. Her sensual living has driven the nations to jealousy and madness. God now uses her as a *"golden cup"* to bring about His ultimate purpose. This nation's demise will drive Israel to Antichrist, who in turn drives Israel, by means of persecution, to the Lord.

25. In verse 12 the Lord says, "Place men in ambush against her."

We have another **telltale sign** of this nation's identity. In part, her enemies are within her borders. These *"in ambush"* manage to get her defenses down and her destruction rolling. It isn't hard to place *"men in ambush"* in a land of a *"mixed multitude."* That, of course, would be most especially true if that nation lacked a desire to enforce immigration laws, showed a reluctance to build defensive barriers, and a refusal to remove millions of *illegal* aliens.

26. In verse 13 the Lord identifies her as one "who dwells by many waters."

That does not mean she is surrounded by water as is the case of a continent nation such as Australia, but she does have an abundance of water to the east, west, north and south.

27. Again in verse 13 the Lord says she is, "abundant in treasures."

She is well endowed in natural resources and wealth of all forms.

28. Verse 41 says, "how Sheshak (a Cryptic name for Babylon) has been captured, and the praise of the whole earth been seized!"

This nation, this end time Babylon, in her day is the most praised nation in the world. The phrase used here denotes her *"capture"* as an unimaginable act.

29. Verse 44 mentions another **telltale sign**; "the nations will no longer stream to him."

This is a nation who, prior to destruction, saw the nations of the world *"streaming to him."* What nation annually receives more visitors and emigrants than any other nation in the world? How about more than all other nations?

30. In verse 50, the Lord describes a previous blessing of this nation's past welfare with the words, "You who have escaped the sword."

Here is another **telltale sign**. Of how many nations can it be said, *"you who have escaped the sword?"* Her people have been spared from the armies of invading nations. With the many waters she is surrounded by, she has had natural protection throughout her history.

31. Verse 53, another **telltale sign,** speaks of the futility of Babylon's defense systems. "Though Babylon should ascend to the heavens. And though she should fortify her lofty stronghold."

Certainly sounds like a national defense shield. *"Lofty stronghold"* literally means, "the height of her strength," and could well refer to a missile defense system. It could also point to her attack being at a time when she is "at the height of her military strength." The most modern defenses and the superiority of her weaponry will not save her. She is fighting God who gives her into the hands of her enemies. The Lord makes certain that is understood. The remainder of verse 53 says, *"From Me destroyers will come to her,"* declares the Lord.

32. Verse 55 says, "The Lord... will make her loud voice vanish from her."

In other words, this nation's *"voice"* was heard throughout the world. Not any more!

Why God Judges The Economic Babylon

There are, as you will see, many reasons her judgment is strong and final. Yet, there is one thing that tips the scale. She forsakes Israel! Forsaking Israel is not necessarily fighting against her. More fully, it means turning her back on Israel, or making demands jeopardizing her safety. You will see that shortly, and then find it repeatedly, in these chapters.

Revelation 18

Verses 2-8 begin a series of statements concerning God's judgment of this end time economic Babylon.

"And he cried out with a mighty voice, saying, 'Fallen, fallen is Babylon the great! And she has become a dwelling place of demons and a prison of every unclean spirit, and a prison of every unclean and hateful bird. For all the nations have drunk of the wine of the passion of her immorality, and the kings of the earth have committed acts of immorality with her, and the merchants of the earth have become rich by the wealth of her sensuality.' And I heard another voice from heaven, saying, 'Come out of her, my people, that you may not participate in her sins and that you may not receive of her plagues; for her sins have piled up as high as heaven, and God has remembered her iniquities. Pay her back even as she has paid, and give back to her double according to her deeds; in the cup which she has mixed, mix twice as much for her. To the degree that she glorified herself and lived sensuously, to the same degree give her torment and mourning; for she says in her heart, "I sit as a Queen and I am not a widow, and will never see mourning." For this reason in one day her plagues will come, pestilence and mourning and famine, and she will be burned up with fire; for the Lord God who judges her is strong.'"

Verse 5 above mentions, "Her sins have piled up as high as heaven, and God has remembered her iniquities." God is a forgiving God, forgetful of all that is cleansed by the blood of the Lord Jesus Christ. "As far as the east is from the west, so far has He removed our transgressions from us," Psalm 103:12. Where sin is not turned from, however, forgiveness is not possible. The *"blood"* of Christ Jesus has been rejected by this city, nation and culture. Her sins, uncleaned, have *"piled up as high as heaven."* In other words, she has gone without judgment for her many sins. Forsaking Israel becomes her final straw. Judgment becomes imminent and inescapable.

But what if this nation has known the Lord, printed Bibles, sent missionaries and accomplished many other wonderful works in her history? "How about some credit for all that?" That was in the past. This is now. She may have church steeples on every street corner, and may have been blessed greatly in days gone by. That was the past. This is now! She has forsaken her heritage and turned from vast privileges to her own ways. "From everyone who has been given much shall much be required," Luke 12:48. The *requirement* is about to be exacted from this nation in full measure.

What tipped the scale? Why has she not been judged already? The late Mrs. Ruth Graham said it best in voicing her thoughts concerning America with this statement, "If God does not judge America, He will have to raise Sodom and Gomorrah and apologize to them." America's judgment, due to her many great sins, have been put on hold for some reason. They have gone without judgment, I believe, because she has not turned from her backing, her support and her defense of Israel. Only for that reason has she not been judged already. Should she forsake that charge, there is nothing to hold back the judgment of God on *all* her sins.

Indeed, this is the devastating curse that breaks the back of the end time economic, *"Babylon the Great."* She *"pillages"* Israel through strong demands backed up with military and monetary support, or the withholding of that necessary support in such a hostile area. Israel is indeed surrounded by Islamic fascists on all sides, crazed by their murderous thoughts of her annihilation. Revelation 18:20, 21 states, "'Rejoice over her, O heaven, and you saints and apostles and prophets, because God has pronounced judgment for you against her.' And a strong angel took up a stone like a great millstone and threw it into the sea, saying, 'Thus will Babylon, the great city, be thrown down with violence, and will not be found any longer.'"

The Revelation's two companion chapters in Jeremiah make it crystal clear that Babylon's judgment is due to her stripping Israel of her defenses. She believes her support of Israel has brought her only ridicule, derision and pain. The severity of her judgment for *"pillaging"* Israel, however, is seen in her complete and forever destruction.

Jeremiah 50

Verse 11 begins with the Judge of Heaven voicing His accusation against Babylon. "Because you are glad, because you are jubilant, O you who pillage My heritage." That *"heritage"* is Israel, the people and the land. "And He gave their land as a heritage, a heritage to Israel His people," Psalm 135:12. See also Psalm 136:21, 22 and Isaiah 41:8-16. To pillage Israel is to pillage the people and nation God often refers to as His *"special treasure!"*

Verse 14 says, "Draw up your battle lines against Babylon on every side, all you who bend the bow; shoot at her, do not be sparing with your arrows, for she has sinned against the Lord."

Verse 24 reveals God's avenue of bringing about Babylon's judgment. "I set a snare for you, and you were caught, O Babylon, while you yourself were not aware; you have been found and also seized because you have engaged in conflict with the Lord." Babylon may have thought her support of Israel brought only hardship and little gain. Turning against Israel, however, *"engaged her in conflict with the Lord."*

Conflict is one thing, but the root of conflict is the age-old sin of arrogance and pride. Verse 29 declares this last days' nation's arrogance from heaven. "Summon many against

Babylon, all those who bend the bow: Encamp against her on every side, let there be no escape. Repay her according to her work; according to all that she has done, so do to her; for she has become arrogant against the Lord, against the Holy One of Israel."

Jeremiah 51

Verse 5 says, "For neither Israel nor Judea has been forsaken by his God, the Lord of hosts." This is a rebuke of Babylon's belief she could *"pillage"* Israel in that dangerous part of the world and not suffer retribution (see 51:56).

In verse 10, Israel replies to Babylon's treachery, "The Lord has brought about our vindication; come and let us recount in Zion the work of the Lord our God."

Verse 11 clearly states the mind of God. "Because His purpose is against Babylon to destroy it; for it is the vengeance of the Lord, vengeance for His temple." The nations' treatment of Israel has been the measure of God's dealings with them. Individual judgment has never been according to the number of sins an individual or a nation commits. Judgment is based on the amount of truth one has, but rejects. Rejection of truth determines the extent of individual judgment. The same goes for nations. See Matthew 11:20-24 for an incontestable example. The *"daughter of Babylon"* is judged severely and quickly. Again, her judgment is not due to the number of her transgressions; they were even put on hold. Her judgment is due to light received, but rejected. She once had great light. That light was rejected, deliberately spurned and despised. Judgment is, therefore, imposed on all her sins.

Jeremiah 51:15-18 distinctly states God's power and His ways are not as man's ways. In verse 19 He tells us, "The portion of Jacob (Israel) is not like these. For the Maker of all is He, and of the tribe of His inheritance; the Lord of hosts is His name." In other words, Israel is different. God chose Israel as *"His inheritance."* As acceptance or rejection of the Lord Jesus Christ is the measure of God's judgment in the lives of individuals, so also the treatment of Israel is the measure of God's dealings with the nations. Be absolutely certain of this, whether it be an individual, or be it a nation, our disposition toward God and His Word is always reflected in our actions. We do what we do because we are what we are.

Therefore, God says in verses 20-24: "'You (Israel) are my war-club, My weapon of war; and with you I shatter nations, and with you I destroy kingdoms. And with you I shatter the horse and his rider, and with you I shatter the chariot and its rider, and with you I shatter man and woman, and with you I shatter old man and youth, and with you I shatter young man and virgin, and with you I shatter the shepherd and his flock, and with you I shatter the farmer and his team, and with you I shatter governors and prefects. And I will repay Babylon and all the inhabitants of Chaldea (the heart of those who rise up against Me) for all their evil that they have done in Zion before your eyes,' declares the Lord."

In verse 35, Israel cries out for vengeance for the evils committed against her. "'May the violence done to me and to my flesh be upon Babylon,' the inhabitant of Zion will say; and, 'May my blood be upon the inhabitants of Chaldea.' Jerusalem will say." These cries are for the atrocities done to her. These acts of violence are possibly being played out on the stage of world events today. Anything that would harm Israel's right or ability to defend herself in that hostile area of the world will clearly qualify as pillaging Israel and Jerusalem. Such ravaging could include removing financial support for her defense, requiring protective walls to come down, the demands of relinquishing portions of her small nation to the Palestinians (especially Jerusalem), demanding the "right of return" of pre-1948 Palestinians who fled Israel proper during the war, and her right to target those murdering her people.

The Lord responds to Israel's cry in verse 36: "Therefore thus says the Lord, 'Behold, I am going to plead your case and exact full vengeance for you; and I shall dry up her sea (broad river) and make her fountain dry.'" Droughts experienced in the past will be insignificant compared to that which is in store for Babylon under the mighty hand of God's judgment.

Verse 49 sums up God's judgment of Babylon in language no one can mistake. "Indeed Babylon is to fall for the slain of Israel, as also for Babylon the slain of all the earth have fallen." It's pay back time.

Who Attacks The Economic Babylon?

The first rule of war is, "know your enemy!" With the end of the cold war and the breakup of the Soviet Union, Russia rather quickly sank to a second world nation. We have already seen how she and her Arab/Muslim confederacy will lead the attack on Israel shortly after Antichrist confirms Israel's peace agreement, perhaps the Quartet's *Roadmap to Peace in the Middle East*. Yet, there seems to be a pressing matter that needs to be taken care of *before* Russia's Middle East excursion.

Jeremiah 50

Verse 3 pinpoints the nation that attacks the economic Babylon. "For a nation has come up against her out of the north; it will make her land an object of horror, and there will be no inhabitant in it." Remember, directions in Scripture are given from Jerusalem, *"the center (or navel) of the world,"* Ezekiel 38:12. This nation's coming *"out of the north,"* makes it clear this attack comes from the same group of nations that will attack Israel at the beginning of the Tribulation, the *"red horse rider"* of Revelation 6:4. Here, as in her attack on Israel, she will have many nations under her command.

Verse 9 gives greater detail of the aggressor nations. "For behold, I am going to arouse and bring up against Babylon a horde of great nations from the land of the north." A "horde of great nations?" Russia does not act alone, but as a *"commander"* (Ezekiel 38:7) for the Muslim nations in her attack on Israel. She bears the same *"commander's"* role in the attack on this last days' economic Babylon, as she will have in her attack on Israel.

After describing the devastation of Babylon, Jeremiah 50:41, 42 again designates the lands of the attackers. "Behold, a people is coming from the north, and a great nation and many kings will be aroused from the remote parts of the earth. They seize their bow and javelin; they are cruel and have no mercy, their voice roars like the sea, and they ride on horses, marshalled like a man for the battle against you, O daughter of Babylon."

Jeremiah 51

Verses 27 and 28 name specific Arab and Muslim nations aligned in this battle with Russia against Babylon. "Lift up a signal in the land, blow a trumpet among the nations! Consecrate the nations against her, summon against her the kingdoms of Ararat, Minni and Ashkenaz; appoint a marshal against her, bring up the horses like bristly locusts. Consecrate the nations against her, the kings of the Medes, their governors and all their lieutenants, and every land of their dominion."

Verse 48 sums up God's judgment of Babylon and ordains her attacker. "Then heaven and earth and all that is in them will shout for joy over Babylon, for destroyers will come to her from the north, declares the Lord."

How Babylon's Attack Occurs

Throughout the passages we are studying much is said about this *"daughter of Babylon's"* destruction. From the *"Fallen, fallen is Babylon the great"* of Revelation 18:2, to "A strong angel took up a stone like a great millstone and threw it into the sea, saying, 'Thus will Babylon, the great city, be thrown down with violence, and will not be found any longer,'" of Revelation 18:21, we know her fall will be complete, decisive and final.

The descriptives of Babylon's doom are far more complete in these two chapters of Jeremiah 50 and 51. They are heart wrenching, and so completely devastating as to horrify the hardest of individuals or nations. Yet, the God of all compassion and knowledge is ever righteous in His dealings with men and nations. Babylon's judgment, therefore, harmonizes with her schemes against God.

Descriptions of her devastation are too numerous to list here. However, a few demand our attention.

First, God describes her attack as being by, *"a horde of great nations,"* Jeremiah 50:9.

Second, this *"horde (is) cruel and have no mercy,"* Jeremiah 50:42.

Third, the battle is over almost as it begins. Men will be placed in *"ambush,"* (Jeremiah 51:12). The devastation of their acts is Herculean. It seems nuclear weapons are detonated in her major cities and strategic points around the country, such as military installations, nuclear plants and areas of dense population. The invading forces are as much a mopping up operation and a slaughter of suburban and rural areas outside the above target arenas as anything else.

Fourth, the Scripture states, "The king of Babylon has heard the report... and his hands hang limp; distress has griped him, agony like a woman in childbirth," Jeremiah 50:43. In other words, there is nothing he can do; there is nothing anyone can do.

Fifth, of her fighting men the Bible says, "The mighty men of Babylon have ceased fighting, they stay in the strongholds; their strength is exhausted, they are becoming like women," Jeremiah 51:30.

Sixth, "Babylon will become a heap of ruins, a haunt of jackals, an object of horror and hissing, without inhabitants," Jeremiah 51:37.

Seventh, she will *"be desolate forever,"* 51:26, and *"it (the land) will be a perpetual desolation,"* Jeremiah 51:62.

Babylon will be so devastatingly and utterly destroyed no inhabitant will ever live in her again, not even during the thousand-year reign of Christ. She will be a scar upon the earth, a permanent testimony of the ravages of sin to any people.

When Babylon's Attack Occurs

The Bible says nothing conclusive about the time of Babylon's attack, but something of a timeline can be gleaned from what Scripture records.

We know Russia and her Arab/Muslim friends (Ezekiel 38:1-7) will attack Israel shortly after she confirms a peace agreement with the head of the reconstituted Roman Empire, known today as the European Union, and her strongman, Antichrist. We also know when Russia attacks Israel at the Battle of Gog and Magog, she and her Arab/Muslim counterparts will be destroyed, *"on the mountains of Israel,"* Ezekiel 39:4.

Therefore, since it is the same Russian confederacy that attacks *"the daughter of Babylon,"* the world's economic center and military powerhouse, her attack on *"Babylon"* must be prior to her attack on Israel.

Now, think about this. Russia and her Muslim/Arab cohorts are no friends of Israel. If the Lord's coming is soon, and America is the economic Babylon, Russia's destruction of her prior to the Tribulation would force Israel to seek the protection of another. That protection will come from Antichrist head of the European Union, i.e. the revived Roman Empire. The seven-year peace agreement he confirms with Israel *is* the beginning point of the Tribulation. A *confirmed agreement* between the European Union and Israel would propel Russia and her confederacy to attack Israel swiftly from the north and south, hoping to catch Europe off-guard and ill-prepared to fully defend the Middle East (Daniel 11:40; Ezekiel 38, 39). A Russian surprise attack at this point would be tremendously advantageous for her and bolstered by her resounding victory over the economic *"daughter of Babylon."*

Russia's ability to gather such a large number of Arab/Muslim nations will be aided by her willing promise to help in the destruction of Israel and the push of the Jewish people into the sea. In all likelihood, Russia's Arab counterparts in this conspiracy will barter for Russia a warm-water port in the Mediterranean in exchange for her help in eliminating the Big and Little Satans, America and Israel. Russia is no friend to Islam either. However, such a uniting fits Islam's centuries' old philosophy, "The enemy of my enemy is my friend." In other words, Islam will welcome Russia's material, logistical and military support. The matter of dealing with the atheistic state of Russia can come on a more opportune day.

Talk around the world is Islam plans to take on Israel first, and then America. Yet, if the economic Babylon were today's America, she would certainly counterattack Russia for her attack on Israel. As a nation we have a military defense agreement with Israel. I believe it is one that will stand up, at least as of this writing. The Islamists are crazy enough to do anything. But Russia wants to survive. They don't have the promise of seventy-two black-eyed virgins and all the grapes they can eat in paradise. Russia, as we know from Scripture, is *"the commander"* for this group of murderous Russian and Islamic fascists. Russia will insist upon a surprise attack on the Great Satan first, then the Little Satan. Not the other way around!

I personally believe this plan is already in the Kremlin's war-room in Moscow. I certainly believe it has been shared with the leadership of the key nations that will be involved. I have no hard proof of either of the above statements apart from analyzing the days in which we live and Scripture's unfailing prophesies of the past leading to their consequent reliability in the future. I'll pit this scenario against any other. Perhaps the major factor behind America not being hit hard since 9/11/01 is the Muslim leaders under Russian encouragement have held back on their insurgents so as not to sound an early alarm in the Oval Office, CIA, Homeland Security or Pentagon.

Observe this also. I've heard from a number of people, "Oh well, we don't have to worry about that. We have the rapture to take us out first." Let's see if that is true. There might be a taking us out first, but is the rapture the means of doing so?

It is not Christians alone who are encouraged to come out of the *"daughter of Babylon,"* but also the Jewish inhabitants of the end time's world economic center. Listen to Zechariah 2:7, 8, "Ho, Zion! Escape, you who are living with the daughter of Babylon. For thus says the Lord of hosts, 'After glory He has sent me against the nations which plunder you, for he who touches you, touches the apple of His eye.'"

Here's a sobering thought! For those of us who believe the rapture takes place just before or near the signing of Israel's peace covenant, no passage in the Bible can be found insuring the economic Babylon is not destroyed prior to the rapture. For no other reason would God so often in these chapters encourage His people to come out of this end time *"daughter of Babylon."*

Listen to Revelation 18:4, 5: "And I heard another voice from heaven, saying, 'Come out of her, My people, that you may not participate in her sins and that you may not receive of her plagues, for her sins have piled up as high as heaven, and God has remembered her iniquities."

"Wander away from the midst of Babylon, and go forth from the land of the Chaldeans; be also like male goats at the head of the flock. For behold, I am going to arouse and bring up against Babylon a horde of great nations from the land of the north," Jeremiah 50:8, 9.

"There is the sound of fugitives and refugees from the land of Babylon," Jeremiah 50:28.

"Flee from the midst of Babylon, and each of you save his life! Do not be destroyed in her punishment for this is the Lord's time of vengeance; He is going to render recompense to her," Jeremiah 51:6.

"We applied healing to Babylon, but she was not healed; forsake her and let us each go to his own country, for her judgment has reached to heaven and towers up to the very skies," Jeremiah 51:9.

"Come forth from her midst, My people, and each of you save yourselves from the fierce anger of the Lord," Jeremiah 51:45.

Through the prophet Zechariah to the Jewish people living in Russia and to those in the economic Babylon of these days God says, "'Ho there! Flee from the land of the north,' declares the Lord, 'for I have dispersed you as the four winds of the heavens,' declares the Lord. 'Ho, Zion! Escape, you who are living with the daughter of Babylon.' For thus says the Lord of hosts, 'After glory He has sent me against nations which plunder you, for he who touches you, touches the apple of His eye,'" Zechariah 2:6-8.

Babylon's demise is certainly declared to be prior to the rapture. Apart from unbelieving Jews, if the attack on economic Babylon were after the rapture, God's call to His own to come out of her would be futile. They would already have been *"caught up."*

Why Such A Devastating Judgment?

The better question might be, "Why hasn't God already destroyed us? God, in all His righteousness, is simply being true to Himself and to His holy nature. If peace and love are to be sustained in eternity, righteousness must be maintained. For righteousness to be maintained, there must be a standard clearly set before all. The Ten Commandments are that standard. Yet, godless and evil men and women have forced from America's classrooms and from our governmental facilities those very Commandments. Nevertheless, the standard must be upheld if only by the exercise of Divine judgment. That judgment is established, "The wages of sin is death." Thankfully that verse does not end on that bitter note for all of us sinners. "But the free gift of God is eternal life through Jesus Christ our Lord," Romans 6:23. He knocks at the door of one's heart, but the individual himself must open the door and invite Him in.

The above is in reference to individual salvation or judgment. Every country will also receive its just recompense, the judgment of the nations. America's founders fully understood this tenet.

Patrick Henry, one of America's Founding Fathers, certainly understood it when he said, "It cannot be emphasized too strongly or too often that this great nation was founded, not by religionists, but by Christians; not on religions, but on the Gospel of Jesus Christ."

George Mason, the Father of the Bill of Rights certainly understood it when he proclaimed, "As nations cannot be rewarded or punished in the next world, they must be in this. By an inevitable chain of causes and effects Providence punishes national sins by national calamities."

Thomas Jefferson, of the same mindset declared, "Can the liberties of a nation be thought secure when we have removed their only firm basis — a conviction in the minds of the people that these liberties are the gift of God? That they are not to be violated but with His wrath? Indeed, I tremble for my country when I reflect that God is just; that His justice cannot sleep forever."

John Adams pointedly added, "We have no government armed with power capable of contending with human passions unbridled by morality and religion... Our constitution was made only for a moral and religious people. It is wholly inadequate to the government of any other."

Benjamin Franklin, while Ambassador to France, said to a French audience in 1774: "He who shall introduce into public affairs, the principles of primitive Christianity will change the face of the world."

Perhaps the severity of this country's judgment is because it purposefully allows the crumbling of its foundational principles, the teachings of the Old and New Testaments. Perhaps it is because this nation, having been more blessed in her lifetime than all other nations, has shaken a fist in the face of the Author of her blessings. Perhaps it is because she has had judgment of her sins withheld more than all other nations. Maybe it is because she has been spared from the sword due to the faithfulness of her forefathers more than all other nations. And, maybe it is because all the above demands responsibility. The Lord Himself laid down the principle, "And from everyone who has been given much shall much be required; and to whom they entrusted much, of him they will ask all the more. I have come to cast fire upon the earth; and how I wish it were already kindled!" Luke 12:48, 49. Who knows how soon it may be *"kindled?"*

Now, for the big question. What if this is America? Nations, as is true of people, act out only that which is permitted. The voting booth is the public voice of the good or bad character of a nation's people. It is the church that is the appointed great divide between righteousness and wickedness. She is the one through whom the Holy Spirit *"restrains"* the powers of darkness (II Thessalonians 2:7). But what if the church in general is anemic? Yes! What if she is "wretched and miserable and poor and blind and naked," Revelation 3:17? She is near bankrupt. She is sick and has been her own doctor. What she needs is the wealth and the covering of Another, and the *"eyesalve"* of the Great Physician (vs. 18). What if the church of America, **from the heart**, humbles herself, prays, seeks God's face and turns from her wicked ways," (II Chronicles 7:14)? What then might be her fate?

Is it too late for revival? Internationally, the institutionalized church is on the way to oblivion by way of the one-world church. That includes the vast majority of the World Council of Churches. The one-way church is deemed a culprit by society, as was and is her risen Lord. She is too narrow, too bigoted, too anti this and anti that. Preach a positive message and it is seen in the most negative way. Preach judgment with passion and conviction and the world rises up in arms.

But let me soften the question. Is this not the Lord Jesus' prevailing forecast concerning the days of His return? Then why should any Bible believing person forecasting Christ's soon coming be the enemy of the church and society rather than the harbinger of glad tidings? Jesus is coming!

The Lord's coming is good news, and should not be an undesirable anticipation. The child of God should embrace the Lord Jesus' return with jubilant expectation. In the world's viewpoint it is understandably and expectantly the last word it wants to hear in spite of how bad things might become in this world. Christ's return to those who have rejected Him is proof positive He is alive. And they're in a whole lot of trouble.

Let me combine a couple questions I posed and answer them from my perspective of Scripture. "What if the economic Babylon is America?" And, "Is it too late for revival?"

Every descriptive given of the last days economic and military Babylon perfectly describes the United States. Of no other country in the world today can it be said that all of these descriptives fit. For those who do not believe this world is heading for certain disaster, or that Christ's coming is not imminent, the hope that they are right must lie in the Lord's return being pushed into the future many decades, probably a century or more. And all that would do is momentarily delay the inevitable. It would take quite a number of years for another country to rise to the position of America's economic superiority. The nations already mentioned along with their Scripturally prophesied places in history soon to surface such as Russia, the Arab/Muslim nations, the European Union and China, of course, cannot be the economic Babylon of the last days. They have a different role to play. Some other country will have to rise from among the nations not mentioned in Scripture. Meanwhile something must also happen to America removing her from today's position as military and economic kingpin of the world. She must be reduced to a position of being non-consequential.

One thing more needs to be emphasized. God sent certain Old Testament prophets to the nations with a message of repent or be judged. Jonah was one such prophet. Under his preaching Nineveh repented and God turned from her destruction. Noah was another such prophet. He preached for one hundred and twenty years with no converts apart from members of his own family. The unchanged world died in the flood.

There were also prophets God sent to certain nations with a message of judgment. That is, a message of judgment and judgment only. No opportunity of repentance was to be mentioned. Judgment was certain and was rapidly approaching. They had gone too far in their rebellion against the God of heaven. Some individuals hearing the message might well come out of her, but the city or nation was under the clear-cut judgment of God. Jeremiah was one such prophet sent with a message of judgment against Jerusalem and Judah. No message of repentance was to be issued. She had gone too far. God as much as told His messenger, "Oh, by the way, Jeremiah. They won't listen to you, but will fight against you," (Jeremiah 1:13-19).

Pore over Revelation 18 and Jeremiah 50 and 51 for any message of the last days' economic Babylon being offered the opportunity of repentance. No message of turning by the economic Babylon is to be found. Instead, there is an encouragement to "come out of her" in six different passages in these chapters.

God does not change! Here is the appropriate question. Will the Laodicean church of America in the obedience of faith repent of her sins and return to God? I need not answer that question. Jeremiah asked the same question of his nation with the words, *"Is there no balm (healing) in Gilead? Is there no physician (savior) there? Why then has not the health of the daughter of my people been restored,"* Jeremiah 8:22? The balm and the physician were there, but the people had turned their backs on God.

Concerning the last days' economic Babylon, Jeremiah records: *"We applied healing (balm) to Babylon, but she was not healed; forsake her and let us each go to his own country, for her judgment has reached to heaven and towers up to the very skies,"* Jeremiah 51:8.

Chapter Nine

A Place Prepared

The Dead Can Hear!

Things Of Eternal Value

We have been observing Biblical prophecy concerning earth's coming attractions and comparing them with today's news headlines and world events. The events we have looked into have or will all work out in that span of history called time. We now come to things of eternal value. These values include a few things that occur before time expires and the many things that shall come to pass after time draws to a close. You didn't think you would have to wear a watch forever did you? So many Rolexes will go up in the smoke of this world's grandest makeover.

There are events between the Millennial Reign of the Lord Jesus and entrance of the redeemed into their eternal homes that apply primarily to those without Christ. These are what I call negative truths. Negative to the unredeemed but not to redeemed. There are also positive truths that apply for all entering into God's newly prepared eternity.

The Scriptures do not bring up these negative and positive truths in chronological order. But, I will seek to do so as much as is possible. Prayerfully, the result will help you keep these truths in the order they will occur. Prepare to be presently satisfied though with only a glimpse of eternal things belonging to the redeemed! Insight into eternity is scattered throughout the Bible, but only two chapters in the entirety of God's Word are devoted to the saints' everlasting future. Much of that which God has laid up for you and for me and for all in His forever family is lost in the inadequacies of present day language and from comprehension by our finite intellects. For those who do not like change, prepare yourself. This will definitely be a new paradigm for all God's children. Yet, that which God has chosen to share with us in this day is enough to cause us to pant after Him, "as *the deer pants for the water brooks,*" (Psalms 42:1).

Words Have Meaning

The Lord spoke to the Jewish people of *"a resurrection to life, (and)... a resurrection to judgment,"* John 5:29. Most everyone is involved in one of these two *"resurrections."* There is also a sizable number among the redeemed that are translated and will therefore have no need for a resurrection. These would include those taken up at the rapture and the Millennial Kingdom saints. We will shortly see the three phases of the first resurrection. The third and final phase is between the close of the Tribulation period and the beginning of the Millennial Reign of Christ Jesus. The Millennial saints and their godly offspring will not see death. They will live throughout Christ's entire reign and will be translated at the close of that reign in much the same order, I am guessing, as those raptured. Scripture is silent on that detail. We will cover each of these three resurrections of the righteous shortly. Before going further, it will be helpful to understand terms in the Bible dealing with the realities of those who already have, or will at their appointed time, departed this life. Resurrection has to do with the body coming back from the grave. Be it an earthy grave, a watery grave or a scattering of ashes to the winds grave, every person will arise at their appointed time. So let's get a little insight into what is behind that mysterious door called death and the netherworld.

Death

The word *"death"* in Scripture has a frightening and mysterious undertone for those without Christ. It can even give hesitation to some in Christ who have walked a guilty distance from their Lord. *"Death"* in the Bible is more than one's last breath. Essentially death is what we call the grave. The grave holds the body of the departed person — saint and sinner alike. Paul softens the word *"death"* for the Christian by using the term, *"sleep."* He applies it in I Corinthians 15:20 to the children of God who have passed on from this scene: "But now Christ has been raised from the dead, the first fruits of those who are asleep." To the church at Thessalonica he wrote: "For if we believe that Jesus died and rose again, even so God will bring with Him those who have fallen asleep in Jesus," I Thessalonians 4:14. The idea is, "Yes, they have died, but in reality their bodies are simply asleep to be awakened on the day Christ comes for His own." The bodies of those who have *"fallen asleep"* in Christ come forth on the resurrection day as *"imperishable"* and *"immortal"* bodies (I Corinthians 15:51-55). Compare the eternal state of a child of God to an acorn planted in the ground. The seed, a seemingly insufficient thing, is placed in the earth but comes forth as something all together miraculous. *"Death,"* for the Christian, says Scripture, *"is swallowed up in victory."*

My grandmother had a great outlook on death. She used to say of a Christian coming to death's door, "God gave her *dying grace*." By that she meant God imparted to that deceased Christian the desire and the power to go through death's door. He meets the demands of life with His grace. That is what grace is. It is the desire and the power to do the will of God. Would that we live more in the center of God's grace today.

For those without Christ, there is no hope or encouragement after death (I Thessalonians 4:13). Their bodies are securely held by *"death,"* only to *"come to life"* (Revelation 20:5) that the *"second death"* might have *"power"* over them in eternity future (Revelation 20:6, 14). A thousand and seven years after the redeemed are raised from their *"sleep,"* *"death"* relinquishes its relentless grip on the bodies of the unrighteous. Each person's resurrected body is then reunited with his or her eternal soul. The "soul" is the actual person: the mind, emotions and will. Relief from suffering punishment, however, is only long enough for eternal judgment to be pronounced at the Great White Throne. *"The second death"* has an eternal chokehold, a terrifying grip on the bodies and souls of the unregenerate for an eternity of separation from God. That is what they wanted. Therefore, God gives them the desire of their rebellious hearts. Thus, it is called *"the second death."* It is an eternal death. One is forever dying, but never consciously dead.

Gehenna

Gehenna is a transliteration (brought directly into English) of the Valley of Hinnom where worshippers of Hinnom placed into the fires of his altars their first-born male child. Such idolatry had ceased prior to the Lord's days on earth, but the term Gehenna was often used in reference to the *fires* in the valley outside Jerusalem. It was the city's landfill. The carcasses of dead animals were forever being thrown there. Here the *"fire"* was said to never be quenched, worms continuously crawled in and out of the rubbish stench, and flies were so thick they could darken the sky. The smoke of Gehenna never ceased rising to the heavens. Such a horrible site was it the Lord Jesus referred to it as being similar to punishment in Hell. This word *"Gehenna"* is used in Scripture for the fires of eternal destruction. See Matthew 5:22 where *"fiery hell"* is the word *"Gehenna."* The same word is used in Matthew 5:29, 30; 10:28; 18:9; 23:15, 33; Mark 9:43, 45, 47; Luke 12:5; and James 3:6. Running these verses will allow you to trace the symbolism *"Gehenna"* powerfully portrays. But keep in mind; a symbol is never as vivid or as authentic as the reality it foretells.

Hell and Hades

The word *"Hades"* comes straight into our English language from the Greek without even a vowel change: *"Hades."* The word *"Hell"* is a translation of the same word and is used interchangeably with it. They both refer to the same place. *"Hades"* or *"Hell"* is the equivalent of the Old Testament Hebrew word *"Sheol."* In fact, Peter in his first sermon quotes David as saying, "Because Thou wilt not abandon my soul to Hades," Acts 2:27. That is a direct quote from Psalm 16:10 where the Hebrew word *"Sheol"* is used. *"Sheol, Hell and Hades"* all refer to one specific *place.* Nowhere can this be found more clearly than in Luke 16:23 where the Lord speaks of the rich man and Lazarus. Lazarus died and was carried away (soul and spirit) to *"Abraham's bosom."* The rich man also died and, "in Hades he lifted up his eyes, being in torment, and saw Abraham far away, and Lazarus in his bosom." *"Hell"* or *"Hades"* holds the souls of the deceased and forever lost, awaiting the Great White Throne Judgment.

This "soul-prison" for the unredeemed deceased is an intermediate place between death and judgment, and is as close as it gets to our Catholic friends' unscriptural doctrine of Purgatory. There is no praying of someone out of an intermediary state, in this case Hell, between death and judgment. It is a deprived religion that charges her constituents money to pray them out of Hell. But then not to have the ability to do so is criminal. Here is the Bible's take on this reality, "… it is appointed for men to die once and after this comes judgment," Hebrews 9:27. There is no second opportunity after death's deed is done. A decision for Christ must be in this life as the Holy Spirit deals with the individual, or not at all. That is why the Apostle Paul taught, "… behold, now is 'the acceptable time,' behold, now is 'the day of salvation,'" II Corinthians 6:2. The message is unmistakably clear from Scripture's standpoint, "Don't wait!"

"Heaven" is a place and not simply a figment of one's imagination. So also *"Hell, Hades or Sheol"* is a real place. *"Gehenna"* defines this *"place of torment"* as a condition of unspeakable misery (Luke 16:28); a place of suffering in *"eternal fire,"* (Matthew 25:41); a place *"where their worm does not die, and the fire is not quenched,"* (Mark 9:48); an *"outer darkness,"* (Matthew 8:12); a place of *"weeping and gnashing of teeth,"* (Matthew 8:12); a place of *"unquench-able fire,"* (Luke 3:17); a *"furnace of fire,"* (Matthew 13:42); a place of *"black darkness,"* (Jude 13); a place where *"the smoke of their torment goes up forever and ever; and they have no rest day and night,"* (Revelation 14:11).

As far as friends and company in this place of eternal destruction is concerned, one may joke about it now but will find eternity to be foolproof in that coming Day of Judgment. With never ending torment, black darkness, and all the weeping and gnashing of teeth, there will be no occasion for fellowship, or the desire of such. No teas will be served. No parties attended. No sports events enjoyed. Yet, should one want to know his neighbor, they can become acquainted right now. Revelation 21:8 reveals the companions of all assigned to *"the second death's"* eternity: "the cowardly and unbe-lieving and abominable and murderers and immoral persons and sorcerers and idolaters and all liars, their part will be in the lake that burns with fire and brimstone, which is the second death." See also I Corinthians 6:9, 10; Galatians 5:19-21; and Revelation 21:27. These do not normally constitute a friendly, loving, caring and longed for neighborhood.

Until judgment day, *Sheol, Hades, or Hell* is the *place* where the souls of the unrighteous dead are held in check in the *fires of Gehenna*. Whether on land, in space or in the deepest sea, *"death"* holds the bodies of the forever lost until called forth on Judgment Day for eternal execution.

The Lake of Fire

"The lake of fire" is the final destination of "unrest" for fallen angels and unregenerate men and women alike. One's eternal company just gets better all the time, doesn't it? The words *"lake of fire"* are used in only two chapters in the Bible. They designate the *place* of separation of sinners from God and His offered, but spurned, mercy and love. On judgment day time closes up shop. Grace has run its course. There is no "pause or mute" button to stop the real life action and horrifying screaming. Judgment is imminent and menacingly near. The beast and the false prophet await the rest of the eternally damned as they were the first to experience this *"lake of fire."*

Revelation 19:20 informs us these two who tormented the earth for seven years have an early and irrevocable invitation to this pit of black darkness and eternal torment. Just dues! "And the beast was seized, and with him the false prophet who performed the signs in his presence by which he deceived those who had received the mark of the beast and those who worshiped his image; these two were thrown alive into the lake of fire which burns with brimstone."

After Satan is *"released for a short time"* from the *"abyss"* where he is imprisoned during the Millennial reign of Christ, he is recaptured and eternal doom is exacted. We read in Revelation 20:10, "And the devil who deceived them was thrown into the lake of fire and brimstone, where the beast and the false prophet are also; and they will be tormented day and night forever and ever."

Finally, *"the lake of fire"* is also brought into view as the eternal abode of the unrighteous among men and women alike. It is the same prison as is the residence of Antichrist, the false prophet, Satan and the fallen angels. Revelation 20:14, 15 are instructive: "And death and Hades were thrown into the lake of fire. This is the second death, the lake of fire. And if anyone's name was not found written in the book of life, he was thrown into the lake of fire."

At the resurrection of those without Christ, *"death"* will give up the bodies of all Earth's unredeemed. *"Hell"* brings forth her *"souls"* to be reunited with their former *"bodies."* After each person appears before the Great White Throne Judgment he or she will be eternally cast into *"the lake of fire."* No probation, no vacation, no sick days, no time outs. It is an eternity from the peace, the joy, the presence, the glory and the blessings of God. On several occasions in Scripture, the words *"weeping and gnashing of teeth"* are mentioned concerning those in this eternal place of dark banishment. The *"weeping"* is due to the torments and sufferings for which each person has been eternally judged. The *"gnashing of teeth"* is doubtlessly due in part to the anguish in this place of torment. Yet, most incidents where this term is used, it is the *"gnashing of teeth"* toward God brought about by hatred and everlasting defiance. In this instance without doubt it is focused upon God Himself. Judgment forewarned is now justly carried out in its due course. Many will cry out, "Who is He to judge me anyway?" God's name has never been more cursed anywhere or at anytime than it will be for an eternity in *"the lake of fire."* Yet, those cries can only be echoed in the blackened, cavernous eternity of those divorced from Almighty God. There will be no repentance and no commuting of sentence throughout eternity in *"the lake of fire."*

"Who is He to judge me?" My friend, He is the Great I Am, the Ancient of Days, the King of Glory, the Creator and Maker of all, The Word of God, the One who has the keys of death and of Hades. He is the King of kings and the Lord of lords. Who are you?

Others will take a less defiant stance. Matthew records their deceitfulness in chapter 7, verse 22 with these words: "Many will say to Me on that day, 'Lord, Lord, did we not prophesy in Your name, and in Your name cast out demons, and in Your name perform many miracles?'" These were the religionists. They had a form of godliness. That is they liked playing the part; and many were very good at it. Some held various ministry positions. Some preached. Some served. Some fooled themselves. But none in repentance and faith had ever turned over the controls of their lives to the Lord Jesus Christ. Many even fooled others. Of these the Lord says, "And then I will declare to them, 'I never knew you; depart from Me, you who practice lawlessness,'" Matthew 7:23.

Resurrection To Life Or Judgment?

One day in the earthly ministry of the Lord Jesus, the religious leaders were seeking to kill Him. So it was a fairly ordinary day. But He was about to bring up an extraordinary subject. John records the Lord's shocking words. "Truly, truly, I say to you, he who hears My word, and believes Him who sent Me, has eternal life, and does not come into judgment, but has passed out of death into life. Truly, truly, I say to you, an hour is coming and now is, when the dead shall hear the voice of the Son of God; and those who hear shall live... Do not marvel at this; for an hour is coming, in which all who are in the tombs shall hear His voice, and shall come forth; those who did the good deeds to a resurrection of life, those who committed the evil deeds to a resurrection of judgment," John 5:24-29.

From this passage we find that every person will be raised from the grave. Some will come forth to a resurrection of eternal life. Others will come forth to a resurrection of judgment, the result of which is called, *"the second death,"* Revelation 20:14. Yes, the dead can hear.

The First Resurrection

The resurrection to life has to do with the saints' future bodies. Revelation 20:4-6 speaks of the "souls of those who had been beheaded because of the testimony of Jesus and because of the Word of God...." These are those who *during the Tribulation* refused to worship the beast or receive his mark. They publicly proclaimed the name of Jesus and were martyred for their faith in Him. Unlike the previous Old and New Testament saints, the bodies of these in view here have not yet been raised. They will now! Coming forth from the grave at the close of the Tribulation, they go on to reign with Christ for the next one thousand years. The Scripture call this, *"the first resurrection,"* verse 6. That is the resurrection of these Tribulation martyrs *completes* the first resurrection.

We might think the "second resurrection" is for those without Christ after the Lord's millennial reign of righteousness. And the Lord Himself did call it *"a resurrection of judgment,"* in John 5:29. The Bible generally calls that resurrection, *"the second death."* We will look into the resurrection to judgment when we come to The Great White Throne Judgment.

The first resurrection, which is for the redeemed, is in three stages. These stages, called *"orders, ranks or files,"* are given to us in I Corinthians 15:22-24. Paul taught the church at Corinth that, "in Adam (our old nature) all die (physically), so also in Christ (our new nature) all shall be made alive (resurrected)," verse 22. *"But each in his own order."* That is, the resurrection of God's own is in different *"orders."* That word *"order"* is a military term meaning order or rank or file, such as you would see when soldiers march by in parade formation. So it shall be with the resurrection of the saints. The saints' bodies will be raised according to *"(their) own order."* Now there are three such *"orders,"* says Paul, connected with the first resurrection of Christ's own.

"(1) Christ the first fruits, (2) after that those who are Christ's at His coming, (3) then comes the end..." I Corinthians 15:23, 24.

The First Order: *"Christ the first fruits"* is the first *"order"* of the first resurrection. This *"order"* has already taken place. Matthew pictures it in Chapter 27:50-53 of his book. When the Lord Jesus rose from the grave, "the tombs were opened; and many bodies of the saints who had fallen asleep were raised; and coming out of the tombs after His resurrection they entered the holy city and appeared to many," verses 52, 53. *"Many bodies of the saints who had fallen asleep"* accompanied Christ's resurrection. They too were raised; that is, they received their resurrection bodies.

These are called *"the first fruits;"* the promise of more to come. Their resurrection is the guarantee, the assurance and the pledge that all others in Christ shall also be raised. This *"order,"* and the two orders that follow comprise the first resurrection, and are pictured for us in the offerings of Leviticus 23. The *"first fruits"* are represented by the waving of the *"sheaf of the first fruits of (the) harvest,"* verses 9-14. That was an offering of faith and thanksgiving for the main harvest to come. This first *"order"* of the resurrection is the promise that all *"in Christ"* will also be raised in immortality.

[NOTE OF INTEREST] These *"first fruits"* were Old Testament saints who received their resurrection bodies.

Most Old Testament saints did not receive their immortal bodies at that time. The souls and spirits of all departed saints prior to the resurrection of Christ Jesus went to a place called *"Paradise,"* also referred to as Abraham's bosom. No person prior to the cross, resurrection and ascension of Christ could go into the presence of God until the blood of the Lamb of God had been offered. How that relates to Enoch and Elijah we are not told. I'm sure there will be no sin in asking when we go home. On the resurrection morning, the Lord Jesus emptied Abraham's bosom and took all those held in captivity there into the very presence of God. When Jesus went marching home, behind Him were the saints who had received their resurrection bodies as *"first fruits;"* that is, the promise of more to come.

Behind them were myriads of disembodied souls and spirits of departed Old Testament saints who made up the remainder in Abraham's bosom. They are still without their immortal bodies as they receive their imperishable, immortal and eternal body when you and I receive ours. For more light on this first order of the first resurrection read through Matthew 27:45-53 and Psalm 68:17, 18.

Paradise, formerly in Abraham's bosom, on Christ's resurrection day was moved to Heaven. Since then, the soul and spirit of every departed child of God goes directly into the presence of God. "To be absent from the body (is) to be at home with the Lord," II Corinthians 5:8.

The Second Order: The second *"order"* of the first resurrection is the main body of the harvest. Paul described this *"order,"* as "after that those who are Christ's at His coming," I Corinthians 15:23f. His *"coming"* is *"in the clouds"* and is the resurrection day spoken of in I Thessalonians 4:16, 17. "For the Lord Himself will descend from heaven with a shout, with the voice of the archangel, and with the trumpet of God; and the dead in Christ shall rise first." Here is the second order of the first resurrection, when Christ comes *"in the air."*

The resurrection of those who have died in Christ is accompanied by a transformation of those who are *"alive"* in Christ at the moment of His *"shout."* "Then we who are alive and remain shall be caught up together with them in the clouds to meet the Lord in the air, and thus we shall always be with the Lord." *"Alive"* or *"dead"* at the *"trumpet's"* sound, described by John in Revelation 4:1, all *"in Christ"* will go to be with their Lord. Where the resurrection bodies of the *"dead in Christ"* are raised from the earth, we who are living and are *"in Christ"* shall "all be changed, in a moment, in the twinkling of an eye, at the last trumpet," I Corinthians 15:51, 52. Their bodies are *"raised"* first; ours bodies, if we are here when Christ comes *"in the clouds"*, are *"changed (metamorphosed)"* forever into Christ's likeness.

That order used to puzzle and slightly agitate me. Why do the *"dead in Christ"* get to go *"first?"* They were already out of this world. I'm still treading through this old sinful dirt. Why do they get to go first? After much study I finally figured it out. Their bodies are in the grave. They have six feet further to go. We'll then be hot on their heels.

This *"order"* of the first resurrection is also pictured as the, *"new grain offering to the Lord"* in Leviticus 23:15-21. This is the Feast of Pentecost and shows God receiving us today just as we are (a leavened loaf). He then cleanses us and makes us acceptable as is pictured in the Livitical prescribed offerings of verses 18-21. Praise God! There is no other way we could ever come into the presence of our Holy God apart from the reality pictured in those prescribed offerings. But with them we stand in the presence of God fully acceptable and eternally loved. In Old Testament days no person could come before God without a blood offering. Today the blood of Christ is their and our offering, given by

Jesus on our behalf. Enter the throne room of God any time you care. Care often! Lots of blessings are bestowed there.

The Third Order: The third *"order"* of the first resurrection Paul describes as, *"then comes the end,"* I Corinthians 15:24. Often misinterpreted as the judgment of the dead, this is the final order of the first resurrection and is for those who perish during the Tribulation, "because of the testimony of Jesus and because of the word of God, and who (did) not receive the mark of the beast or his image," Revelation 20:4. *"This (completes) the first resurrection,"* verse 5.

This final order of *"the first resurrection"* is also pictured for us in Leviticus 23:22. "When you reap the harvest of your land, moreover, you shall not reap to the very corners of your field, nor gather the gleaning of your harvest; you are to leave them for the needy and the alien. I am the Lord your God." God's provision for the Tribulation saints is pictured in the *"gleaning."* It is as if He says, "There is salvation, even to the edge of time for man." This truth will doubtlessly offer comfort and strength to many during the sufferings of the Tribulation, and a steadfast hope in their deaths.

The Millennial Kingdom

The Millennial Kingdom refers to the coming one thousand year reign of Christ on the throne of David. This kingdom age is the literal fulfillment of all Old Testament expectations. It will be an earthly kingdom superintended by none other than the God of creation, and the Lord Jesus is His name. This is the time of Israel's manifested glory. A perverted concept of The Kingdom, held by Israel, was one of the chief reasons she did not recognize her Messiah at His first coming. She was not looking for a Servant. She desired and expected One who would exalt her over her national rivals. One of the basic fundamentals of godliness, Old and New Testaments alike, is found in God's word to

Solomon, "If My people who are called by My name will humble themselves and pray, and seek My face and turn from their wicked ways, then I will hear from heaven, will forgive their sin, and will heal their land," II Chronicles 7:14. In the words of Peter, "Humble yourselves, therefore, under the mighty hand of God, that He may exalt you at the proper time," I Peter 5:6.

Never is the humility of the saints taught more prevalently than in the teachings of Jesus. At the disciples' question, "Who then is greatest in the kingdom of heaven?" the Lord answered by calling a child to Himself. "Whoever then humbles himself as this child, he is the greatest in the kingdom of heaven," Matthew 18:1-4. As a reproach to the religious leaders in the days of His earthly ministry, the Lord addressed the multitudes and the disciples with these words: "The scribes and the Pharisees have seated themselves in the chair of Moses; therefore all that they tell you, do and observe, but do not do according to their deeds; for they say things, and do not do them.... But the greatest among you shall be your servant. And whoever exalts himself shall be humbled; and whoever humbles himself shall be exalted," Matthew 23:1-3, 11, 12.

Servanthood in the family of God is both a position one willingly takes and an attitude to be developed. Considering others as more worthy than oneself is the secret to becoming more like Christ. It is the only road that truly leads to God ordained servanthood. This position and attitude does not change during the Kingdom Age on earth, the Millennial Reign of Christ Jesus. It was the requirement for those desiring to enter the kingdom of heaven in Christ's day. It is the same requirement today. It will continue as the way of life throughout eternity.

The first resurrection and the second death (Revelation 20:14) are separated by the one thousand year reign of Christ on Earth. The resurrection to life (John 5:29) will be completed before the Millennial Kingdom begins (Revelation 20:4-6). The resurrection to judgment, for those whose names are not found written in the Lamb's Book of Life (vs. 15), is at the close of the Millennial Kingdom and prior to eternity future.

Numerous passages of Scripture are devoted to describe the Lord's return in power and glory to establish His everlasting dominion. Two such thrilling examples are: "And in the days of those kings (Antichrist and his 10 kings) the God of heaven will set up a kingdom which will never be destroyed, and that kingdom will not be left for another people; it will crush and put an end to all these kingdoms, but it will itself endure forever," Daniel 2:44. "I kept looking in the night visions, and behold, with the clouds of heaven One like a Son of Man was coming, and He came up to the Ancient of Days and was presented before Him. And to Him was given dominion, glory and a kingdom, that all the peoples, nations, and men of every language might serve Him. His dominion is an everlasting dominion which will not pass away; and His kingdom is one which will not be destroyed," Daniel 7:13, 14.

This one thousand year reign of the Lord Jesus Christ on earth, sandwiched between the resurrection of life and the resurrection to judgment, will also be the fulfillment of every earthly covenant with Israel. Still, there is other business that must be attended prior to the establishment of Israel's covenant and the Kingdom's reign. Four promises will be fulfilled according to Scripture:

First, there is the glorious appearing of the promised Messiah (Matthew 24:27).

Second, all Israel will be gathered from the corners of the Earth (Matthew 24:31).

Third, there is the judgment of Israel (Matthew 24:37 – 25:30).

Fourth, there is the judgment of the nations (Matthew 25:31-46).

The Kingdom Pictured

The Millennial Kingdom is a reestablishment of God's original intent as far as creation is concerned. Several passages declaring differing aspects of the Kingdom follow. A good concordance will lead you to many more. You do have a Strong's Concordance, don't you?

The Lord will be there. "And it will come about in that day that living waters will flow out of Jerusalem, half of them toward the eastern sea and the other half toward the western sea; it will be in summer as well as in winter. And the Lord will be king over all the earth; in that day the Lord will be the only one, and His name the only one.... And people will live in it (Jerusalem), and there will be no more curse, for Jerusalem will dwell in security," Zechariah 14:8, 9, 11.

Righteousness will reign. "And He will judge between many peoples and render decisions for mighty, distant nations. Then they will hammer their swords into plowshares and their spears into pruning hooks; nation will not lift up sword against nation, and never again will they train for war. And each of them will sit under his vine and under his fig tree, with no one to make them afraid, for the mouth of the Lord of hosts has spoken," Micah 4:3, 4.

Truth and joy will reign. "Thus says the Lord, 'I will return to Zion and will dwell in the midst of Jerusalem. Then Jerusalem will be called the City of Truth, and the mountain of the Lord of hosts will be called the Holy Mountain.' Thus says the Lord of hosts, 'Old men and old women will again sit in the streets of Jerusalem, each man with his staff in his hand because of age. And the streets of the city will be filled with boys and girls playing in its streets,'" Zechariah 8:3-5.

The curse on creation of Genesis 3:17-19 will be removed. "For the anxious longing of the creation waits eagerly for the revealing of the sons of God. For the creation was subjected to futility, not of its own will, but because of Him who subjected it in hope, that the creation itself also will be set free from its slavery to corruption into the freedom of the glory of the children of God. For we know that the whole creation groans and suffers the pains of childbirth together until now," Romans 8:19-22. "The wilderness and the desert will be glad, and the desert will rejoice and blossom like the rose," Isaiah 35:1

Disease and despair will be done away. "Then the eyes of the blind will be opened, and the ears of the deaf will be unstopped. Then the lame will leap like a deer, and the tongue of the dumb will shout for joy. For waters will break forth in the wilderness and streams in the Arabah (desert)," Isaiah 35:5, 6.

Change in the animal kingdom. "And the wolf will dwell with the lamb, and the leopard will lie down with the kid, and the calf and the young lion and the fatling together; and a little boy will lead them. Also the cow and the bear will graze; their young will lie down together; and the lion will eat straw like the ox. And the nursing child will lay by the hole of the cobra, and the weaned child will put his hand on the viper's den. They will not hurt or destroy in all My holy mountain, for the earth will be full of the knowledge of the Lord as the waters cover the sea," Isaiah 11:6-9.

The above passages and many more give us but a taste of life on earth when the Son of God sits on the throne as promised to Israel. "He will be great, and will be called the Son of the Most High; and the Lord God will give Him the throne of His father David; and He will reign over the house of Jacob forever; and His kingdom will have no end," Luke 1:32, 33.

The Inhabitants of the Kingdom

It is interesting to note who will inhabit the earth during the Millennial Reign of Christ. The church age saints are already immortal beings. The Old Testament saints, including the Tribulation saints who lost their lives over their testimonies of Christ, are also immortals. Remember, this group is linked with Israel in that they came out of the Seventieth Week of Daniel. So, since we are all immortals, who are the mortals that inherit the earth during the Kingdom Age?

There are not an abundance of passages addressing this question. And there need not be. Here is what we can know from Scripture. Not including the Lord Jesus and whatever He may have the angels cooking up, there will be three categories of people on earth, some will be mortal and some will be immortal. This is not a game show, but "The three categories are:

The mortals who inherit the Kingdom. Do you remember the *"one like a son of man"* in Revelation 14:14. He is seen sitting on a cloud with a golden crown on His head and a sickle in His hand. It is none other than the Lord Jesus Himself. He is superintending the safety of His own during the waning days of the Tribulation. Suddenly, He puts His sickle in and *"gathers the harvest of the earth."*

Those *"gathered"* are men and women who have come to a saving knowledge of Christ Jesus during the Tribulation and whose lives have been spared Antichrist's murderous ways. These Jews and Gentiles alike will inherit the Kingdom with Christ, the one thousand year reign of Christ. Passages concerning Jewish inhabitants of the Kingdom can be found in Deuteronomy 30:3-6; Isaiah 11:11-12; 14:1-3; 60:1-22; Jeremiah 23:6-8; and Micah 4:6-8. The following passages deal with Gentile inhabitants of the Kingdom: Psalm 72:11, 17; 86:9; Isaiah 45:6; Daniel 7:13, 14; Zechariah 8:22; and Amos 9:12.

(Come on now. You've got to look some of these up. If I printed them all out the Lord might sound His trumpet before the publisher can crank up his printing press.)

These children of God, as mortal beings, will repopulate the nations of the Earth. They have eternal life with Christ, as they confessed Him during the Tribulation. Their children, however, birthed during the Millennial Age, must also have opportunity to place personal faith in Christ. Their occasion of doing so does not arrive until the end of the Millennial Reign. Those living in outward obedience to the Lord Jesus Christ will live throughout the coming Millennium. Those openly rebelling against the Lord will die at the young age of one hundred and go to their appointed place. Apart from the death of the rebellious, sickness, sorrow and weeping will never enter the Millennial Kingdom.

"No longer will there be in it an infant who lives but a few days, or an old man who does not live out his days; for the youth will die at the age of one hundred and the one who does not reach the age of one hundred shall be accursed," Isaiah 65:20.

What would cause a *"youth"* to die at the then young age of one hundred? Open rebellion against Christ is the answer. Judgment is always according to light received, but rejected. In the Millennial Kingdom, Christ Jesus is living among the inhabitants on earth. They see Him in perfect light and in all His glory (as did the angels of old). Yet, hidden in the flesh of man is a sin nature. Even with Satan bound and kept from his enticements toward evil, the human heart will occasionally spit out its own venom. It will be dealt with swiftly.

The immortal Old Testament saints. Old Testament saints, including saints having given their lives for Christ during the Tribulation (the 70th week of Daniel), will *"reign with Christ for a thousand years,"* Revelation 20:4.

The Lord's Apostles seem to be given a special place in the Kingdom of Christ. "And Jesus said to them, 'Truly I say to you, that you who have followed Me, in the regeneration when the Son of Man will sit on His glorious throne, you also will sit upon twelve thrones, judging the twelve tribes of Israel," Matthew 19:28.

How all this *"reigning"* actually plays out we are not told. Betcha we'll find out. But we'll have to wait and see first hand. I suppose we'll have time to nose-in and see what others are doing. Believe it though; you'll have a full plate before you as well.

The immortal bride and a rod of iron. Once the Lord calls the church to Himself, the Scripture informs us, *"and thus we shall always be with the Lord,"* I Thessalonians 4:17f. Revelation 20:6 confirms the fact we are indeed *"with the Lord"* and "will be priests of God and of Christ and will reign with Him for a thousand years."

There is also a new task given us. The Bible speaks that upon the Lord Jesus' returning, He "comes with a sharp sword, so that with it He may smite the nations; and He will rule them with a rod of iron..." Revelation 19:15. The *"rod of iron"* indicates that obedience sometimes must be enforced. The *"rod,"* during the Millennial Reign also seems to be passed to the church age saints. "And he who overcomes, and he who keeps My deeds until the end, to him I will give authority over the nations; and he shall rule them with a rod of iron, as the vessels of the potter are broken to pieces, as I also have received authority from My Father," Revelation 2:26, 27.

It seems we will be ruling with the authority of Christ in His Kingdom. Perhaps we will be stationed over various worlds, countries, states, cities or streets. As we observe and care for the children of those who inherit the Kingdom, we will learn first hand the depths of depravity born in the human heart. Eternal values, better than any university's postgraduate degree, will be extensively learned as we administer the Law of Righteousness for a thousand years. Maybe I'll get that PHD after all.

The Final Revolt

The Millennium will be a school for the saints of Old and New Testaments alike. It will be a place of unparalleled advance for the mortal human race. Nothing but righteousness checks the advances in science, math and engineering coupled by a walk with our ever-present Lord Jesus Christ. There will be trials though. As new generations are birthed and grow, they will have little personal experience of the disastrous effects of sin, though doubtlessly taught and often recalled by their parents and former generations. Yet, as will be clearly evidenced in the course of the Millennium, the sin nature is still passed from father to child.

As is the habit with time, the thousand years also will eventually come to its end. With it time must close its eyes and pass into history gone by. But hold on! There is an invitation that must first be given. The many born during the past one thousand-year reign of righteousness and peace have not been given opportunity to receive or reject Christ Jesus the Lord. Satan was not thrown into the lake of fire into which the beast and false prophet were thrown — and for this very reason. He would provide a perfect opportunity for everyone born over the past millennium of his incarceration to nail down his or her eternal stake.

Will they accept Christ Jesus as their eternal Lord and Savior? They have gotten to know Him well. Surely, no one would refuse Him. Yet, His Law is supreme and unbending. Perhaps it does require too great a limitation to live under for ages without end? Will the grass seem greener on the dark side for millennial inhabitants as it has for so many before them? Time will shortly tell. Before a man can be a saint, he must have opportunity to be a sinner. The choice is imperative for every man, woman and child. When Satan is released from the abyss, gloves come off, deceitfulness struts, anger spews and the inhabitants of the world move with lightening quickness toward the final revolt.

Satan is *"released from his prison,"* Revelation 20:7. The *"bottomless pit"* hasn't changed his mindset of overthrowing God Almighty. He comes out swinging and ranting, plans well drawn, schemes all in place. Off to the *"nations which are in the four corners of the earth, Gog and Magog,"* he goes disastrously and with cunning guile (verse 8). Will he find enough followers to overthrow the Lamb of God? No, certainly not. Not even if everyone joined his feeble fray. Sadly he finds more than enough to attempt his wicked plan. History has already been written, my friend. It is terrible that so many never learned to read, hear and heed (Revelation 1:3). He goes forth gathering men and women for war, and *"the number of them (that follow) is like the sand of the seashore,"* verse 8f. How sickening! How deceitful and desperately wicked is the human heart (Jeremiah 17:9)!

This is God's battle alone. How dare anyone once again lift a hand against His resurrected Son. The saints of God are as determined as the devil's children. They gather in defense around the city of Jerusalem. However, they are told to stand back and watch. We all become spectators from the sidelines of this coming scene. And what a scene it will be! The Second Battle of Gog and Magog pits the millions of Satan's followers against the One. That is hardly an evenhanded fight! "Lord, are you sure you can't use some help?" we might ask. "I'm sure," will come His reply. "It's a stacked deck — on My side."

Preview the eve of eternity: "And they came up on the broad plain of the earth and surrounded the camp of the saints and the beloved city, and fire came down from heaven and devoured them. And the devil who deceived them was thrown into the lake of fire and brimstone, where the beast and the false prophet are also; and they will be tormented day and night forever and ever," Revelation 20:9, 10.

How's that for a resounding victory?

The Great White Throne Judgment

What a contrast between the *"The Judgment Seat of Christ,"* where members of God's forever family will stand, and *"The Great White Throne of Judgment"* at which those who have followed Satan, sin and self will reluctantly and rebelliously bow knee and head. Believers are no better people in many instances than unbelievers. That's a shame, but it is a fact. The truth is some believer's have not lived as good a life as many unbelievers. It must be remembered, however, that living a good life saves neither them nor anyone else. It is faith not works that saves. That's just too simple for some people. And it doesn't seem fair to others believing good works ought to count for at least a sundeck in Heaven. Nevertheless, believers are forgiven and therefore incomparably better off because of the righteousness of Another. Each of the redeemed has inherited an eternity of bliss and joy acquired by childlike faith in Christ Jesus. The destiny of the believer was settled as the Holy Spirit drew him or her to faith in Christ Jesus. The destiny of the unbeliever was also settled as he or she rejected God's offer of love and forgiveness in the Lord Jesus Christ. One's eternally blessed future is due all to the mercy and grace of God as shown through the shed blood of Christ Jesus the Savior. Just as sure as *"The Judgment Seat of Christ"* is the awarding bench of the saints, so also *"the Great White Throne of Judgment"* is the judgment bar for unbelievers waiting just around life's most jolting corner.

John brings the Day of Judgment to our attention in Revelation 20:11-15. "And I saw a great white throne and Him who sat upon it, from whose presence earth and heaven fled away, and no place was found for them." You might want to go back to Revelation 1:9-18 and review the unnerving site of the One John sees as the coming again Lord and Judge. Remember, John the beloved Apostle upon seeing the returning Lord, *"fell at His feet as a dead man,"* verse 17. If John, whom the Lord loved and who loved his Lord, over fear *"fell at His feet as a dead man,"* what do you think the lost among humanity will do when they see the resurrected and coming again Son of God, their Lord and Judge. I'll tell you what they *will seek* to do. They seek to *"(flee) away, (but) no place was found for them."* Where can anyone flee from the Lord of Creation? The Psalmist knew the answer to that. Check out Psalm 139:7-12 for a blessing.

John continues, "And I saw the dead, the great and the small, standing before the throne, and books were opened; and another book was opened, which is the book of life, and the dead were judged from the things which were written in the books, according to their deeds." The Lord Jesus called this *"the resurrection of judgment"* in John 5:29. No one standing without the robe of righteousness of Christ Jesus will be excused from this judgment bar. Kings and queens of nations, presidents of countries, ambassadors, tyrants, men and women of every social strata, religious and non-religious alike, poor, middle class, and wealthy, every race, every tribe, every people on the face of the planet without Christ will *"stand before the throne."*

As they *"stand"* before the Creator and Judge, *"books are opened."* These are the *"books"* with the names of the unredeemed throughout the seven millenniums of human history. In the pages of these *"books"* are written the names of those who have died without Christ. (God is an omniscient God. He can do things like that.) I imagine under each name is detailed information logged in on every thought, every act and every word spoken by that individual. Actually, I don't have to imagine. I read the Book and He tells us so. "And I say to you, that every careless word that men shall speak, they shall render account for it in the Day of Judgment," Matthew 12:36.

Every act of disobedience, every lie, every evil thought, every corrupt imagination, every word spoken, every sin ever committed still sits solidly on the pages of the records of one's life and on the shoulders of those having refused the gift of Calvary's forgiveness. Far worse, recorded is every witness of Christ rejected, every Bible verse scorned, every testimony of God's love refuted, every Spirit-filled sermon despised, every conviction of the Holy Spirit squelched, every song lifting high the name of Jesus Christ disputed, every star that ever twinkled reminding of the presence of God repudiated, every "No, no, no!" defiantly shouted at God's offer of forgiveness and eternal life. Everyone *"standing"* before this judgment bar is declared, *"without excuse,"* Romans 1:20. This is the moment of which the Apostle Paul spoke, "... every knee should bow, of those who are in heaven, and on earth, and under the earth, and that every tongue should confess that Jesus Christ is Lord, to the glory of God the Father," Philippians 2:10, 11.

"And another book was opened, which is the book of life." The recordings in this *"book"* are presented as an unconditional all-condemning witness. Doubtlessly it will be needed. As Christ mentioned, many will say on that day, "Lord, Lord, did we not prophecy in Your name, and in Your name cast out demons, and in Your name perform many miracles?" Matthew 7:22. Then they will hear the Lord's pronouncement of the most awful words in any language, "I never knew you; depart from Me, you who practice lawlessness," verse 23. Notice the word *"practice"* is in the present tense. Though dead in the water before Christ, they have not ceased to *"practice lawlessness."* Through all the pleading, arguing and crying no mistakes will be found in the *"books"* of Heaven's record. The *"voice like the sound of many waters"* (Revelation 1:15) on the Great White Throne of Judgment will be obeyed on this day.

Thus, "... the dead were judged from the things which were written in the books, according to their deeds." "For *all* their sins?" Yes, for every one of them. Every sin could have been washed in the blood of the Lamb of God. Christ rejected, however, leaves one with the weight of sins for which just payment is now due. *"The wages of sin is death,"* Romans 6:23. Always has been, always will be. Judgment is *"according to their deeds."* Every sin's judgment is fault-lessly rendered. Eternity can never render the slate, "Paid in full." These are for sins that can only be paid with one's life. Remembered by all experiencing this day will be another life, a sinless one, and therefore one qualified to die for another. Those sins would have been paid in full. That offer, however, was refused one time to many.

Nevertheless, there is one sin, I am convinced, that brings about the most austere judgment of all. This sin deter-mines the severity of eternal punishment. I mentioned it a little earlier. Throughout the Bible we find judgment will be apportioned according to light received, but rejected. Another way to say that is, truth discerned but disdained, taught but trampled, received but refused will receive the harshest punishment. The Bible says, *"from everyone who has been given much shall much be required,"* Luke 12:48. Those having received the most truth, the most light, the most opportunity will be held most accountable. Such is the background behind which we find some of the Lord's most devastating statements.

"Then He began to reproach the cities in which most of His miracles were done, because they did not repent. Woe to you, Chorazin! Woe to you, Bethsaida! For if the miracles had occurred in Tyre and Sidon which occurred in you, they would have repented long ago in sackcloth and ashes. Nevertheless, I say to you, it shall be more tolerable for Tyre and Sidon in the day of judgment, than for you. And you, Capernaum, will not be exalted to heaven, will you? You shall descend to Hades; for if the miracles had occurred in Sodom which occurred in you, it would have remained to this day. Nevertheless, I say to you that it shall be more tolerable for the land of Sodom in the day of judgment, than for you," Matthew 11:20-24.

Satan's degree of eternal torment and suffering will be the most severe in *"the lake of fire."* His sin was committed in perfect light. He dwelled in the very presence of God. His position was to *"cover,"* that is to "protect and grace" the throne of God. He was the *"anointed cherub who covers,"* Ezekiel 28:14. When he sinned against God, it was in perfect light, against perfect truth.

Therefore, his punishment will be far greater than that of all others. God says, *"... you will be thrust down to Sheol, to the recesses of the pit,"* Isaiah 14:15. That is the place from which the fires of judgment issue. Satan will not rule in that forever netherworld. No one will. It is an unruly situation. That's why it is sealed for eternity.

After Satan, in degree of punishment, will be the fallen angels, also known as demons. These are those who revolted against God under Satan's leadership. Just above the fallen angels will be all those men and women, boys and girls who sat in Bible believing and teaching churches, in Spirit-filled Sunday School classes, who having heard much and having been convicted often, will be condemned all the more for refusing to turn from sin and self to the Lord Jesus Christ. Remember, judgment is due to light received, but rejected. Above them will be those who have heard less, but rejected nevertheless. And just above them will be found those who had little opportunity, yet rebuked the outstretched nail-scarred hand of Jesus Christ.

Paul's words concerning the nation of Israel have a ring of warning for everyone, "Behold then the kindness and severity of God; to those who fell, severity, but to you, God's kindness," Romans 11:22.

John continues relating the Lord's revelation to him, "And the sea gave up the dead which were in it, and death and Hades gave up the dead which were in them; and they were judged, every one of them according to their deeds," Revelation 20:13. *"Death"* empties itself of the *"dead which were in it."* *"Hades"* brought forth, bound and shackled, the souls which were in it. These souls and bodies raised and reunited are *"judged, every one of them according to their deeds."* After sentencing, "death and Hades were thrown into the lake of fire. This is the second death, the lake of fire," Revelation 20:14.

The *"book of life"* may on request be checked, but when their names cannot be found they are *"thrown into the lake of fire,"* verse 15. The names of those at this bar of judgment will not be found in the Lamb's book of life, and there will be no appeals. Forever and ever is the pronouncement of eternal judgment!

The New Heaven And The New Earth

There are *"new"* things God has declared He will fashion for eternity. Most of what lies ahead is beyond our present day comprehension. Yet, in figurative language He gives us a glimpse of what is in store for His family. One of the over-riding truths of Scripture is that God has a place prepared for His own.

There will be a *"new heaven."* There are three heavens in our present day. The first heaven is where we dwell, the earth and the atmosphere that envelops our world. This heaven is the primary habitation of man. The second heaven is that vast universe beyond earth's atmosphere. The stars, planets, moons, suns and galaxies so majestic on any clear night. These luminaries have always brought thinking people in awe and wonder of the Creator. The third heaven is beyond the universe. It is the dwelling place of God. Into this third heaven Paul was summoned, later to call it his *"third heaven"* and *"caught up to Paradise"* experience (II Corinthians 12:2, 4). What an experience that must have been!

God tells us He will make *"a new heaven... for the first heaven... passed away,"* Revelation 21:1. The words *"passed away"* do not mean they will be destroyed or annihilated, or that they cease to exist. "Purged" gives us a better understanding of these words in today's language. As the world was renovated by water in days gone by, so it shall yet be renovated once again. This time it is renovated by fire. Peter speaks of the same day in II Peter 3:10-13. It is the time spoken of when God makes *"all things new,"* Revelation 21:5. Regeneration is the best word to identify God's re-creation. It will be a remaking, a rebirth in much the same way as an individual is born-again today. Don't worry about it now. You can explore this *"new heaven"* for endless ages to come. Gravity will not hold you down.

There is also coming in the same manner, *"a new earth."* The Starship Enterprise has never seen such a scrambling of molecules as the Lord of heaven will perform before our eyes. He shares with us a little about it; such as *"there is no longer any sea."* We will just have to wait and see what all is in store. I sure hope there are golf courses. But how much fun would it be if God decides to play? It'd be hard to beat a perfect score of 18. This making of *"all things new"* has been a greatly sought after expectation of many godly men and women. Isaiah long ago quoted God concerning eternity's new things, "For behold, I create new heavens and a new earth; and the former things shall not be remembered or come to mind," Isaiah 65:17. This is that city Abraham sought so long ago. We will call it home one day.

Some interpreters of Scripture believe the *"new heaven and the new earth"* means the old heavens and earth are not used in making the new, but that they are completely destroyed and altogether new ones are created. I don't care! Do you?

The New Jerusalem And Eternity

Revelation 21:2 focuses in on our new dwelling place for the ages to come. "And I saw the holy city, new Jerusalem, coming down out of heaven from God, made ready as a bride adorned for her husband." Again, the mind swirls when considering this sight. This city, *"New Jerusalem, coming down out of heaven from God,"* is linked not only with our eternal home, but also with the dwelling place of God. Today we are *"the temple of the living God,"* II Corinthians 6:16. Yet, this is going to take on a whole new meaning when, *"He dwells among (us),"* (Revelation 21:3). It all begins when, "the saints go marching home."

Revelation 21:9 - 22:5 pictures the New Jerusalem in language that is dazzling, but at the same time mystifying. It is as if He is saying, "Wait until you see this!" Once again, the language used depicts the *"New Jerusalem"* and *"the bride"* as one and the same. Observe, "And one of the seven angels who had the seven bowls full of the seven last plagues, came and spoke with me, saying, 'Come here, I shall show you the bride, the wife of the Lamb.' And he carried me away in the Spirit to a great and high mountain, and showed me the holy city, Jerusalem, coming down out of heaven from God, having the glory of God," Revelation 21:9-11.

The angel invited John to see *"the bride,"* and then showed him *"the new Jerusalem."* The *"bride"* and *"Jerusalem"* are one, and she is the dwelling place of God.

Thus, in speaking of the *"New Jerusalem"* in verse 3, we are told, "... the tabernacle of God is among men, and He shall dwell among them, and they shall be His people, and God Himself shall be among them."

Let it boggle your mind in amazement. Our best guesses and imaginations fall so far short of the wonder, the glory and the majesty to be revealed. We will doubtlessly stand in shocked marvel, wonderment and awe in that coming day. You have just got to be there!

Here is something else for which we all look forward. "And he shall wipe away every tear from their eyes; and there shall no longer be any death; there shall no longer be any mourning, or crying, or pain; the first things have passed away," Revelation 21:4. That will be a glorious day for all in God's forever family. But, I want you to dwell with me on this for a fleeting moment or two.

The redeemed are caught up to meet the Lord just before the beginning of the Tribulation. The next seven years were spent with Him *"in the air."* We went before the Judgment Seat of Christ where rewards for faithfulness were given. We danced in our wedding dress with our eternal Bridegroom at heaven's most marvelous marriage feast. We then returned with our Lord to put down earth's revolt at Armageddon. We were with the Lord Jesus throughout the judgment of Israel and the judgment of the nations. The one thousand year reign of Christ on earth found us reigning alongside Him. We saw Satan loosed for a short time to gather the nations for the Second Battle of Gog and Magog. We were at our Savior's side when time came to an end with God purging creation of His enemies. We were with Christ throughout the Great White Throne Judgment and the sealing of the lake of fire.

We watched as He made the new heaven and a new earth and then brought New Jerusalem down out of heaven. Now we find ourselves walking through the gates of the New Jerusalem. Then, and mark this, not until then, it is not until this point the Lord will *"wipe away every tear from (our) eyes."*

We have been with the Lord as immortals for better than 1,007 years. All this time we lovingly worshiped Him and served Him. Perhaps, without realizing it we were in heaven's prep school for dwelling and reigning with God throughout eternity. We were assigned responsibility and used the rod of iron in gentle discipline. We have looked into the faces of many who in their hearts harbored anger and rebellion against our Bridegroom. Tears in abundance flowed from our eyes as we reigned, served and walked with the Lord. We have seen others through the eyes and wisdom of Christ, and tears have flowed. We recognized our former selves in the lives of so many enslaved to self, and tears again poured. We identified in people the hardened hearts we once harbored, and tears certainly streamed. We sought to minister, often without success, to those in rebellion, and tears cascaded over our immortal cheeks.

I believe God will be using these years in our lives in preparing us to reign with Him throughout eternity. But more importantly, I believe God will use all these experiences to teach us the utter sinfulness of sin. No one after walking through those gates of pearl and having their tears wiped dry will ever desire to sin against so great and loving a God as ours. Yes, tears will flow for a time. But, they will be *"wiped away"* by God Himself as we enter the New Jerusalem and an eternity with Him forever at our side.

You might want to familiarize yourself with some of the details of the New Jerusalem, your eternal residence. Here are some quick facts. Now, if some of this sounds expensive, don't worry. God can afford it. And He never passes on a bill.

1. The brilliance of your new home is dazzling. See Revelation 21:11.

2. The city has a great and high wall with twelve gates. At the gates twelve angels are stationed. The names of

the twelve tribes of Israel were written on the gates. See Revelation 21:12. Let us never forget, it was through Israel God gave the Covenant, the Law, the Word of God and the Son. Israel paid dearly over the millennia as Satan sought to destroy the plan and purpose of God by destroying her. The names of the twelve tribes of Israel written on the gates will forever be a memorial to that tiny nation bringing praise to God from the lips of all who pass through these gates for endless ages ahead.

3. The wall also has twelve foundation stones with the names of the twelve apostles of the Lamb. See Revelation 21:14. My, what we owe to these Apostles, and so many others. They too have an eternal memorial!

4. "The city is laid out as a square, and its length is as great as the width; and he measured the city with a rod, fifteen hundred miles; its length and width and height are equal," Revelation 21:16. Are you ready for this? Can you take it? Heights don't give you nose bleeds, do they? The city is fifteen hundred miles in every direction. On which floor will your mansion be? A stroll around the block will take.... Oh well, maybe a day will still be as thousand years.

5. The wall of the city is made of jasper. The city itself is pure, transparent gold. The foundation is made of precious stones. The gates are made of twelve pearls, and the streets of the city are pure gold. See Revelation 21:18-21. Have you ever seen such a rich design?

6. There is no temple, church or synagogue. "The Lord God, the Almighty, and the Lamb, are its temple (sanctuary)." See Revelation 21:22.

7. There is no sun or moon, "for the glory of God has illumined it, and its lamp is the Lamb." See Revelation 21:23.

8. "There shall be no night, and its gates shall never be closed." See Revelation 21:25.

9. "Nothing unclean and no one who practices abomination and lying, shall ever come into it, but only those whose names are written in the Lamb's book of life." See Revelation 21:27.

What a place for a permanent address. What a place to call home. What an eternity is before us.

The River Of The Water Of Life

How better could prophecy bring God's Book to a close than by showing us the source of eternal life?

"And he showed me a river of the water of life, clear as crystal, coming from the throne of God and of the Lamb, in the middle of its street. And on either side of the river was the tree of life, bearing twelve kinds of fruit, yielding its fruit every month; and the leaves of the tree were for the healing of the nations," Revelation 22:1, 2.

God's forever family will picnic on these streets of pure gold, which are so perfect they are like transparent glass. The *"tree of life"* forfeited by Adam in the Garden of Eden has been transplanted on both sides of the river, and bears its *"twelve kinds of fruit... every month."* Every need that could ever arise is met before it is ever imagined. That's heaven! And from that *"fruit,"* can't you imagine, is going to be made some mighty good heavenly ambrosia?

More importantly, I want you to look with me briefly as to what is conveyed by *"the river of the water of life."* Obviously, this river is a fountain assuring God's life to all heaven's inhabitants throughout eternity to come. The *"river of the water of life"* speaks of God's never ending life, and points to His abounding nature. All He has He freely gives to the betterment, nourishment and well being of His creation. This river flows *"from the throne of God and of the Lamb."* It is the same *"river of the water of life"* offered in the past, and now throughout eternity future. There will be no thirst there, ever!

The Lord referred to this *"water"* in His instruction to Israel, *"come to Me and drink,"* John 7:37, 38. He explained His life was theirs by personal invitation, and invitations were sent to "whosoever will." Once received this life-giving fluid would become a *"river of living water"* toward others through them. Of course, He was speaking of the Spirit of God, the very life of God, verse 39. In teaching this, the Lord used a common but often overlooked reference when He stated, *"... as the Scriptures have said,"* verse 38. The Old Testament Scriptures foreshadow the reality of the life of God flowing by, to and through His people.

Ezekiel 47:1-12 is the passage. Reading through it you discover a shadow of the truth of Revelation 22, a picture of the substance to come. However, there is much more here. The passage in Ezekiel expounds on the Lord's teaching in John 7:37, 38. And the Ezekiel passage speaks not of eternity, except in its extended greater sense, but of your life and mine today.

In the Ezekiel passage the prophet is in a vision walking through the house of God. There is a Man escorting him through this experience. The Man with Ezekiel foreshadows the Lord Jesus Christ. Ezekiel is representative of you and of me and of all who seek a walk with Christ Jesus the Lord. Having come through the house, and now returning to the door of the house (verse 1), Ezekiel notices God has a leaky faucet. A few drops of water were flowing from the south side of the altar of God — then it turned toward the east. I am going to give you, without all the supporting verses due to space, the meanings tucked away in this tremendous, life changing passage. Study it slowly and thoroughly. The imagery is explosive and meant to be applicable to our lives. And there is so much more to be drawn than I've pulled from the text.

"Water" in the Bible is a picture of the Word of God. But moving water, running water, is a picture of the Spirit of God, the life of God; made clear to us by John 7:39. The *"water"* Ezekiel sees is moving. It is just a few drops. But it is flowing. And, it is flowing from the *"south side of the altar of God."*

Remember, Ezekiel is in the house of God, the place where God dwells. Heaven is somewhere up north. That's why Satan declared: *"I will ascend to heaven... in the recesses of the north,"* Isaiah 14:13. He was speaking of the throne of God. So if heaven is up north and the *"water"* is flowing *"from south of the altar,"* (Ezekiel 47:1) it is flowing toward you and me down here. This *"water"* representing the life of God is coming our way.

But then the *"water"* turns and flows toward the *"east."* *"East"* in the Scripture has the connotation of "ahead of or before me." The life of God flowing from the throne of God is toward us, but then flows from us toward the *"east."* All God has in store for us is intended to flow to us, through us and from us to others. Wow! Now, that sounds downright Christian, doesn't it?

In verse 3, we find the *"man"* with Ezekiel *"measuring a thousand cubits (1,500 feet)"* toward the east. He then came back and brought (or "led") Ezekiel through the *"water"* now *"reaching the ankles."* A *"measuring line"* in the Bible is representative of God's Word. (See Amos 7:7.) This same Word, given in the past and good throughout eternity, is our measuring rod as well. The Word of God is the measuring line by which He will judge each of us to see how we built our lives. The Man *"measured"* a certain distance, came back, got Ezekiel, and helped him through *"the water (now) reaching the ankles."* The *"water"* had supernaturally risen. The lesson is simple. The more we walk in accordance with the Word of God, the deeper become the blessings flowing from the throne of God. These blessings are proportionate to the measure of our walk. The few *"drops"* back at the throne of God have now risen to Ezekiel's *"ankles."* And don't let this escape your attention; knowing the Word of God is one thing. Allowing the Author of the Word to lead us through the reality of it opens a whole new realm of "Christ in you" and "you in Christ."

Never satisfied with anything short of the perfect will of God, the Man measures another thousand cubits, came back for Ezekiel, and assisted him *"through the water, water reaching the knees,"* verse 4a. He measured another thousand cubits, came back for Ezekiel, and brought him *"through the water, water reaching the loins,"* (verse 4b); that is, his waist muscles. It matters not how long we have known the Lord, it is how far we've walked with Him. And a lifetime is not long enough to exhaust the journey. There is always so much more to know concerning this Man. The further we go with Him, the deeper are the blessings of His life in which we are privileged to walk. But He is never satisfied that we remain where we have come. There is always further to go.

"Again he measured a thousand; and it was a river that I could not ford, for the water had risen, enough water to swim in, a river that could not be forded," verse 5. If we allow, He will eventually take us to the point of swimming in a too deep to fathom and too broad to cross *"river of living water."*

I won't take time to address the *"thousand cubits."* Apart from that number of *"cubits"* equaling 1,500 feet, the only thing I know is it represents a "certain distance in a certain direction a certain Man desires we walk." He measures it out and we are to follow in His footsteps. We are to walk in accordance with the *"measuring line,"* the Word of God. Ezekiel was encouraged to walk in that direction. Because of his obedience the Man lent His assistance.

About that time, however, Ezekiel must have come close to a heart attack. "And he said to me, 'Son of man, have you seen (do you comprehended) this?' Then he brought me back to the bank of the river," verse 6.

When I first saw that I asked, "Lord, why? He was out there in a river of water to swim in. Why did You make him come back?" Eventually, the answer came. It always does. We cannot expect to get out there overnight. It takes time to get into the Word of God. It takes time for God's Word to get into us. But if you and I are faithful to walk in truth given, He will assist us along the way. All the way! And one of these days it will be you, way out there in blessings up to your ankles, then to your knees, and on up to your waist. But don't stop! He is never satisfied with drawing short. In this life there isn't enough time to stop and diddle. He has a *"river of living water"* to pour out upon you and through you today to a world of thirsty men and women.

As good as that is, don't miss the most important lesson. There is an eternally vital truth in this passage. The Christian life is not all about our blessings and it is not about us. The more we walk with the Lord Jesus in accordance with His Word, the more blessings flow not only to us, but they also flow from us into the presence of others. I really hope you grasp this! It is not about us! It is all about Him, and because of Him it is all about others. Though the joy and blessings are ours along the way, they have always been intended for those crossing our earthly path.

Determine to walk with Him, and watch the results grow.

Should you dare walk to where you are in *"ankle"* deep blessing of the presence of God, you will bring *"ankle"* deep blessings of the presence of God into the presence of others. Oh, by the way, let Him measure the depth. You just keep your eyes on Him. If we increase our walk He will increase our depth. *"Knee"* deep walking will bring *"knee"* deep blessings of the life of God to others. *"Waist"* deep waters brings *"waist"* deep blessings of the presence of God into the presence of everyone your life touches. They will not all turn to Christ Jesus because of you. But, the opportunity to do so will be there. We are not responsible for the response of others. We are responsible for the opportunity afforded others.

Keep on walking with Him and one day you will be blessed with and be a blessing of *"rivers of living water"* for all to drink.

Would you like to see one of those blessings right now? Look at the closing words of Ezekiel 47:9, *"... so everything will live where the water goes."* My friend, that is a promise from God. *"Everything... lives... where the water goes."* God simply seeks a channel through which His life can flow to others in this world. Ours is the blessed privilege of drinking from this fountain of *"river of the water of life"* for eternity to come.

Don't wait until you get there to drink from this river. The truth is, *"... as He is, so also are we in this world,"* I John 5:17f. If we walk as He leads, He will see that our *"river"* flows to a dying world all around us. To do so, we must dwell near the bank of the river, drink from the source and walk where He leads.

I have no better way to end this book than the Lord's final words to all of us than in the way He wrapped up the closing chapter of the Bible. He is the One who said: "I, Jesus, have sent My angel to testify to you these things for the churches. I am the root and the offspring of David, the bright morning star. Yes, I am coming quickly," Revelation 22:16, 20.

Come, Lord Jesus!

Printed in the United States
125829LV00005B/101/A